DATE DUE

JUN 27 2006	
NOV 13 2013	
DEC 04 2013	
DEC 11 2013	

Controversies
of the
Sports World

The Greenwood Press **Contemporary Controversies** series is designed to provide high school and college students with one-volume reference sources that each explore controversies in seven specific areas important to contemporary life: sports, music, entertainment, medicine, education, business, and law. Students will discover that difficult problems occur across disciplines, that they manifest themselves in many different ways, and that not all of these problems have easy answers. The series' unique focus on those in high-profile professions is designed to help readers consider the importance of ethics in all sectors of society. Students will be encouraged to develop their critical thinking by examining the history of these topics, exploring various solutions and drawing their own conclusions.

CONTROVERSIES
OF THE
SPORTS WORLD

Douglas T. Putnam

Contemporary Controversies

GREENWOOD PRESS
Westport, Connecticut • London

Library of Congress Cataloging-in-Publication Data

Putnam, Douglas T., 1953–
    Controversies of the sports world / Douglas T. Putnam.
      p.   cm. — (Contemporary controversies, ISSN 1522–2047)
    Includes bibliographical references and index.
    ISBN 0–313–30558–7 (alk. paper)
    1. Sports—Social aspects—United States. 2. Sports—Moral and
ethical aspects—United States. I. Title. II. Series.
    GV706.5.P88   1999
    796'.0973—dc21   98–38217

British Library Cataloguing in Publication Data is available.

Library of Congress Catalog Card Number: 98–38217
ISBN: 0–313–30558–7
ISSN: 1522–2047

First published in 1999

Greenwood Press, 88 Post Road West, Westport, CT 06881
An imprint of Greenwood Publishing Group, Inc.

Printed in the United States of America

The paper used in this book complies with the
Permanent Paper Standard issued by the National
Information Standards Organization (Z39.48–1984).

10 9 8 7 6 5 4 3 2 1

In memory of my father,
David Hopkins Putnam
(1924–1995)

Contents

Acknowledgments

The research and writing of this book were completed with the support and encouragement of many friends and colleagues. My thanks go to my mother, Nancy Putnam; my brother and sister-in-law, Jeff Putnam and Martha Morss; my brother, Jonathan Putnam; my sister, Betsy Putnam; and especially Melanie Kaminski Putnam, who injected into my hide a strong dose of Polish stick-to-it-iveness whenever my production ebbed. Special appreciation is extended to Tracey Dils and Robin Charles for showing me that the writing dream is not an impossible dream, and to friends Liz Taylor Cherry, Steve and Mandy Solis, Ralph and Cookie O'Neal, Dave and Patti Seibert, Steve Judy, Liz Gorman, Verna Ellis, and Kacey Calich for walking with me on the long and challenging march.

Emily Birch of Greenwood Publishing Group first approached me with the idea for this project, and her guidance and support have been pivotal. Linda Ellis, my production editor, and Beverly Miller, my copy editor, have been equally helpful in the final stages of the production process.

I have dedicated this book to the memory of my father, David Hopkins Putnam. It is he who implanted in me a passion for clear-headed analysis, a desire to know the ways of the world, a respect for divergent opinions, and, above all, a love of sports as both a spectator and participant. Thanks, Dad, for giving me the courage to compete and the strength to persevere.

Introduction

In the last half of the twentieth century, the wide-ranging enterprise of sports has assumed a hugely prominent role in American society. There are few people in the United States who have not been affected in some manner by the overwhelming increase in televised sporting events, professional team franchises and leagues, media interest, programs for girls and women, youth sports competitions, sports betting, and high-profile athletes and coaches who command multi-million-dollar salaries. As spectators or participants, or both, millions of Americans now view sports as the central, defining activity of their lives.

In its many aspects, the sports world both reflects and influences the larger society of which it is a part. Sports are now deeply entwined with our schools, colleges, and universities, our family lives, our workplaces, our social networks, and our commercial and political systems. Sports even have a place in our religious institutions and in the private, fantasy lives of individuals. Sports are adored by people from all walks of life, and they can offer the opportunity to build bridges between young and old, rich and poor, black and white, and male and female. And because the sports world is connected to so many institutions and traditions, it is an excellent place to study the complicated and often powerful social forces that create controversy.

This book examines sixteen controversies of the sports world—ongoing conditions or sets of circumstances that give rise to drama, conflict, and tension and that illuminate one or more aspects of sports' connection to, and influence on, our society. Within the book, readers will discover tales of garbage-littered inner-city playgrounds and shimmering suburban skating rinks, histories of enduring spectacles like the World Series and the Olympic Games, accounts of courageous athletes in training and competition, and stories of the people who surround athletes and do so much to create and sustain controversies: parents, coaches, agents, team owners, fans, gamblers, doctors, public officials, and corporate sponsors.

Each chapter discusses how a specific controversy has developed in the sports world, with a focus on how it has affected individuals and institutions in one of the major spectator sports. The chapter presents the background of the controversy and traces its evolution over time to the present. In addition to linking past and present, each chapter explores the reasons that the controversy endures, presents opposing viewpoints on its nature and effects, and offers an outlook on the course it may take in the future. The chapter is followed by a list of topics for discussion which teachers can use to initiate dialogue and encourage students to more fully examine the materials. The reader will also find lists of books, magazines, newspapers, and organizations for more detailed information.

America's love affair with sports shows no sign of abating. All of the controversies discussed here have existed for decades, and there is virtually no chance that any of them will be resolved soon. This book is not an attempt to resolve the controversies but to assess the effects of their ongoing presence. To students, teachers, parents, and other interested readers, *Controversies of the Sports World* is presented as a tool with which to learn more about the great influence that the sports world has had, and will continue to have, on our lives and our society.

1

Superstars for Sale

Recruiting high school football and basketball players is a competitive ordeal that generates prestige, success, and millions of dollars for the colleges and universities that are athletic superpowers. The boundaries of legal and ethical behavior are hard for many people involved in the recruiting process to see. Who wins and who loses in this high-stakes game?

It was the first Wednesday of February 1998, and in the communities and states across America that support major college football teams, thousands of fans waited by radios and televisions in anxious anticipation. In some places, like Baton Rouge, Louisiana; Lincoln, Nebraska; and Gainesville, Florida, they assembled in field houses, hotels, and banquet halls, cheering together as news updates arrived through the morning, afternoon, and evening. On signing day—the first day of the eight-week period during which high school football players can make commitments to attend the universities of their choice the following fall—few people go home disappointed. The letters of intent signed by blue-chip athletes and their parents or guardians fuel the hopes and dreams of fans and coaches everywhere. Before they have graduated from high school and before they have even set foot in a college classroom, these seventeen- and eighteen-year-old football stars, as well as their counterparts on the basketball court, have become vital components in the enterprise of big-time college sports.

Tom McMillen, an All-America, Olympic gold medalist, and eleven-year veteran of the National Basketball Association (NBA), remembers his own signing day vividly. In the spring of 1970 he was the finest high school basketball player in the nation, dominating every game he played as a seven-foot center for Mansfield High School in the mountains of northern Pennsylvania. After his freshman year, he drew the attention of sixty colleges with an interest in his roundball skills. After his sophomore year, the number swelled to 150. The coach of one of those institutions, knowing of the young man's interest in politics and public service, arranged a meeting for him with President Lyndon Johnson. By the end of his junior year, McMillen was being pursued by 300 colleges. That spring, a wealthy booster of the University of Kentucky flew McMillen and his high school coach in a private jet to the school's campus in Lexington, where they were greeted by 3,000 fans.

The recruiting experience amazed and depressed the astute eighteen-year-old, who went on to excel at the University of Maryland, earn a Rhodes scholarship, and serve five terms as a member of the U.S. House of Representatives from Maryland's Fourth District:

> The circus atmosphere of my recruiting was destructive not only to my family but also to the youngsters who followed in the media the absurd efforts of colleges to land me. No valedictorian was so hotly recruited nor received 1 percent of the press coverage devoted to me, not in 1970 and not today. It is impossible for me to calculate how much Maryland and other colleges spent to recruit me, but several hundred thousand dollars is a conservative estimate—far more, I imagine, than was normally spent back then to recruit a college president or a top professor. (McMillen 1992: 63)

Indeed, little has changed in the three decades since McMillen stepped aboard the dizzying carousel reserved for America's young football and basketball superstars, where grown men pursue adolescent boys with the vigor of big game hunters on safari. The names are different, the media hype has grown more intense, and boosters—private supporters of a football or basketball program who have no official connection to the university—have been barred from all recruiting activities since 1987. But the controversies and tensions that the process creates remain the same. "Anybody who wants to know about recruiting, who thinks it's a joyous time in your life, I'll tell them another story," says Durrell Price, a stellar running back from Sylmar, California, who signed with the University of California at Los Angeles (UCLA) in 1996. "It's the most stressful thing I've ever been through" (Layden 1996: 27).

HIGH STAKES

The worrisome sentiments of McMillen and Price are shared by many other young athletes seeking glory on campus. Their sentiments arise from the anxiety inherent in the unpredictable nature of high-level sports competition. Beneath the brimming self-confidence of the high school superstar who has excelled since childhood on the playing field lurks a nagging question: Can I succeed? About 1 million boys play high school football each year in the United States; roughly 260,000 of them are seniors. Those seniors seeking to play major college football are competing for 2,600 available scholarships at the 109 Division I-A schools in the National Collegiate Athletic Association (NCAA). For many recruits, college football is not a game played for the vague and lofty ideals of hard work, sportsmanship, and team spirit. Instead, it is the avenue that must be walked to earn a chance to play the game professionally in the National Football League (NFL). For that reason, the college game means wealth, hope, and a future—not only for the athletes themselves but for the family members they want to take with them as they climb the ladder of material success.

The odds of a college player reaching the professional ranks are slim. Each year, the thirty NFL teams draft only about 240 players out of the thousands who compete at all levels in the college ranks. Several hundred more may receive tryouts as undrafted free agents. As rookies, they face intense competition from more experienced veteran players. Hundreds of rookies do not last beyond the summer training camps that precede the season; an NFL team usually carries only five to seven rookies on its forty-eight-man roster. And most of those players who do attain their dream discover that it slips away quickly. The average career in the NFL lasts three or four years.

The coaches, assistant coaches, and athletic department officials who recruit blue-chip athletes face many of the same pressures as the athletes themselves. "I can coach good players, but I can't do a thing with bad ones," wrote former Georgia Tech and UCLA head coach Pepper Rodgers in his book *Fourth and Long Gone*. "No coach is *that* good at his job. . . . In coaching there are three important things: recruiting, recruiting, and recruiting" (Rodgers 1984: 87).

Most coaches face the same slim odds of ultimate success as the players. For the perennial superpowers of college football that are the dream destinations of high school stars—Notre Dame, Ohio State, Michigan, Penn State, Florida, Florida State, Tennessee, Nebraska, Colorado, Alabama, Southern California, and UCLA—the supply of outstanding players greatly exceeds the demand. Those schools acquire the bulk of the bounty. *Super Prep* magazine, a publication that scrutinizes the recruiting process, reported in 1995 that twenty-one superpower schools signed over 80 percent of the blue-chip prospects in that year's senior class (Layden 1996: 23). Those figures change little from year to year, and the remainder of the schools, which must compete against the superpowers on the field, are forced to make do with the prospects who are left over.

Even the superpower schools face strong challenges in maintaining their competitive edge, because recruiting is an inexact science. There is no way to predict with perfect accuracy how a seventeen-year-old high school All-America will perform in college. Standout stars can fail miserably, and players who are overlooked or downgraded in the recruiting process can blossom and excel. "If someone writes that you had a recruiting class in the top 10, people are going to want to know why your team isn't in the top 10," says UCLA assistant football coach Gary Bernardi (Layden 1996: 23). In fact, there may be many reasons for a team to fall short of expectations. Of the eighty-five football players an NCAA Division I-A school may retain on athletic scholarship at one time, many will fall prey to academic failure, injuries, family problems, or poor performance on the field. Some will transfer to other schools.

For the scholarship athletes who arrive on campus with great fanfare for their freshman year, there are no guarantees of success. In the major college programs, they will toil for forty hours each week during the football season, with a schedule that includes daily practice, weightlifting, team meetings, film sessions, community activities, and supervised study periods. Many will see their head coaches earning huge salaries and lucrative promotional endorsements and their schools reaping millions of dollars from television broadcast rights, bowl game receipts, and game ticket sales. Yet the players are entitled to receive nothing beyond tuition, room, board, fees, and textbooks—the benefits provided in their athletic scholarships.

Some of those players think this seems unfair. Their sweat, after all, is the fuel that runs this enormous moneymaking machine. Without players, there would be no television, no bowl games, and no game ticket receipts. Do they deserve something more than what they are getting for their efforts? Today, as in the past, many college athletes think they do, and many supporters of their efforts in the athletic arena are giving them what they ask for.

THE MANY FORMS OF PAY-FOR-PLAY

Paying college athletes for their on-field performances is a tradition that dates back to the late nineteenth century in the United States, when football teams utilized the services of seasoned "tramp" players, who moved from school to school under the guise of academic transfer whenever the offered price seemed attractive enough. The practice continued through the first half of the twentieth century, as football's power center shifted from the elite private schools of the East to the large state universities of the Midwest, the Pacific Coast, and the South. It expanded during the economic boom after World War II, when television, jet air travel, and the nation's unquenchable thirst for winners, losers, and passive entertainment transformed college football and basketball into a multi-billion-dollar business.

In a study of payment schemes conducted by Professor Allen L. Sack of the University of New Haven in 1989, 31 percent of the 1,182 active and former NFL players who responded admitted to accepting improper payments during their college careers. Fifty-three percent of the respondents said they saw nothing wrong with the practice, and 78 percent said college athletes deserve greater compensation than allowed by the NCAA rules (McG. Thomas 1989: A34).

The payments that players receive take a number of specific forms. They may consist of inducements provided to an athlete while he is still in high school, in an effort to obtain his signature on a letter of intent that obligates him to enroll at the university. Inducements may be offered to and accepted by the adults who surround a star player. "A lot of high school coaches have their hands out—a lot of them," Georgetown University basketball coach John Thompson told the *Washington Post*. "I become very suspicious when a kid is in the room with you . . . and the [high school] coach makes a statement that 'I have to talk to John privately. We have to have a conversation.' Right away, you say to yourself, 'Here it comes'" (Brubaker 1988: D9).

The more common forms of pay-for-play consist of rewards for athletes, or their parents—cash, gifts, interest-free loans, automobiles, rent-reduced apartments, access to credit cards and telephones for long-distance calls—after the athletes are enrolled on scholarship and playing as members of their college team:

- In 1997, the *Detroit Free Press* reported that Ed Martin, a sixty-three-year-old retired electrician from Detroit, paid more than $100,000 each to University of Michigan basketball stars Chris Webber and Maurice Taylor during their tenure on the Wolverine basketball team (Taylor and McCabe 1997: 1A). The reports led to the resignation of head coach Steve Fisher.

- Todd Bozeman, the basketball coach at the University of California at Berkeley, was forced to resign in 1996 after he admitted paying $30,000 to the parents of star point guard Jelani Gardner. Gardner himself was unaware of the payments (Wieberg 1997: 1C).

- An All-Southwest Conference wide receiver at the University of Houston told the *Houston Post* that he frequently used a department store credit card supplied by the university. "I could never know who paid for all the stuff," he said. "I guess the football department paid for it. I know I didn't. I never even got a bill for it" (Sperber 1990: 269–270).

- Sixty football players at the University of Nebraska and fifty-four at the University of Tennessee were penalized by the NCAA in

1986 for selling their allotment of game tickets to boosters and pocketing the cash received for personal use (Sperber 1990: 262).

- An assistant coach at a New England school devised a system for renting cars for team members—as long as their performance was satisfactory. "I rent the car, take the maximum insurance, and give the keys to the player. My only worry is that he'll get into a wreck and the newspapers will pick it up. . . . Rent them a Hertz when they're playing well and cooperating. Send them to Rent-a-Wreck on their own money when they're not" (Sperber 1990: 268).

- In his 1989 trial on felony charges for diverting public funds for personal use, Luther Darville, a University of Minnesota academic adviser, cataloged in detail his gifts of cologne, tennis shoes, underwear, and dinners for Gopher basketball and football players and their girlfriends. "I took them to some of the finer places," he told the court. "They enjoy expensive products" (Berkow 1989: 47).

- On his recruiting visit to Indiana University, basketball prodigy Chris Mills told a Hoosier player, "I have to have money. I have to have a car. I have to live in my own place." When Mills was informed that Indiana did not offer illegal inducements to recruits, he seemed confused and disappointed. An assistant coach at the University of Kentucky later sent Mills's father $1,000 in cash in an air freight envelope, a transgression that led to a two-year NCAA probation for the Wildcat basketball program (Sperber 1990: 250).

- The *Dallas Morning News* reported in 1986 that at one time thirty-three University of Texas football players lived in an Austin apartment complex owned by a former player, who provided them with a 30 percent reduction in rent (Sperber 1990: 260).

In fact, the NCAA states in its manual:

The recruiting process involves a balancing of the interests of prospective student-athletes, their educational institutions and the Association's member institutions. Recruiting regulations shall be designed to promote equity among member institutions in their recruiting of prospects and to shield them from undue pressures that may interfere with the scholastic or athletic interests of the prospects or their educational institutions.

It then goes on to prohibit the following financial aid, benefits, and arrangements:

Like many other college superstars, Marcus Camby was showered with gifts, favors, cash, and attention during his stellar career at the University of Massachusetts. It seemed as if nearly everyone—particularly men who were vying for the privilege of serving as his agent—wanted a piece of his remarkable talent. Unlike many other players, however, Camby did not try to conceal his behavior when confronted about it. "People were coming up to me offering me things, trying to get close to me," he confessed to *Sports Illustrated*. "The phone was always ringing. Everything was happening so fast my head was spinning, and I did some things I'm not proud of. I did some things I shouldn't have done." (AP/WIDE WORLD PHOTOS)

(a) An employment arrangement for a prospect's relatives;

(b) Gift of clothing or equipment;

(c) Cosigning of loans;

(d) Providing loans to a prospect's relatives or friends;

(e) Cash or like items;

(f) Any tangible items, including merchandise;

(g) Free or reduced-cost services, rentals or purchases of any type;

(h) Free or reduced-cost housing;

(i) Use of an institution's athletics equipment (e.g., for a high-school all-star game); or

(j) Sponsorship of or arrangement for an awards banquet for high-school, preparatory school or two-year college athletes by an institution, representatives of its athletic interests, or its alumni groups or booster groups.

The difficult task of enforcing the rules against pay-for-play falls to the investigative staff of the NCAA. Recruiting inducements and on-campus payments comprise a sizable portion of the caseload of the nineteen investigators, who receive up to twenty tips each day from players, coaches, parents, reporters, and anonymous callers regarding possible unauthorized activity. Inexperienced, underpaid, and overworked, the investigators who conduct twenty to twenty-five major probes each year operate under a number of institutional restraints that make effective enforcement difficult.

The central obstacle is that the NCAA functions as both the policeman and promoter of college athletics. It must keep the enterprise ethical by regulating the conduct of individual players and coaches and, at the same time, play a pivotal role in generating millions of dollars for its member schools, primarily by selling television broadcast rights to the annual NCAA basketball tournament. In many instances, the regulation of individual conduct becomes the second priority. In an endeavor where as few as forty athletic programs realize a monetary profit each year, there is little demand on the part of member schools for sanctions that can mean the loss of bowl game and television revenue and a reduction in the number of athletic scholarships that a school may offer in its quest for top-notch talent. "Winning is the thing that ensures income," says former University of Maryland chancellor John Slaughter. "Football and basketball have to make money, and they have to win to make money, and that's how the cycle becomes so vicious" (Brownlee 1990: 50).

Critics characterize the NCAA as a trade association run primarily for the benefit of athletic directors and coaches, who prefer a system where only the most egregious offenders are punished while the rest remain free to pursue business as usual: winning games and making as much money as possible. The critics believe that the NCAA's member schools, despite their declarations to the contrary, do not want aggressive enforcement of the rules that they themselves create.

Supporters of the NCAA's enforcement efforts reject that notion as cynical nonsense. They do not accept the view that all programs cheat and break the rules. Instead, they assert, most major football and basketball programs are operated honestly and ethically. "I was in the business for 25 years," says former NCAA executive director Richard Schultz. "Maybe if I had cheated as a coach I would have been a little more successful. But I think as a coach, you've got to live with yourself first. And the first time you offer an athlete something you shouldn't, you are no longer recruiting an athlete, you're buying a witness" (Nuwer 1989: 122).

MOVEMENT TOWARD CHANGE

As major college football and basketball programs accelerate their quest for money and success, they continue to wrestle with the irony that lies at the heart of their enterprise: college athletes are poverty-stricken moneymakers. Their performances generate millions of dollars in revenue for the schools they represent, yet they themselves are entitled to nothing more than the benefits that come with their athletic scholarships. Supporters of the current system say that those benefits—and the chance to earn a college degree—are more than sufficient payment for the services that an athlete provides. Critics counter that thousands of athletes have no meaningful chance to earn a degree because of the overwhelming demands placed on them to make athletics their first, and only, priority. They see major college sports as a place where mercenary professionalism flourishes under the pretense of noble amateurism and commercial exploitation hides behind the veil of academic ideals. In such an environment, the temptation for athletes to accept pay-for-play can become overwhelming.

In 1998, the member institutions of the NCAA took a small step toward redefining the athlete's role on campus: they approved a rule that will allow Division I athletes to work part time during the school year. The practice was forbidden for decades because it was feared that some schools would abuse it by providing frill jobs. Under the new rule, athletes will be permitted to work only after completing their freshman year, and only if they are in good academic standing. In addition, their compensation will be limited to $2,000—the amount of financial obligation that a typical student incurs each year beyond the costs of tuition, room, board, fees, and textbooks.

Supporters of more radical change doubt that many football and basketball players will find time to take advantage of the new rule. They do not believe it goes nearly far enough. Instead of allowing athletes simply to seek part-time employment, they believe that schools should relieve themselves of their heavy burden of hypocrisy by paying athletes for the tasks they perform now, exactly like other students and other workers in the free enterprise system. "It's unfortunate that we should even be asking if everybody in America should be paid for their work," says Dick DeVenzio, a former standout on the Duke University Blue Devils basketball team who today is perhaps the most ardent supporter of paying college athletes. "Of course they should. Look, a university is a wonderful place. It can handle weird artists, weapons research, experiments with animals, and athletes. It can accommodate everybody. So can it easily accommodate players getting paid? Of course. It's a university" (Looney 1996: 41).

Among the supporters of DeVenzio's point of view is Walter Byers, the stern taskmaster who served as the first executive director of the NCAA from 1951 to 1987. In his 1995 book *Unsportsmanlike Conduct* Byers proposed a five-point College Athletes' Bill of Rights:

> Repeal the rule that establishes the NCAA as national arbiter of the term, value, and conditions of the athlete's outside income during his or her college career.
>
> Repeal the NCAA rule that prevents players from holding a job during the school year. The NCAA repealed that rule in 1998 for Division I athletes.
>
> Require repeal of the transfer rule, which unreasonably binds athletes to their current colleges by requiring them to sit out a year of competition after transferring to a new college.
>
> Force the NCAA to allow players, during their collegiate careers, to consult agents in making sports career choices, a practice currently forbidden.
>
> Amend worker's compensation statutes in state legislatures to require major colleges to provide coverage for varsity athletes who are injured during the course of college careers (Byers 1995: 375–384).

In an organization where change comes slowly and painfully, Byers's proposal has little chance of being enacted in the near future, if at all. But Byers's eminence in the field of intercollegiate athletics, and the growing number of players, coaches, and university officials who share his views, will make certain that the issue of paying athletes, both under and over the table, will continue to generate controversy as college sports enters its second century.

A CASE STUDY IN SCANDAL—BIG TROUBLE IN BIG D: SMU GETS THE DEATH PENALTY

No other scandal in college football history was more pervasive than the pay-for-play scheme operated by boosters and officials of Southern Methodist University (SMU) in Dallas in the 1970s and 1980s. As a member of the prestigious Southwest Conference in the football-crazed state of Texas, SMU used illegal inducements, gifts, and cash payments to bolster its effort to achieve competitive parity with Texas and Texas A&M, the state's established gridiron powers. In his 1989 book *A Payroll to Meet*, sportswriter David Whitford presents a detailed portrait of corruption in the SMU football program.

1976: Ron Meyer, a flashy and aggressive Ohio native, debuts as head coach of the SMU Mustangs, guiding them to a victory over Texas Christian. At the time, SMU is serving the final year of its fourth football-related penalty imposed by the NCAA.

1977: Meyer recruits his first blue-chip superstar, quarterback Mike Ford of Mesquite High School near Dallas. SMU establishes a pipeline to Kashmere High School in Houston, which would supply eight stars to the Mustangs over the next three years.

1978: Armed with envelopes of cash, SMU boosters begin the practice of making rounds in the poorer neighborhoods of Houston and providing modest, regular payments to the families of SMU players.

1979: Mustang Mania erupts as SMU signs the two most coveted running backs in Texas, Craig James of Houston and Eric Dickerson of Sealy. From 1980 to 1984, SMU wins three Southwest Conference titles, plays in four bowl games, and finishes in the national Top 10 four times.

1981: The NCAA announces a fifth probation on June 10 for twenty-nine rules violations. The violations involving cash payments to players are examined and dismissed for lack of evidence.

1982: Ron Meyer resigns as head coach at the end of the season to coach the New England Patriots of the NFL. He is replaced by Bobby Collins. SMU boosters continue the practice of paying players under Collins.

1983: The Mustangs recruit a sterling freshman class, with eight of the twenty-two players admitting later that they had been promised monthly salaries of up to $750. The NCAA begins an ongoing investigation of the program. Former Texas governor William Clements becomes head of the SMU board of trustees.

1984: SMU booster and Dallas real estate mogul Sherwood Blount recruits lineman Sean Stopperich by pledging to provide $5,000 in cash, a rent-free apartment, a $300 monthly allowance, and a job for Stopperich's father in Dallas.

1985: Stopperich leaves the team without playing a game and reveals his financial arrangments to the NCAA, which then bans all booster involvement in the SMU football program. In August, the NCAA cites the school for fifty rules violations, including payments to players. Despite the NCAA sanctions, payments continue to thirteen active players.

1986: Former Mustang David Stanley meets with NCAA investigators on October 21 and gives them an envelope of SMU stationery in which his mother received cash. Stanley and his mother pass lie detector tests administered by the NCAA. Stanley discusses his payments in an interview with a Dallas television station on November 12. SMU president Donald Shields, athletic director Bob Hitch, and coach Bobby Collins resign.

1987: On February 25, the NCAA imposes the "death penalty" on SMU, a complete cancellation of the football program for the 1987 season, as well as a shortened season of seven away games in 1988. SMU, acting on its own, later cancels its entire 1988 season. On May 14, Texas governor William Clements, former head of the school's board of trustees, confesses that he personally approved continued cash payments to players in 1985, after the imposition of NCAA sanctions.

1989: The Mustang football program resumes operation under the direction of new head coach Forrest Gregg.

TOPICS FOR DISCUSSION

1. A 1989 study by Professor Allen L. Sack revealed that a large percentage of football players at major universities who went on to play in the National Football League (NFL) took illicit pay during their college careers. Were these players wrong to take payments that they knew were against the rules of the National Collegiate Athletic Association (NCAA)? Or were they simply receiving fair payment for the services they performed on the football field? Explain your answer.

2. The NCAA changed its rules in 1998 to allow student-athletes at Division I schools to hold part-time jobs. Should student-athletes be permitted to work? Why or why not?

3. Boosters of college athletics—private supporters of football and basketball programs who have no official connection to a university—have been barred from all recruiting activities since 1987. Should

boosters be allowed to participate in the recruiting process? Why or why not?

4. Former NCAA executive director Walter Byers is among those who think players should be allowed to hire agents during their college athletic careers, a practice currently forbidden by the NCAA. Should athletics be allowed to hire agents while they are still in college? Why or why not? Explain your answer.

5. Paying athletes for the work they perform during practice and competition would be one of the most significant changes ever instituted in college sports. Is it a change that should be made? Why or why not?

RESOURCES AND REFERENCES

Books

Byers, Walter, with Charles Hammer. *Unsportsmanlike Conduct: Exploiting College Athletes.* Ann Arbor: University of Michigan Press, 1995.
    The man who served as executive director of the NCAA from 1951 to 1987 describes the history and present-day state of college athletics and traces its evolution from a game to a commercial pastime devoted to the pursuit of money and power.
Caryer, Lee. *The Recruiting Struggle: What Athletes and Parents Need to Know, According to More Than 170 Experts.* Columbus, Ohio: Caryer Enterprises, 1996.
    Presents insights on the recruiting process from athletes, parents, coaches, and news reporters. Many case studies of individual experiences are highlighted.
Funk, Gary. *Major Violation: The Unbalanced Priorities of Athletics and Academics.* Champaign, Ill.: Leisure Press, 1991.
    The author, an academic adviser to athletes at Southwestern Missouri State University, focuses on the challenges that athletes face in the classroom as they strive to meet the demands imposed on them by fans, the media, and their institutions.
Knight Foundation Commission on Intercollegiate Athletics. *Keeping Faith with the Student-Athlete: A Solid Start, a New Beginning for a New Century.* Charlotte, N.C.: The Knight Foundation, 1993.
    This hard-bound volume collects three reports issued from 1991 to 1993. The commission has made twenty recommendations for change in college athletics, including five-year scholarships, more control by university presidents, and strengthened academic eligibility requirements for athletes.
McMillen, Tom, with Paul Coggins. *Out of Bounds: How the American Sports Establishment Is Being Driven by Greed and Hypocrisy and What Needs to Be Done About It.* New York: Simon & Schuster, 1992.
    McMillen, a former college and professional star and a former congress-

man, indicts a system he has seen up close and personal—a system that in his mind has turned colleges into "sports factories."

Nuwer, Hank. *Recruiting in Sports*. New York: Franklin Watts, 1989.

Offers a step-by-step analysis of the recruiting process for college athletes, with advice to parents and students on their rights and responsibilities.

Rodgers, Pepper. *Fourth and Long Gone*. Atlanta: Peachtree, 1984.

This novel by a former coach is an insider's look at college football.

Sperber, Murray. *College Sports, Inc.: The Athletic Department vs. the University*. New York: Henry Holt and Company, 1990.

Examines the major college athletic department as a business enterprise and provides in-depth coverage of the financial aspects of coaching, recruiting, scholarships, and revenue sources.

Telander, Rick. *The Hundred Yard Lie: The Corruption in College Football and What We Can Do to Stop It*. New York: Simon & Schuster, 1989.

The former All-Big Ten cornerback at Northwestern University wrote this classic exposé of college football before "turning in his badge" as the sport's beat reporter for *Sports Illustrated*.

Walsh, Jim, with Richard Trubo. *Everything You Need to Know about College Recruiting*. Kansas City, Mo.: Andrews and McMeel, 1997.

Provides the most current comprehensive guide of the recruiting process for parents and high school athletes.

Whitford, David. *A Payroll to Meet: A Story of Greed, Corruption & Football at SMU*. New York: Macmillan, 1989.

An in-depth account of perhaps the most wide-ranging pay-for-play scandal in college football history, the only one for which the NCAA imposed the "death penalty," a total cancellation of the 1987 season for the Southern Methodist University team.

Magazines and Newspapers

Barbash, Louis. "Clean Up or Pay Up: Here's the Solution to the College Sports Mess." *Washington Monthly*, July–August 1990: 38–41.

Urges the adoption of "a system of sports without strings," which would end the pretense that athletes are students and instead pay them for their services.

Berkow, Ira. "Whose Hand Was That, Anyway?" *New York Times*, November 18, 1989: 47.

A commentary on the trial of Luther Darville, a University of Minnesota academic adviser who operated a fund to pay football and basketball players.

Brownlee, Shannon, with Nancy S. Linnon. "The Myth of the Student-Athlete." *U.S. News and World Report*, January 8, 1990: 50–52.

A detailed look at the high costs of running a major college sports program.

Brubaker, Bill. "Top Players Face Recruiting Pressure Early." *Washington Post*, February 7, 1988: D1.

A discussion of basketball recruiting in the Washington, D.C., metropolitan area.

Gough, Russ. "Do As We Say, Not As We Do." *Sporting News*, February 5, 1996: 9.

Lambasts several actions taken at the 1996 NCAA convention, which the author labels perpetuations of the sham of amateurism.

Johnson, Constance. "The Rules of the Game." *U.S. News and World Report*, April 13, 1992: 60–63.

An overview of the NCAA's enforcement role in college sports.

Klein, Frederick C. "For the NCAA, Success Often Isn't Academic." *Wall Street Journal*, January 31, 1997: B9.

Reflects on the NCAA's organizational priorities.

Layden, Tim. "Sign Language." *Sports Illustrated*, February 19, 1996: 21–27.

Profiles signing day, when hundreds of high school football stars excite the passions of coaches and fans by announcing which colleges they will attend.

Looney, Douglas. "Cash, Check or Charge: The Discussion Is No Longer Whether We Should Pay College Athletes, But How. OK, Here's How." *Sporting News*, July 1, 1996: 38–43.

The veteran sportswriter outlines a ten-point plan for compensating college athletes.

McG. Thomas, Robert G. "Illicit Pay in Wide Use, Study Contends." *New York Times*, November 17, 1989: A34.

A look at the study by Professor Allen L. Sack of the University of New Haven that documented extensive payments to college athletes.

Rushin, Steve. "Inside the Moat." *Sports Illustrated*, March 3, 1997: 68–83.

Rushin visits the NCAA headquarters in Overland Park, Kansas, and describes the inner workings of the organization and the day-to-day lives of its employees.

Taylor, Jeff, and Mike McCabe. "Fast Wealth for U-M Stars: Taylor, Webber Linked to Large Cash Payments." *Detroit Free Press*, May 31, 1997: 1A.

An exposé of the activities of Ed Martin, a booster of the University of Michigan basketball program, who was investigated by the NCAA, at the request of the university, for making cash payments to players.

Taylor, Phil. "Tangled Web." *Sports Illustrated*, September 15, 1997: 66–76.

Chronicles the illicit activities of basketball star Marcus Camby during his years at the University of Massachusetts.

Wieberg, Steve. "Bozeman Left with Tenuous Future." *USA Today*, July 18, 1997: 1C.

Discusses the dismissal of Todd Bozeman as basketball coach at the University of California at Berkeley.

Organizations to Contact

Center for the Study of Sport in Society
Northeastern University
316 Huntington Avenue, Suite 161 CP
Boston, MA 02115
Phone: 617–373–4025

Fax: 617–373–4566 or 617–373–2096

Internet Web Site: www.sportinsociety.com

Founded in 1984, the organization is dedicated to the idea that the sports community can, and should, take a lead role in bringing about positive social change in the world.

National Collegiate Athletic Association (NCAA)

6201 College Boulevard

Overland Park, KS 66211–2422

Phone: 913–339–1906

Fax: 913–339–0030

Internet Web Site: www.ncaa.org

The NCAA is a national body that oversees the athletic programs of more than 900 member schools. The Web Site contains excellent, up-to-date information on student-athlete graduation rates and the recruiting process.

2

Breaking Down Barriers

African American athletes have made enormous strides in the twentieth century and integrated many playing fields that were once exclusively white domains. But racism remains alive in the sports world today, and the struggle for respect and recognition by African American athletes continues.

The tumultuous scene at Augusta National Golf Club in Georgia in April 1997 bordered on dangerous: on the final hole of the Masters Tournament, Tiger Woods walked down the fairway toward the eighteenth green protected from a swarming throng of admirers by deputy sheriffs and tournament marshals. So hungry were the fans to touch a piece of history that it seemed for a moment as if Woods actually might be mobbed as he finished a record-breaking performance to earn his first major title as a professional golfer. No other winner of the prestigious Masters, created in 1934 by golfing legend Bobby Jones, has produced as much admiration and awe as the sensational golfer who joined the professional ranks in 1996 after a sterling amateur career in which he won three consecutive U.S. Amateur titles.

There was admiration because Woods was merely twenty-one years old, one of the youngest competitors ever to win one of golf's four major titles: the Masters, the United States Open, the British Open, and the Professional Golfers' Association (PGA) Championship. There was awe because of the manner in which he dispatched his opposition, using mammoth drives off the tee to shoot four rounds in eighteen under par. Woods humbled the fabled Augusta National course, winning by a monstrous margin of twelve strokes, the greatest in major tournament play this century. "He's more dominant over the guys he's playing against than I ever was over the guys I played against," said Jack Nicklaus, the

At Augusta National Golf Club in Georgia, 1997 Masters champion Tiger Woods slips into the coveted green jacket with assistance from defending champion Nick Faldo. Woods became the first golfer of color to win one of this sport's four major championships. He achieved victory in a tournament that did not even invite an African American to participate until 1975, the year of his birth, and he did so in spectacular fashion, winning by a record-setting margin of twelve strokes and shooting all four rounds under par. Woods does not describe himself as an African American. Instead, he says he is "Cablinasian," a word of his own invention that stands for Caucasian, black, Indian, and Asian—the four groups that comprise his racial heritage. (AP/WIDE WORLD PHOTOS)

winner of eighteen major professional titles whose course record at Augusta was broken by Woods (Reilly 1997: 37).

Neither Woods's age nor his talent, however, seemed as important as the color of his skin, because he became the first nonwhite to win what has been among the whitest of all sporting events. He triumphed in a bastion of Caucasian supremacy that did not admit its first black member until 1991, in a city where slavery and racial segregation flourished from the Revolutionary War until the civil rights revolution of the 1960s. In an African American neighborhood a few miles south of Augusta National, a dozen caddies from the course assembled outside a tavern to watch the scene on an old black-and-white television set. "Am I excited?" one of them was asked. "If golf was all black and one white guy was doing this, wouldn't *you* be? Hell, yes, I'm excited" (Rushin 1997: 42).

Woods's win in Augusta and his burgeoning career on the PGA Tour have had the same effect on millions more throughout the world, many of whom had no previous interest in golf or even in any other sport. To those millions, however, he is more than simply an African American athlete shattering another racial barrier. In fact, that is a description that Woods himself dislikes and downplays, because he believes it fosters an inaccurate understanding of his ethnic heritage. His mother, Kutilda, is half Chinese and half Thai, and his father, Earl, is half black, one-quarter white, and one-quarter Native American. Woods says he just is who he is—the person you see in front of you. His parents dubbed him the Universal Child, and that nickname comes as close as any other to describing his seemingly limitless appeal, based as much on his poise, wisdom, and humility as on the color of his skin or his immense talent. The young golfer seems to satisfy what sportswriter Gary Smith describes as "a communal craving, a public aching for a superstar free of anger and arrogance and obsession with self" (Smith 1996: 38).

Earl Woods understands the public's desire for a sport hero like his son. It was Earl's iron-handed discipline and tireless support that laid the foundation for Tiger's success. Earl believes his son's temperament will be the pivotal component in a long, successful career. "So many athletes who reach the top had things happen to them as children that created hostility, and they bring that hostility with them," he says. "But that hostility uses up energy. If you can do it without the chip on the shoulder, it frees up all that energy to create" (Smith 1996: 50).

There was a time in America when athletes of color did not have the opportunity to pursue careers in sports with the absence of hostility that seems so remarkable in Tiger Woods. The venues of sport have not always been as welcoming as they are today. On April 15, 1997, just two days after Woods's victory in Augusta, the nation honored one of those athletes of color on the fiftieth anniversary of his most remarkable feat.

When Jack (Jackie) Roosevelt Robinson took the field in 1947 for the Brooklyn Dodgers at Ebbets Field and broke the color barrier in major league baseball (MLB), he had already endured a steady stream of racial animosity. He lived in a society in which white and black were treated separately and unequally in virtually every respect. African Americans suffered crippling discrimination in nearly every facet of life.

Unlike Woods, who had the strong support of two loving parents, Robinson was raised by a mother who worked as a domestic maid after her husband, a Georgia sharecropper, abandoned the family when Jackie was an infant. Although Woods has endured his fair share of racial antagonism, including numerous death threats, he grew up in relative stability in the middle-class suburb of Cypress in southern California. After leaving Georgia, Robinson and his family found a home in an all-white neighborhood in Pasadena, California, where they faced continual harassment, especially after they resisted neighbors' efforts to evict them from their house. And while Woods left Stanford University to pursue a lucrative career on the PGA Tour, Robinson left UCLA after two years as a four-sport star to earn money for his family, convinced that a college degree would be worthless to a black man in America in the 1940s. His only early opportunities in professional sports came as a running back for the Honolulu Bears and the Los Angeles Bulldogs, minor league football teams.

Drafted by the army in 1942, Robinson was barred from the officers' candidate school and the baseball team at Fort Riley in Kansas. At Fort Hood in Texas in 1944, he faced a court-martial for refusing to step to the back of the bus to make room for a white soldier. In 1945, after he signed a contract for $600 a week and a $3,500 bonus to play for the Montreal Royals, a Brooklyn Dodger farm team, Montreal manager Clay Hopper voiced his opinion bluntly to Dodger owner Branch Rickey: "Do you really think that a nigger is a human being?" (Robinson 1995: 17–21, 49).

Robinson's ordeal continued during his ten-year career with the Dodgers. All of the nicknames bestowed on him by the press reflected his skin color: the Ebony Ty Cobb, the Dark Destroyer, the Jim Thorpe of His Race. And because he had notably dark skin, described by one observer as "imperial black," Robinson faced added insults. In the first two months of his first season, he was hit by pitches six times—as many times as any other player in the National League had been hit in the entire 1946 season. He also endured high-flying spikes from malicious base runners.

A proud and fiercely competitive man, Robinson was ordered by Branch Rickey to ignore the silent stares, physical abuse, death threats, and verbal taunts that he endured from fans, reporters, opponents, and even his own teammates. He obeyed those orders only with great difficulty. Instead of retaliating, his natural inclination since childhood, he focused on becoming the best player he could. He won the 1947 Rookie of the Year award and the 1949 Most Valuable Player award and played in six World Series and six All-Star games. When he died of diabetes in 1973 at age fifty-three, his legacy was assured. "Jackie Robinson stands for bravery, dignity, intelligence, intensity," said outfielder Willie McGee of the St. Louis Cardinals in 1997. "He changed baseball and America. I wish he was still here to change them some more. As far as I'm concerned, he is the man of the century" (Wulf 1997: 86).

As athletes of color and champions, Jackie Robinson and Tiger Woods stand half a century apart. Robinson struggled in an era of entrenched segregation, when most of society's institutions, and virtually all of the venues of sports competition, were white domains. Woods is beginning his career in a time when America has lived for a generation with the Civil Rights Act of 1964, busing to achieve racial balance in public schools, and affirmative action programs to promote minority hiring and educational opportunities. The nation also has seen the full racial integration of most of its playing fields. On the surface, it appears as if African Americans have made significant strides in the five decades between Robinson's first game with the Brooklyn Dodgers and Woods's triumphant victory march at the Masters. But beneath the surface, away from the pomp and glitter of high-profile superstardom, their struggle for respect and recognition continues.

PROGRESS ON AND OFF THE FIELD

The large number of black athletes in the three major professional sports—football, baseball, and basketball—is an ongoing source of pride and inspiration for the African American population. African Americans make up about 13 percent of the population of the United States, but they are a dominant presence in major league stadiums, ballparks, and arenas. In the National Football League (NFL), 67 percent of the 1,815 players in 1996 were black. In MLB in the same year, 17 percent of the players were black, and 20 percent were Latino. And in the National Basketball Association (NBA), 80 percent of the 361 players in 1996 were black (Simons 1997: 54).

African American athletes who succeed in professional sports are rewarded handsomely for their efforts. In the NFL in 1996, the average annual player salary was $767,000; the minimum salary permitted under the players' collective bargaining agreement with the owners was $131,000. In MLB, the average annual salary was $1.1 million and the minimum salary $150,000. In the NBA, the average salary was $2 million, the minimum $247,500 (Simons 1997: 47–48). The most talented and successful athletes also reap rewards off the field in the form of commercial endorsements. In the upper echelon of earners is home run slugger Ken Griffey, Jr., of the Seattle Mariners, one of baseball's most charismatic performers. In addition to his $8.5 million annual salary, which he will earn every year from 1997 to 2000, Griffey now earns about $5 million annually in endorsements. Among the major companies receiving Griffey's endorsement in 1997 were Nike, Pizza Hut, Nintendo, General Mills, Rawlings, Gargoyles eyewear, and Upper Deck baseball cards (Simons 1997: 54).

In addition to their prominent presence as players in professional football, baseball, and basketball, African Americans in the 1990s made notable advances in several other parts of the sports world:

- In 1997, Orlando Henry (Tubby) Smith signed a five-year contract to coach basketball at the University of Kentucky, which has fought the stigma of racism since the long coaching tenure of the legendary Adolph Rupp from 1930 to 1972. Rupp waited forty years before recruiting an African American to play for the Wildcats. Head coach Rick Pitino, who guided the school to its sixth national title in 1996 with five black starters, did much to erase the stigma. But some doubt that Smith, the sixth of seventeen children born into a Maryland farming family, will be embraced warmly as the first black coach in Lexington, where two statues of Confederate soldiers still stand on the lawn of the Fayette County courthouse. The former assistant coach of the Wildcats, who also headed teams at the University of Georgia and the University of Tulsa, downplayed those concerns. "It's more important to be competent and to be judged on the content of my character and not the color of my skin," he said on the day of his appointment. "I expect to be here a long time. We want to put down deep roots" (Weir 1997: 2C). When Smith guided the Wildcats to their seventh NCAA title in 1998 in his first year at the helm, he took a giant step toward his goal of remaining in Lexington.
- In 1995, Mike Grier of the Edmonton Oilers became the first American-born and -trained black to play in the National Hockey League (NHL). The six-foot, 230-pound right wing starred at Boston University before entering the professional ranks (Wallace 1995: B14).
- In 1997, brothers Kevin and Carl Poston, owners of Professional Sports Planning of Farmington Hills, Michigan, became the first African American sports agents to represent a first-round pick in the NFL draft. They negotiated a contract with the St. Louis Rams on behalf of Ohio State University tackle Orlando Pace. The Pos-

Once regarded as too big and slow for the sport, Edmonton Oilers' right wing Mike Grier is the first black American to play in the National Hockey League. Grier joined the Oilers after a strong career at Boston University. The first minority player in the NHL was Willie O'Ree, a black Canadian who played from 1958 to 1961. In 1998, there were nine black players in the NHL: Grier, Anson Carter (Boston Bruins), Jarome Iginla (Calgary Flames), Kevin Weekes and Peter Worrell (Florida Panthers), Nathan Lafayette (Los Angeles Kings), Grant Fuhr (St. Louis Blues), Sandy McCarthy (Tampa Bay Lightning), and Donald Brashear (Vancouver Canucks). (AP/WIDE WORLD PHOTOS)

tons' feat was a milestone because sports agents, particularly those who represent high-profile players, are overwhelmingly white. Only 45 of the 320 active agents registered with the NFL in 1996 were African American (Shropshire 1996: 132).

- In 1996, Jackson State University in Mississippi became the first historically black college to send a team to the National Collegiate Athletic Association (NCAA) golf tournament in the ninety-nine-year history of the event (*Sports Illustrated* 1996: 21–22).

These success stories, and others like them, have contributed greatly to the view that the sports world in America is free, open, and democratic—that it is, indeed, the place in our society where the truest and most inspiring enactments of the American dream can be found. But the acceptance of African American athletes, coaches, owners, and agents does not mean that skin color has lost its relevance in sports or the rest of society.

A DREAM DEFERRED

The progress made and status attained by African American athletes in the 1990s has not created a sports world free of the taint of racism. In the view of those who see the sports world as an extension of society at large, that may be an ideal that is impossible to achieve. Several prominent sports figures in recent years have made statements that reveal both conscious and unconscious racial attitudes that continue to permeate much of the sports world:

- In 1987, on the television news show *Nightline* honoring the fortieth anniversary of Jackie Robinson's entry into MLB, Los Angeles Dodgers general manager Al Campanis discussed the lack of black managers and executives in the sport with interviewer Ted Koppel. "I truly believe that they may not have some of the necessities to be, let's say, a field manager or perhaps a general manager," Campanis said. Although Campanis insisted that he did not intend to stereotype or demean African Americans, he was fired by the Dodgers after the strong and nearly universal negative public reaction (Shropshire 1996: 21–22). Soon after, Toronto Blue Jays manager Cito Gaston exploded the myth of the incompetent black manager when he piloted his team to World Series titles in 1992 and 1993.
- In 1997, golfer Fuzzy Zoeller traded quips with reporters after Tiger Woods's Masters victory and joked about the upcoming 1998 dinner at Augusta for past tournament winners where

Woods, according to Masters tradition, would select the menu as defending champion. "Tell him not to serve fried chicken next year ... or collard greens, or whatever the hell they serve," Zoeller said. When tapes of the exchange were broadcast on the Cable News Network one week later, Zoeller faced a storm of criticism and lost his sponsorship and promotion contracts with Kmart Corporation (*Sports Illustrated* 1997: 24).

- Football commentator Jimmy "the Greek" Snyder, in an interview with a Washington, D.C., television reporter on Martin Luther King Day in 1988, offered this explanation for the dominance of black athletes in professional football: "The difference between blacks and whites goes all the way back to the Civil War when, during the slave period, the slave owner would breed his big black [man] with his big [black] woman so that he could have a big black kid—that's where it all started. The black is a better athlete to begin with because he's been bred to be that way because of his thigh size and big size." Like Campanis, Snyder was dismissed from his job for his comments (Shropshire 1996: 23).

- In 1993, several offensive remarks made by Marge Schott, the owner of the Cincinnati Reds baseball team, were exposed during a wrongful dismissal suit filed against the team by a former employee. According to testimony in the case, Schott described two of her players as "million-dollar niggers" and said she would "rather have a trained monkey working for me than a nigger." Schott also complained about "money-grubbing Jews" and said, "Hitler had the right idea for them, but went too far." Her fellow team owners fined Schott $25,000 and barred her from overseeing the day-to-day operations of her team for one year (Shropshire 1996: 24).

- In 1997, the NHL suspended Chris Simon of the Washington Capitals for three games after he directed racial slurs at Mike Grier during a game in Landover, Maryland. Florida Panthers winger Peter Worrell was the target of racial insults on the ice in the same year.

These remarks, as well as those of others that are not reported or publicized, indicate that although America is half a century removed from the toxic racial atmosphere in which Jackie Robinson made his major league debut, there exists a stubborn resistance to full acceptance of African Americans in all facets of the sports world. In his provocative study *In Black and White: Race and Sports in America*, Kenneth L. Shropshire describes the situation as one grounded in a reluctance to part with privilege and prerogative:

For African-Americans to attain a greater role in the power positions in sports, a representative role, some people—*white* people—will have to give something—white power—up. In sports what must be sacrificed is the right of whites, primarily white men, to attain top-level management positions and sell franchises to their white friends. Since the beginning of sports in this country, private personal networks have controlled the power positions. The sacrifice is not so much giving up one's own job as it is giving up the power to give a job to someone else. This power has real, practical importance when the economy of the sports world is taken into account. The business of sports is not downsizing but expanding. Each year at least one of the professional sports leagues adds or contemplates adding a new franchise. Jobs continue to emerge in sports while they disappear from other industries. To begin to do business in a different way is an almost unthinkable sacrifice. All of the parties need to remove their color blinders and recognize the harm of discrimination and the positive value that diversity brings. (Shropshire 1996: 34)

Nowhere else has Shropshire's concern been more boldly illuminated than in the NFL, where African Americans have struggled for decades to gain head coaching positions in a system that is an excellent example of what he calls a "private personal network." After the 1996 season, there were ten openings for head coaching positions in the league. Twenty-four candidates were interviewed for those positions, and only one—Philadelphia Eagles defensive coordinator Emmitt Thomas—was black. He did not receive an employment offer.

Among those bypassed completely for interviews were Johnny Roland, an assistant coach for twenty-two years with the Green Bay Packers, Philadelphia Eagles, Chicago Bears, New York Jets, and St. Louis Rams; and Sherm Lewis, offensive coordinator of the Super Bowl champion Green Bay Packers. When the Rams fired head coach Rich Brooks, Roland was ignored as a potential successor while the team's management hired Dick Vermeil, a white man who had been out of coaching for fifteen years. Lewis was ignored despite his four coaching appearances in the Super Bowl and his guidance of the league's most potent offense. "Most people draw from organizations that are successful," he said. "If they ran it like any other big business they'd look at the successful organizations and go get one of their top people. That's what IBM would do" (Guss 1997: 56).

At the beginning of the 1998 season, the thirty-team league had three African American head coaches: Dennis Green of the Minnesota Vikings, Ray Rhodes of the Philadelphia Eagles, and Tony Dungy of the Tampa Bay Buccaneers. They followed in the footsteps of Art Shell, the first coach to break the NFL color barrier. He assumed the helm of the Los Angeles Raiders in 1989 and is now the offensive line coach for the Atlanta Falcons. All four men are deeply aware of the obstacles that qualified African American coaching candidates face in the NFL, where many team owners, members of the media, and fans continue to believe that blacks make better running backs, wide receivers, and defensive backs than head coaches.

Dungy tried twice for the head coaching job in Philadelphia that now belongs to Rhodes. He also rejected a 1993 offer to lead the Jacksonville Jaguars, an expansion team. He was once told by a team executive that he would never get a head coaching job in the league until he shaved his goatee, which the executive thought made him look too much like an angry black radical from the 1960s (Chappell 1996: 150). After Buccaneer owner Malcolm Glazer offered Dungy a six-year, $3.6 million contract in 1996, he responded by molding the team into a serious title contender for the first time in its history. "I don't think anyone is going to say, 'This guy's good but he's black, so I can't hire him,' " says Dungy. "But the thought process is, Is this what I really want? This isn't what I perceive the coach to be. And many times the owner may not even know why. So the reason becomes: He's too soft-spoken or too young or too old" (Price 1996: 70).

It is this subliminal perception that lies at the heart of the coaching controversy. Team owners and general managers, as businesspeople, prefer to hire candidates who are similar to coaches who have already achieved success or are similar to coaches they have known personally and admired. Those coaches invariably have been older, conservative white men who had reputations as strong leaders and strict disciplinarians: Vince Lombardi of the Green Bay Packers, Paul Brown of the Cleveland Browns and the Cincinnati Bengals, Tom Landry of the Dallas Cowboys. Consequently, team owners and general managers often pass over qualified blacks and hire whites with whom they are familiar through business, social, and family connections—and who conform to their long-held ideal about what a successful coach should be.

In an effort to promote minority hiring, the NFL established the Coaches Fellowship Program in the late 1980s. The program allows entire coaching staffs, primarily from the historically black colleges and universities of the South, to work with NFL coaching staffs during preseason training camp and the regular season. About twenty of the 200 participants have been hired as assistant coaches in the league. The program has its critics, who ask why it is necessary only for black coaches, and not white ones, to prove their talent and worth during a four-week internship program. But even its critics do not deny that the program has quickened the pace of minority hiring in the NFL coaching ranks.

"I think it's a matter of commitment," says Rachel Robinson, the widow of the baseball pioneer who has herself become a vibrant spokes-woman for racial justice in the years since her husband's death. "I think it's a matter of people in leadership positions deciding that they're not going to discriminate. They are going to open up opportunities to the best available candidate, including minorities. And I don't think we're there yet" (Guss 1997: 84).

There are few people in the sports world of any color who would disagree with Rachel Robinson's assessment. In spite of Tiger Woods, Tubby Smith, and all the other African Americans who have broken barriers in recent years, nearly all would agree that the words of her husband, Jackie, in his autobiography still describe the situation of African Americans in sports today: "I know that I am a black man in a white world. In 1972, in 1947, at my birth in 1919, I know that I never had it made."

AFRICAN AMERICAN ATHLETES: A CENTURY OF FIRSTS

1908: First black man to win an Olympic gold medal: John Baxter (Doc) Taylor, a sprinter who ran the third leg of the 4×100-meter relay for the American team in London.

1920: First black men to play in the National Football League: Frederick Douglas (Fritz) Pollard of the Akron Pros and Robert W. (Rube) Marshall of the Rock Island Independents, who played in the league's inaugural season.

1947: First black man to play for a major league baseball team: Jackie Robinson of the Brooklyn Dodgers.

1948: First black woman to win an Olympic gold medal: Alice Coachman, who captured the high jump competition at the Summer Games in London.

1950: First black man to play in the National Basketball Association: Earl Lloyd of the Washington Capitals.

1957: First black woman to win the Wimbledon singles tennis crown: Althea Gibson. She also won the U.S. national title that year at Forest Hills. She repeated the two-title sweep in 1958.

1960: First black woman to win three Olympic gold medals: Wilma Rudolph, a polio survivor, who won the 100-meters, 200-meters and 4×100-meter relay at the Summer Games in Rome.

1967: First black man appointed head coach in the National Basketball Association: Bill Russell of the Boston Celtics. He served as player-coach on the Celtics' title teams of 1968 and 1969.

1968: First black man to win the U.S. Open tennis crown: Arthur Ashe.

In 1975, he became the first black man to win the Wimbledon singles title in England.

1975: First black man to manage a major league baseball team: Frank Robinson of the Cleveland Indians. He also managed the San Francisco Giants and the Baltimore Orioles.

1988: First black woman to win four Olympic medals in one Olympics: Florence Griffith Joyner, who earned three golds and one silver in the Summer Games in Los Angeles.

1989: First black man appointed head coach in the National Football League: Art Shell of the Los Angeles Raiders.

1991: First black man to race in the Indianapolis 500: Willy T. Ribbs.

1996: First black woman to win an Olympic gold medal as a gymnast: Dominique Dawes, a member of the American women's team in Atlanta.

1997: First black man to win one of the four major professional golf titles: Tiger Woods, who won the Masters Tournament in Augusta, Georgia, by a record margin of twelve strokes.

TOPICS FOR DISCUSSION

1. Many African American athletes and coaches say skin color has not lost its relevance in the sports world; they still face discrimination on the playing fields. Do you agree with this point of view? Explain your answer.

2. Professional golfer Fuzzy Zoeller was criticized in 1997 for making joking references to fried chicken and collard greens when discussing Tiger Woods. Critics thought he was demeaning African Americans with stereotyped comments about the type of food they eat. Others say Zoeller's remarks were harmless. Which view do you think is more accurate? Why?

3. Marge Schott, the owner of the Cincinnati Reds baseball team, was barred from operating the Reds for one year after her remarks about "million-dollar niggers" and "money-grubbing Jews" were exposed in the media. Was Schott's punishment too harsh or too light? Should she be allowed to continue as the Reds' owner, or should she be forced to give up her position?

4. Attorney and author Kenneth Shropshire believes that no significant racial changes will occur in the sports world until more African Americans attain top-level management positions with teams and actually own teams. Do you agree with Shropshire's point of view?

5. Some researchers and commentators now believe it may be possible to demonstrate that black athletes are genetically superior to their

white counterparts. Is the athletic superiority of blacks a myth and/
or a stereotype, or is it something that can be objectively measured
and determined to be accurate?

RESOURCES AND REFERENCES

Books

Ashe, Arthur. *A Hard Road to Glory: A History of the African-American Athlete*. New
York: Warner Books, 1988.
Ashe's three-volume work is a comprehensive compilation of African
American athletes in America from 1619 to the present. It contains little
analysis but includes career statistical records of numerous athletes, as
well as team-by-team listings.
Early, Gerald. *Tuxedo Junction: Essays on American Culture*. Hopewell, N.J.: Ecco
Press, 1989.
In a book dealing with broad issues of American culture, Early offers
cogent essays on African American sports heroes Joe Louis, Paul Robeson,
and Jackie Robinson. For advanced readers.
Lapchick, Richard. *Five Minutes to Midnight: Race and Sports in the 1990's*. Lanham,
Md.: Madison Press, 1991.
The son of St. John's University basketball coach Joe Lapchick recounts
his youth and his experiences as a social activist seeking justice for African
American athletes. Lapchick is director of the Center for the Study of Sport
in Society at Northeastern University.
Robinson, Jackie. *I Never Had It Made*. New York: Putnam, 1972; Hopewell, N.J.:
Ecco Press, 1995.
The autobiography of the Brooklyn Dodgers second baseman who broke
the color barrier in major league baseball.
Shropshire, Kenneth L. *In Black and White: Race and Sports in America*. New York:
New York University Press, 1996.
Shropshire, a practicing sports attorney and former general counsel for
major league baseball, provides in-depth analysis of nearly all of the issues
affecting race and sports, including hiring practices, the roots of racism,
and team ownership by minorities.
Sifford, Charlie, with James Gallo. *"Just Let Me Play": The Story of Charlie Sifford,
the First Black PGA Golfer*. Latham, N.Y.: British American Publishing, 1992.
An engrossing testimonial of the struggles and prejudices Sifford faced as
a pioneer black golfer in the 1950s and 1960s.
Strege, John. *Tiger: A Biography of Tiger Woods*. New York: Broadway Books, 1997.
Chronicles the personal and professional life of the young golf superstar.
Wiggins, David K. *Glory Bound: Black Athletes in a White America*. Syracuse, N.Y.:
Syracuse University Press, 1997.
Eleven essays exploring the tumultuous relationship between mainstream
white America and African American athletes. Subjects include the
nineteenth-century jockey Isaac Murphy, racial unrest in college campuses
in the 1960s, and the debate over black athletic superiority.

Magazines and Newspapers

Anderson, Dave. "The System the NFL Must Change." *New York Times*, March 25, 1997: B9.

A commentary on the persistent refusal of NFL owners to hire African American candidates for head coaching positions in the league.

Blum, Debra E. "Commission's 'Fairness Index' Rates 152 Colleges in NCAA's Division I." *Chronicle of Higher Education*, November 24, 1995: A32.

A discussion of the survey of university graduation rates and hiring practices conducted by the Rainbow Commission on Fairness in Athletics.

Blum, Debra E. " 'Eyes on the Prize': Leader of Black Coaches Sees Fight to Get Athletes into College as Part of Broader Struggle." *Chronicle of Higher Education*, July 13, 1994: A33–34.

A profile of Rudy Washington, founder of the Black Coaches Association.

Chappell, Kevin. "The 3 Coaches." *Ebony*, November 1996: 144–50.

Profiles three African American head coaches in the NFL: Dennis Green of the Minnesota Vikings, Tony Dungy of the Tampa Bay Buccaneers, and Ray Rhodes of the Philadelphia Eagles.

Deford, Frank. "Crossing the Bar." *Newsweek*, April 14, 1997: 53.

The veteran sportswriter comments on Jackie Robinson's achievement, calling him a "gifted and complicated man" who helped "set the table" for the civil rights revolution of the 1960s.

Guss, Greg. "Skin Games." *Sport*, May 1997: 53–58, 84.

An examination of the state of race in sports, fifty years after the breaking of baseball's color barrier.

Hatfield, Dolph. "The Jack Nicklaus Syndrome." *Humanist*, July–August 1996: 38–39.

Discusses comments concerning African American athletes by golfer Jack Nicklaus and baseball executive Al Campanis.

Nack, William. "The Breakthrough." *Sports Illustrated*, May 5, 1997: 56–67.

A detailed account of Jackie Robinson's first months as a major league baseball player with the Brooklyn Dodgers.

Nance, Roscoe. "Thomas' Ownership Move Bridges Color Barrier." *USA Today*, May 2, 1997: 4C.

A report on former NBA star Isaiah Thomas's efforts to become majority owner of the Toronto Raptors.

Price, S. L. "About Time." *Sports Illustrated*, June 10, 1996: 68–74.

A profile of Tampa Bay Buccaneers head coach Tony Dungy and his football odyssey.

Reilly, Rick. "Strokes of Genius." *Sports Illustrated*, April 21, 1997: 34–45.

A report on Tiger Woods's victory at the Masters Tournament in 1997.

Rushin, Steve. "Black and White: As They Watched Tiger Woods Make History, Some Augustans Were Reminded of Progress Yet to Be Made." *Sports Illustrated*, April 21, 1997: 42.

Several African American caddies at Augusta National Golf Club reflect on Tiger Woods's Masters victory.

Simons, John. "Improbable Dreams: African Americans Are a Dominant Presence in Professional Sports. Do Blacks Suffer as a Result?" *U.S. News and World Report*, March 24, 1997: 46–54.

A discussion of the fixation on sports success in the African American community and the negative repercussions that it creates in other aspects of life and the work world.

Smith, Claire. "A Grand Tribute to Robinson and His Moment." *New York Times*, April 16, 1997: A1.

A report on the fiftieth-anniversary celebration of Jackie Robinson's entry into baseball at Shea Stadium in New York, an event attended by President Bill Clinton and Rachel Robinson, the player's widow.

Smith, Gary. "The Chosen One." *Sports Illustrated*, December 23, 1996: 28–52.

Profiles Tiger Woods, the magazine's 1996 Sportsman of the Year, with an accent on the role his parents played in preparing him for life as a professional athlete.

Sports Illustrated. "Teeing Up for History." May 20, 1996: 21–22.

A brief report on the Jackson State University golf team.

Wallace, William N. "To Be Young, Black and Gifted on Ice." *New York Times*, February 7, 1995: B14.

A profile of hockey player Mike Grier.

Walsh, Bill. "Reaching across the N.F.L.'s Color Line." *New York Times*, January 23, 1998: A19.

The Hall of Fame coach discusses ways to promote minority hiring in the NFL.

Weir, Tom. "Kentucky, Smith Forge New Beginning." *USA Today*, May 13, 1997: 1C.

An account of the hiring of Tubby Smith, the first African American basketball coach at the University of Kentucky.

Wulf, Steve. "The Lion and the Tiger: A Golfer Teaches Us a Lesson We Should Have Learned 50 Years Ago from a Baseball Player." *Time*, April 28, 1997: 86.

Discusses the common ground created among disparate members of society when they rally around the achievements of sports pioneers like Jackie Robinson and Tiger Woods.

Organizations to Contact

Black Coaches Association
6601 Center Drive West, Suite 500
Los Angeles, CA 90045
Phone: 310–342–8253
Fax: 310–342–8254
Internet Web Site: www.bca.org
The association promotes the creation of a positive environment in which issues related to minority coaches in sports can be exposed, discussed, and resolved.

National Baseball Hall of Fame and Museum
P.O. Box 590

25 Main Street
Cooperstown, NY 13326
Phone: 607–547–7200
Fax: 607–547–2044
E-mail: info@baseballhalloffame.org
Internet Web Site: www.baseballhalloffame.org
The Hall of Fame Library includes a significant collection of materials on the history of the Negro Leagues and the history of African American players in the sport.

3

Slaves to the Scale

The compulsion to stay thin can become an overwhelming force in the lives of many athletes, especially females who compete in gymnastics and figure skating. Athletes who become slaves to the scale place themselves at serious risk of injury and even death. What are the forces in sports and society that demand such dangerous sacrifices?

The deaths came with alarming swiftness at the end of 1997, and for a brief moment they turned the attention of the sports world away from Tiger Woods and Michael Jordan and the upcoming Winter Olympic Games and Super Bowl, and toward a much more obscure activity. Amateur wrestling, one of the oldest and most elementary of all sports, and one that is steadily disappearing from America's college campuses, was rocked to its embattled core by the passing of three competitors. All three had exercised themselves to death in the midst of strenuous physical workouts, consumed by an urgent desire to lose weight in order to gain a competitive advantage over their opponents.

The fact that the three young men died within a span of one month may have been a freakish coincidence, but it forced a hard and direct look at a host of controversial training techniques. Those techniques, in all of what one coach called their many "hideous forms," require athletes to become slaves to the scale and make weight reduction the top priority of their athletic lives. In wrestling, as well as in other sports as varied as horse racing, swimming, diving, distance running, figure skating, and gymnastics, competitors risk their health and lives to get thin and stay thin.

Billy Saylor, a freshman at Campbell University in Buies Creek, North Carolina, was the first of the three wrestlers to die. He suffered cardiac arrest on November 9 after riding an exercise bicycle in a rubber suit as he tried to drop his weight from 201 to 195 pounds. Twelve days later, Joseph LaRosa, a senior at the University of Wisconsin-LaCrosse, died of heat stroke wearing a rubber suit and two sweatsuits. By the time he collapsed, his body temperature had reached 108 degrees. Like Saylor, LaRosa was riding a stationary bicycle. And on December 9, University of Michigan wrestler Jeff Reese died trying to shed seventeen pounds in preparation for a meet against Michigan State University. Clad in a rubberized wet suit inside a training room at Crisler Arena heated to 92 degrees, Reese collapsed and died after becoming dizzy and lightheaded. The medical cause of death was listed as rhabdomyolysis—the cellular breakdown of skeletal muscle. That breakdown, coupled with extreme dehydration due to lack of water intake, caused Reese's heart and kidneys to fail.

What force compelled these three athletes to do something that they knew was not only abnormally stressful but downright dangerous? The goal for each was to become a better wrestler. Like boxing, the sport is contested in weight classes. A wrestler who drops his weight to the highest number of pounds permitted in a particular class is believed to have an advantage over a wrestler who is competing at his natural weight within that class. That advantage arises because when the heavier wrestler loses weight, he lowers his percentage of body fat, which increases aerobic capacity. Successful weight reduction requires the wrestler to maintain his natural strength advantage as he sheds pounds and lowers his percentage of body fat.

That requirement is not always met. There are those who believe that only the most physically gifted can accomplish the trick without weakening themselves to the point where they gain no advantage over their opponents. But that belief is not common in the world of college wrestling. There, a wrestler's ability to lose a large amount of weight quickly is viewed as a badge of machismo. Many go through rapid weight loss cycles as many as thirty times in a single season (Thompson and Sherman 1993: 48). The activity is tacitly endorsed by many coaches, who often lecture against radical weight cutting but then ignore it when it actually takes place (Fleming 1998: 134). The same point of view was apparent for many years in the rules of the National Collegiate Athletic Association (NCAA). The NCAA strongly advised wrestlers against using a number of weight loss techniques but did not ban them.

The death of Jeff Reese exposed the trauma of weight cutting at its most extreme. Saylor and LaRosa were trying to lose relatively small amounts of weight. But Reese's goal was to earn the open spot on the Michigan roster in the 150-pound weight class. To do that, he had to drop 17 pounds, nearly 10 percent of his body weight. Reese's father complained that Michigan wrestling coach Dale Bahr gave his son only four days to accomplish the task. Bahr responded that he issued no such order. He compared Reese to a student who waits until the night before a final exam to review an entire semester of academic work (*USA Today* 1997: 3C).

Reese's death also raised the specter of drug use. No steroids, alcohol, or other drugs were found in his body, but tests did reveal the presence of creatine, a legal substance that has been used by thousands of athletes, including sprinters Michael Johnson and Linford Christie and swimmer Amy Van Dyken. Produced by the liver and kidneys, creatine is an organic compound found naturally in muscle tissue. It increases physical strength and enhances speedy recovery from strenuous workouts. A synthetic version that is billed as a supplement to the natural substance can be obtained without a medical prescription. Sports physicians measure the improvement in muscular strength provided by creatine at between 5 and 10 percent. There is no way to determine if the creatine found in Reese's body was natural or synthetic, but he apparently suffered from its most negative side effect: creatine keeps water inside muscles and causes the rest of the body to overheat. When the substance is produced or ingested in large amounts, the overheating can be drastic.

In January 1998, the NCAA took action in response to these deaths. The organization, which has monitored deaths in college sports since 1982, did not document a fatality in wrestling until the three in 1997. The new rules were designed to prevent any further deaths. They banned the use of saunas, rubber suits, and diuretics, drugs taken to increase urination and reduce body weight. They also banned the use of exercise rooms with temperatures above 79 degrees. Existing rules already barred laxatives, fluid restriction, self-induced vomiting, and steam rooms. Perhaps most important, the new NCAA rules established the weigh-in time for wrestlers as two hours before the match, not twenty-four hours before, as under the previous rules. The point of the change is to prevent wrestlers from using that twenty-four-hour period between weigh-in and match to "recover" from the negative effects of drastic weight cutting. That chance for recovery often promotes even more extreme actions by wrestlers. The new weigh-in time is designed to prevent wrestlers from entering matches in an even more weakened condition.

The University of Michigan made changes in its own training procedures that went beyond those made by the NCAA. Athletic director Tom Goss, who considered dropping the sport completely after Reese's death, banned all plastic, rubber, and nylon exercise suits. He also required daily weigh-ins by all wrestlers and participation in a nutrition education program by coaches, student-athletes, and athletic trainers.

The steps taken in college wrestling to confront and reduce the dangers of weight reduction far exceed those taken in other sports where low body weight is a priority. Indeed, in most other sports no steps are taken

University of Michigan wrestler Jeff Reese grapples with his opponent during a college meet. The twenty-one-year-old from Wellsburg, New York, died on December 9, 1997, from dehydration and trauma suffered during intensive weight loss. After his death, the National Collegiate Athletic Association imposed strict new weight-cutting rules to prevent further injuries and deaths to wrestlers. Coach Greg Strobel of Lehigh University says that educating coaches and wrestlers is the key to implementing the new rules effectively. (AP/WIDE WORLD PHOTOS)

at all, and many competitors suffer the consequences. Like wrestlers, jockeys can become obsessed with their weight and sit for hours in saunas and hot boxes to melt away the excess pounds that can send them to the unemployment office. They often use appetite suppressants, diuretics, and laxatives (Thompson and Sherman 1993: 51–52). Steve Cauthen, the star jockey who guided Affirmed to horse racing's Triple Crown in 1978, has said that a major reason for his retirement from the sport in 1983 was his unwillingness to continue the ordeal of weight reduction. Greg LeMond, the cyclist who captured the Tour de France title three times, believes that his failed efforts to lose weight greatly hindered his ability to compete in the later stages of his career.

For male athletes, the process of radical weight reduction can lead to shortened careers, damaged health, and death. As perilous as the process is in the sports of wrestling, horse racing, and cycling, it bears only a limited resemblance to the situation faced by many female athletes in the sports of figure skating, gymnastics, diving, and distance running. In those arenas, the compulsion to stay thin can overwhelm even the strongest personalities. One of those was gymnast Christy Henrich. Nicknamed Extra Tough because of her spartan work ethic and physical courage, Henrich became an elite gymnast in her teens and barely missed making the 1988 Olympic team. Henrich paid the ultimate price for her success. In 1994 she starved herself to death in a tragic effort to maintain her competitive edge. "It feels like there's a beast inside of me, like a monster," she once said. "It feels evil."

BEAUTY AND THE BEAST

The beast inside Christy Henrich was anorexia nervosa, a disease estimated to affect 7 to 8 million people in the United States. Nearly 90 percent of its victims are female, and the majority of those females are between the ages of fourteen and twenty-five (Sirimarco 1994: 14). *Anorexia* means "without appetite," and it bluntly describes the most visible behavior of the disease's victims: they stop eating. The lack of food intake spawns a host of physical problems that include abnormal thyroid function, impaired breathing, erratic heart rhythms, hypothermia, weakened bones, and amenorrhea, the cessation of the menstrual cycle. As an anorexic's body battles the cold that becomes an enemy to its survival, it often grows lanugo—fine hair that develops on the face and arms to provide an extra layer of warmth. After a victim has suffered the disease for four or five years, X-rays of her body can resemble those of an eighty-year-old. The bones look like hollowed honeycombs, sapped of the calcium that has been shipped to other parts of the body to compensate for the acute shortage brought on by malnutrition.

Bulimia is the other major eating disorder that afflicts young women.

Bulimics achieve and maintain low body weight not by self-starvation but by binge eating, which is followed by purging through self-induced vomiting, excessive exercise, fasting, or the ingestion of laxatives or diuretics. Bulimics generally suffer the same physical degradation as anorexics. Those who practice self-induced vomiting also face additional problems, including swollen salivary glands, gum disease, gastrointestinal disorders, increased tooth decay, and the loss of tooth enamel.

Anorexia and bulimia are extremely difficult to cure, because the medical community has never been able to determine precisely what causes them and because the diseases in their early stages often are not recognizable by the afflicted individuals or those who surround her. But researchers have identified a number of factors that seem to encourage their development. Young women who develop eating disorders often are raised in families that display a preoccupation with body weight and physical appearance, rely on external standards of self-worth and success, and include a history of depression and drug and alcohol abuse. The victims themselves often display low self-esteem, a strong fear of disapproval, a preoccupation with food, and an irrational belief that their bodies are unattractive (Thompson and Sherman 1993: 4–8).

The young women who are psychologically susceptible to eating disorders receive little support from society's elders or institutions. Indeed, physical thinness in females is generally considered a prime virtue in America. Joan Jacobs Brumberg, a professor of history and women's studies at Cornell University, asserts that girls in the twentieth century "have come to believe that the body is the ultimate expression of the self." In her book *The Body Project* (1997), Brumberg writes that skin, breasts, hair, eyes, legs, and, above all, low body weight have become the dominant preoccupation of adolescent females. Spurred by a ravenously commercial culture that celebrates physical form, young females succumb to the pressure to maintain the perfect body.

Nowhere is that pressure more intense than in the so-called appearance sports—those in which winners and losers are determined not by objective, numerical standards but by the subjective appraisals of judges. It is no surprise that in the two most popular appearance sports—gymnastics and figure skating—the most famous athletes are not men, but women. Very few women have earned places in the pantheon of American sports heroes, and a sizable number of them have been tennis and track and field stars such as Billie Jean King, Chris Evert Lloyd, Wilma Rudolph, and Florence Griffith-Joyner. But a nearly equal number have been Olympic medalists in gymnastics and figure skating: Cathy Rigby, Mary Lou Retton, Shannon Miller, Peggy Fleming, Dorothy Hamill, Kristi Yamaguchi, and Tara Lipinski.

In her powerful book *Little Girls in Pretty Boxes* (1995), sports columnist Joan Ryan shines a revealing light on the ordeals of young gymnasts and

Figure skater Michelle Kwan is a superstar in a so-called appearance sport, where body weight and physical looks often make the difference between winning and finishing second. She won her first world figure skating championship in 1996 at age fifteen and earned a silver medal in the 1998 Winter Olympics at age seventeen. Kwan says going through puberty can damage the careers of young women in her sport. She says she began to experience problems on the ice when she "got hips." "Even if your body is just a little bit different, it throws you off," she told *USA Today*. "Even if you gain one pound, it makes you lopsided." (AP/ WIDE WORLD PHOTOS)

figure skaters. The goal in each sport is to be decidedly feminine. Figure skating in particular rewards competitors who pay close attention to hair style, makeup, music, and costumes. At the same time, the athletes strive to be champions in the grand male tradition: physically tough and mentally focused on achieving the highest level of performance possible. Gymnasts and figure skaters are more likely than those with less driven personalities to be victimized by anorexia or bulimia. In fact, in the course of writing her book, Ryan found only a handful of elite gymnasts who did not have a history of some form of eating disorder (Ryan 1995: 5).

A second contributing factor is that, as in other sports, weight often needs to be lost quickly. In gymnastics, that can be difficult because it is primarily an anaerobic sport in which athletes do not expend the levels of energy needed in running and swimming. And unlike male wrestlers, who usually regain the weight they lose to prepare for matches, figure skaters and gymnasts do not feel that they have that option. An official at the 1984 Olympics told Mary Lou Retton, "You know, if I could, I'd take half a point off because of that fat hanging off your butt" (Ryan 1995: 59). Retton laughed off the barb. Unfortunately, there are many competitors who lack the confidence and self-esteem to do the same. The biggest fear of young female gymnasts striving to achieve world-class status is the arrival of womanhood. Today, more than ever before, it can signal the beginning of the end of their careers. When Czech gymnast Vera Caslavska won Olympic gold medals in 1964 and 1968, she was five feet, three inches tall and weighed 121 pounds. Three decades later, the typical elite gymnast had shrunk six inches and forty pounds.

The pressure to stay young, small, and thin is the driving force behind what Ryan characterizes as a tradition of "legal, even celebrated, child abuse" (Ryan 1995: 4). Among those applying the pressure are parents, who often have invested thousands of dollars and hours in promoting the careers of their daughters, and coaches, whose reputation and livelihood depend on producing champions. Indeed, the coaches are often as intensely driven as the athletes they instruct (Ryan 1995: 141–71, 197–238). Al Fong, a former college gymnast who trained Christy Henrich, stands out in a sport full of domineering men. "I work at this seven days a week," he told *Sports Illustrated*. "And I look forward to doing it for the next 25 years. It's an obsession with me" (Nordan 1994: 58). Fong demands the same level of intensity from his charges. Workouts at his Great American Gymnastics Express in Blue Springs, Missouri, run from six A.M. to nine A.M. and five P.M. to nine P.M., six days a week. Equally demanding is Bela Karolyi, the native of Romania based in Houston, Texas, at a gym known as the Factory. Karolyi, who coached Olympic gold medalists Nadia Comaneci and Mary Lou Retton, has no qualms about driving athletes to their breaking point and pitting them against one another in the quest for success. "These girls are like little scorpions," he once said. "You put them all in a bottle and one scorpion will come out alive. That scorpion will be champion" (Ryan 1995: 22).

Gymnastics coaches need no special training or education to practice their craft, nor are they subject to child labor laws that protect others who are as young as aspiring gymnasts. The reasoning behind the lack of oversight is that gymnastics is not a true occupation and that the competitors are in the sport by their own choice. In fact, many gymnasts earn financial stipends that are based on competition results. And there is no way to determine with any accuracy the difference between a gymnast's personal choices and the choices of the parents, coaches, and others who are promoting her career. In the end, the young athletes carry on in a world that is both highly rewarding and bitterly cruel, and one that operates with little interference from outsiders.

Today, the rules of that world are more demanding than ever. When figure skaters and gymnasts fail, the whole word watches. For those who come up short, there is rarely another shot at the prize. Very few compete at the highest level of their sports for more than four years. For those who do succeed, the television ratings are high, the endorsement possibilities are numerous, and the promise of future earnings is assured—as long as they stay thin. The beast that lived inside Christy Henrich—and that lives inside so many other young athletes—will always be a dangerous one.

TOPICS FOR DISCUSSION

1. Many wrestlers and other athletes who engage in weight reducing use creatine, a strength-building substance that is created naturally in the body but also can be bought and used as a supplement. The health risks of creatine are largely unknown. Should athletes be allowed to use creatine? Why or why not?

2. After the death of wrestler Jeff Reese, the University of Michigan required all of its coaches, student-athletes, and athletic trainers to participate in a nutrition education program. Is mandatory participation in such a program a good or bad idea? Explain your answer.

3. Professor Joan Jacobs Brumberg believes that, for American girls in contemporary society, "the body is the ultimate expression of the self." Is Brumberg's claim accurate, or is it exaggerated? Describe the pressures that many adolescent girls feel to maintain the perfect body.

4. Gymnastics and figure skating coaches do not need licenses or specialized training to practice their profession. Should these coaches be subject to more intensive scrutiny and regulation? If so, by whom?

5. Girls and women who participate in gymnastics and figure skating have a strong chance of falling victim to eating disorders. What positive steps can be taken by parents, coaches, and the athletes themselves to avoid the trauma of anorexia and bulimia?

REFERENCES AND RESOURCES

Books

Brennan, Christine. *Inside Edge: A Revealing Journey into the Secret World of Figure Skating*. New York: Scribner, 1996.
The veteran *Washington Post* sportswriter chronicles a season on the figure skating circuit.

Brumberg, Joan Jacobs. *The Body Project*. New York: Random House, 1997.
The author studies the diaries of adolescent girls from the 1840s to the present to trace the rise of body consciousness.

Claude-Pierre, Peggy. *The Secret Language of Eating Disorders: The Revolutionary Approach to Understanding and Curing Anorexia and Bulimia*. New York: Times Books, 1997.
A renowned medical doctor offers a program for battling anorexia and bulimia.

Hesse-Biber, Sharlene. *Am I Thin Enough Yet? The Cult of Thinness and the Commercialization of Identity*. New York: Oxford University Press, 1996.
An advanced look at the many social and psychological forces that compel American women to pursue thinness.

Miller, Shannon. *Going for the Gold*. New York: Avon Books, 1996.
The autobiography of the champion gymnast.

Ryan, Joan. *Little Girls in Pretty Boxes: The Making and Breaking of Elite Gymnasts and Figure Skaters*. New York: Doubleday, 1995.
The noted sports columnist unveils the often grim reality behind the fairytale facade of world-class gymnastics and figure skating.

Sirimarco, Elizabeth. *Eating Disorders*. North Bellmore, N.Y.: Marshall Cavendish Corporation, 1994.
An excellent overview of the causes and effects of eating disorders.

Strug, Kerri, with John Lopez. *Landing on My Feet: A Diary of Dreams*. Kansas City, Mo.: Andrews and McMeel, 1997.
The 1996 Olympic champion tells her story.

Thompson, Ron A., and Roberta Trattner Sherman. *Helping Athletes with Eating Disorders*. Champaign, Ill.: Human Kinetics Publishers, 1993.
Information on identifying and treating athletes who suffer from eating disorders.

Magazines and Newspapers

Becker, Debbie. "Skating's Great Leap: USA Women Could Sweep Medals." *USA Today*, March 21–23, 1997: 1A, 2A.
Discusses the explosive growth of American figure skating.

Fleming, David. "Wrestling's Dirty Little Secret." *Sports Illustrated*, December 29/ January 5, 1998: 134.

Criticizes the college wrestling world for failing to address the dangers of radical weight reduction.

Litsky, Frank. "Collegiate Wrestling Deaths Raise Fears about Training." *New York Times*, December 19, 1997: A1, C20.

A detailed report on the fears raised by the 1997 deaths in college wrestling.

Nordan, Merrell. "Special Report: Eating Disorders." *Sports Illustrated*, August 22, 1994: 55–60.

Recounts the career of Christy Henrich, who died of anorexia in 1994.

Patrick, Dick. "Notre Dame Runner Battles Eating Disorder." *USA Today*, October 8, 1997: 9C.

Profiles cross-country runner JoAnna Teeter's battle against anorexia.

Plummer, William. "Dying for a Medal." *People*, August 22, 1994: 36–39.

A report on the life and death of gymnast Christy Henrich.

Smith, Eileen. "Bodybuilders' Fret 'Flip Side' of Anorexia." *USA Today*, November 24, 1997: 1A.

A note on muscle dsymorphia, a psychiatric disorder in male weight lifters who become obsessed with building muscles.

Sports Illustrated. "The Right Mat Moves." January 26, 1998: 33.

A short commentary on the NCAA's response to the three college wrestling deaths in 1997.

Stroh, Mackenzie. "Anorexia." *Cosmopolitan*, October 1997: 218–21.

One woman's chilling tale of her battle against anorexia and the self-hatred that triggered it.

USA Today. "NCAA Troubled by Wrestlers' Deaths." December 2, 1997: 3C.

A note on the deaths of wrestlers Billy Saylor, Joseph LaRosa, and Jeff Reese.

Organizations to Contact

American Anorexia/Bulimia Association (AABA)
165 West 46th Street, Suite 1108
New York, NY 10036
Phone: 212–575–6200
Internet Web Site: members@aol.com/amanbu
AABA provides information on eating disorders for professionals, victims, and friends and families of those suffering from the diseases. An ongoing discussion of issues related to eating disorders can be found on the World Wide Web in the newsgroup at alt.support.eating-disord.

National Association of Anorexia Nervosa and Associated Disorders
P.O. Box 7
Highland Park, IL 60035
Phone: 847–831–3438
Fax: 847–433–4632

The association is a national clearinghouse of information on eating disorders for health professionals and the general public. It maintains chapters in forty-five states and fourteen countries.

National Institute of Mental Health (NIMH)
NIMH Public Inquiries
5600 Fishers Lane, Room 7C-02 MSC 8030
Bethesda, MD 20892–8030
Phone: 301–443–3673
E-mail: nimhinfo@nih.gov
An agency of the U.S. Department of Health and Human Services, NIMH has taken a lead governmental role in the fight against eating disorders.

National Mental Illness Screening Project
One Washington Street, Suite 304
Wellesley Hills, MA 02181–1706
Toll-free phone: 800–969–6642
Internet Web Site: www.nmisp.org
This nonprofit organization was founded to coordinate nationwide mental health screening programs, including those for eating disorders. Locations for free, anonymous screenings are listed in the site locator on the project's Internet Web Site.

4

Under Pressure

The careers of many young athletes begin as soon as they are old enough to walk, often under pressure from parents and coaches. Millions of kids reach for the dream of superstardom, but few achieve it. Is victory all that matters in youth sports competition, or can a balance be struck between winning and having fun?

The referee knew something was wrong when he saw the blood. In a high school football game, it is not unusual for players to leave the field with injuries. But in the game between St. Pius and Academy high schools in Albuquerque, New Mexico, on October 12, 1996, the Academy players who streamed steadily to the sideline were not suffering from the usual assortment of bumps and bruises. Blood flowed from their necks, arms, and legs. One Academy senior had a deep slice on his forearm that took twelve stitches to close. In all, at least five Academy players were cut.

When the officials stopped the game in the first half and checked the uniforms and equipment of the players on both teams, they made a surprising discovery. Mike Cito, one of the St. Pius players, was sporting a buckle on his helmet that had a razor-sharp edge—sharp enough to shred a magazine cover. At first, the officials thought the sharpened edge was a manufacturing flaw, and they ordered Cito to replace his helmet with a new one. When they took a closer look after the game, their surprise turned to horror. The buckle had been deliberately sharpened. "There was no question it was milled," said Jeff Turcotte, the activities director of St. Pius. "Mike didn't admit to doing it, but he admitted he knew it was sharpened" (Associated Press 1996: 1D).

There seemed to be only one reason that anyone would commit such an act: to draw the blood of any Academy player who came into contact with Cito's helmet during the game. When it was discovered that the person who had sharpened the helmet was Albuquerque dentist Stephen Cito, Mike's father, the surprise and horror of the city's athletic community turned to outright disbelief. The coaches and players had seen many aggressive and overbearing parents who seemed capable of doing nearly anything to help their children achieve success on the playing field. But the thought of any individual's crafting a razor-sharp edge on the buckle of a football helmet seemed too outrageous to be true.

Mike Cito was dismissed from the St. Pius team, placed on probation, and forced to apologize to the Academy players. His father faced a lawsuit from one of the injured players and his parents. The message that the player and his parents were trying to send to both father and son was "Play fair." Unfortunately, that message is falling on deaf ears all too frequently in youth sports leagues, middle schools, and high schools. Examples of bad behavior abound. A high school basketball player takes issue with a referee's call and plants a punch on his jaw that sends the referee to the hospital emergency room. A football game for eleven- and twelve-year-olds in Belleville, Illinois, ends with an on-field donnybrook between coaches and parents. In the Northwest Valley Conference outside Los Angeles, the traditional postgame handshake between football players, a long-standing symbol of good sportsmanship, is abandoned after a series of fights erupt between opposing teams. "If we're that far gone, we shouldn't be playing at all," says coach Daryl Stroh of Granada Hills High School in the San Fernando Valley in Los Angeles. "If kids can't handle losing we aren't doing our job. Overcoming the adversity of losing is part of growing up" (*Executive Educator* 1994: 15).

Who is responsible for the decline in sportsmanship and the selfish attitude that seems so prevalent in today's young athletes? There are plenty of parties to blame. One is society at large, where doing whatever it takes to achieve success and earn material rewards is widely viewed as a cardinal virtue. Another is the atmosphere in the professional sports world, where fighting, taunting, trash talking, and grandstanding have become so common that they barely raise an eyebrow. Then there are the sports figures who do more than fight and talk trash: Roberto Alomar of the Baltimore Orioles, who spit in an umpire's face; Dennis Rodman of the Chicago Bulls, who kicked a photographer; Latrell Sprewell of the Golden State Warriors, who put a choke hold on his coach during practice; and figure skater Tonya Harding, who became involved in her husband's plot to hire a gang of thugs to shatter the knee of Harding's archrival on the ice, Nancy Kerrigan.

The misdeeds of professional athletes and the casual attitude that society sometimes seems to take toward them clearly are factors in the decline of sportsmanship among young people. But most experts who study the lives of young people—psychologists, psychiatrists, educators, and pediatricians—place the bulk of the blame on a group of people much closer to home: the parents and coaches of young athletes, who create the atmosphere of tension and anxiety that leads to poor sportsmanship. Nothing can put a damper on a soccer game between seven-year-olds like an irate father bounding onto the field to deliver an obscenity-laced tirade in the face of a referee who has made a bad call. The only thing that might be worse is a hyperventilating coach heaping abuse on a nine-year-old who hasn't put on his "game face." About 25 million boys and girls participate in team or individual sports in the United States each year. By the time they reach age fifteen, nearly three-quarters of them have quit, according to a survey of 26,000 kids by the Institute for the Study of Youth Sports at Michigan State University (Dash 1996: 94).

The kids who quit invariably offer two reasons. First, the sport is no longer fun because they feel pressure to meet the expectations of their parents. Second, they can no longer tolerate the verbal, emotional, and physical abuse they receive from their coaches. The prime lesson to be learned from this massive retreat is simple. If the games are no longer fun, the kids are going to go home. It may take them weeks, months, or years to make that choice, but when joy disappears from the playing fields, the kids will too.

The world of youth sports has traveled far from the days before World War II, when there were few organized leagues, and most games were contested by boys—and boys alone—in streets, sandlots, and backyards, while girls watched from the sidelines. When Carl Stotz founded Little League Baseball in 1939 in his hometown of Williamsport, Pennsylvania, he envisioned an atmosphere in which young athletes could be instructed and nurtured, not pressured and intimidated. In millions of individual cases, Stotz's vision has been realized. In millions of others, that vision has turned empty and bitter. "We have a sportsmanship problem in youth sports," says Art Taylor of the Center for the Study of Sports in Society at Northeastern University. "That said, we can't just cry in our beer. We've got to solve the problem" (White 1997: 1).

FOLLOWING THE STARS

Mothers and fathers seeking to be positive influences in the lives of the young athletes in their families can look to the parents of several star performers for advice and instruction. The most prominent parental role model today probably is Earl Woods, the father of golfer Tiger Woods. The love and affection they share for one another is genuine and inspirational. Their embrace after Tiger's triumph at the 1997 Masters Tournament, described by President Bill Clinton as the best shot of the day, warmed the hearts of even the most hard-bitten and cynical souls. It was

Shortstop Daniel Baca of Guadalupe, Mexico, fielding a grounder in the 1997 Little League World Series, is one of millions of youths who participate in organized team or individual sports. But 75 percent of the kids who play sports quit by the age of fifteen because, they say, sports are no longer fun, and they face pressure and abuse from parents, teammates, and coaches. Playing by the rules, respecting teammates and opponents, and valuing the enjoyment of the game over victory all seem to have taken a back seat to the desire of adults to see kids finish first at any cost. (AP/WIDE WORLD PHOTOS)

Earl, a native of Kansas who served two tours of duty in Vietnam as a Green Beret officer, who gave Tiger his first golf lesson at the Navy Golf Club in southern California when Tiger was eighteen months old. Earl has been his son's confidant, taskmaster, and strongest supporter ever since, teaching him not only the physical skills of golf but also the emotional control needed to compete at the game's highest level.

The parents of figure skater Tara Lipinski provided her with the same level of devotion. Jack and Pat Lipinski paid nearly $75,000 each year to support Tara's dream of becoming an Olympic gold medalist, a dream that came true at the 1998 Winter Olympics in Nagano, Japan. At age fifteen, Tara became the youngest figure skater ever to win gold. When she began the pursuit of her dream at age eleven, the Lipinskis could have allowed Tara to move away from their Sugar Land, Texas, home by herself and live with a host family in the city where she trained. That arrangement is common for elite athletes. But no one in the family wanted Tara to be on her own. Instead, they decided to keep the family together. While Jack remained in Texas and continued to work as the vice president of an oil-refining company, Tara and Pat moved together to Delaware and then to Michigan as Tara advanced to the top. They maintained their sense of togetherness, but the price was high: monthly telephone bills of one thousand dollars or more, forty airplane flights each year to allow Jack to see his wife and daughter on weekends, and a sense of loss that the telephone calls and airplane flights could never quite undo. The lives of the Lipinskis show that it is not only the young athletes themselves who must make sacrifices to pursue their dreams. Their parents must sacrifice too.

When Tara decided after her Olympic triumph to become a professional skater, she was criticized for bowing out of future Olympic Games, which do not allow professionals to compete in her sport. Why, the critics asked, would she be willing to accept a life of relative obscurity? The answer was easy. At age fifteen, after five years of grueling demands, she longed for a more normal life. She wanted to hang out with her friends, shop at the mall, watch television, eat pasta with marinara sauce and brownies with ice cream, and be with her dogs and her dad. Her parents were thrilled with her decision (Kelly 1998: D1).

Another set of parents working to provide a balanced life for their athletic children are Richard and Oracene Williams. Their daughter Venus is a teenage tennis prodigy. She made her professional debut at age fourteen and in 1997 became the first African American woman since Althea Gibson in 1958 to reach the finals of the U.S. Open. The six-foot, two-inch performer with beaded braids and a mile-wide grin won her first professional title in 1998 at age seventeen. In her younger years, she played infrequently. Richard Williams, the son of a Louisiana sharecropper who raised his family in the impoverished city of Compton, California, resisted the persistent efforts of players, agents, sponsors, and tournament officials to push Venus and her sister, Serena, onto the women's professional tour. For Richard and Oracene, family and school came before tennis. If Richard had to lock up his daughters' balls and rackets to emphasize the point, he did so. "He has done what he thought in his heart was best for his girls," says Rick Macci, who coached Venus for four years. "He gets an A-triple plus for being the type of parent he is. He's got educated, well-mannered kids who have their priorities in line" (Nelson 1998: 5).

Producing children with their priorities in line also is the goal of Chris Evert, the great tennis champion who won 157 tournaments in her eighteen-year professional career, including three Wimbledon and six U.S. Open titles. In elementary school, she wanted to be a social worker, missionary, or teacher. "Then I got involved in tennis and everything was just me, me, me," she says. "I was totally selfish . . . because if you let up for one minute, somebody was going to come along and beat you" (Heilbroner 1996: 244). She is not promoting athletic careers for her three young sons. Evert says she wants them to use their brains instead of their bodies to make their mark in the world. In the household of Evert and her husband, Andy Mill, a former Olympic skier, sports will be played for fun and fitness only.

DON'T DO IT FOR DAD

Fun and fitness sounds like a promising combination. They are the goals of nearly all children when they first become involved in sports. Unfortunately, those goals can become obscured once some young athletes enter the world of competition for the first time. Too often they end up playing not for fun and fitness but to please the adults in their lives.

One group the young athletes seek to please is parents. Sports columnist Joan Ryan says that, despite our best intentions, there is a bit of the stage mom or dad in every parent, and "we cover it up under the guise of 'wanting the best for our children' " (Ryan 1997: 8). Too many parents see their children as a way to rekindle their own failed dreams of athletic glory or to enhance their own prestige or reputation within a community. They fail to provide their sons and daughters with the element most necessary to achieving athletic success: the ability to develop ambition on their own, separate and distinct from the ambitions of adults. Parents can help develop that ambition by focusing on basic athletic skills while their kids are under the age of ten, and by showing their kids how much they themselves enjoy sports.

As young athletes grow older, the process can become more complicated. The peer pressure of adolescence arrives, the level of competition increases, and the emotional and financial investments of parents can become deeper. Most important, a coach can emerge as a key influence. That is not always a positive development. When Nicolas Clark, a Little League Baseball player in Crown Point, Indiana, won a trophy in 1995 as a member of a championship team, he instead handed the trophy back to the league's board of directors. "The coaches treated me like scum," he said. "I don't want this" (Dash 1996: 94). Clark's coaches had stood idly by as Clark's teammates taunted him relentlessly for his lack of skill. And when his mother complained to the coaches and said all her son wanted to do was have fun, she was informed that the game was about winning. If Nicolas wanted to have fun, he was advised to do so elsewhere.

Many coaches engage in even worse behavior. One coach in a coeducational hockey league in Minnesota launched a "get the girl" strategy and ordered his thirteen-year-old team members to slam the lone female on the opposing team into the boards until she collapsed and had to be taken to the hospital (Dash 1996: 94). Others specialize in verbal abuse of a sexist nature, berating their charges by calling them sissies, girlies, mama's boys, babes, bimbos, and worse. Coaches also practice less graphic forms of abuse: using alcohol and tobacco during games and practices, giving more playing time to their own sons or daughters, relegating lesser talents to the bench, providing special favors for talented stars, harassing officials and umpires, and manipulating or "stacking" team rosters to ensure themselves better players.

Some coaches change their ways, like Peter von Allmen, the girls' basketball coach at Fort Atkinson High School in Wisconsin. In 1992, he was forced to resign as coach at another high school because of his repeated verbal abuse of players. "I thought if we were winning, the girls must be having a good time," von Allmen said. "I was so wrong. Over 17 years, we won 85 percent of our games, including two state championships. But we didn't have fun. My ego put winning ahead of everything. The parents were right to want me gone" (Dash 1996: 123).

Parents are indeed the major source of pressure for coaches in youth leagues, middle schools, and high schools. They have the power to remove abusive or incompetent coaches. At the same time, pressure from parents can force many good coaches to step down, usually because they do not lead their teams to enough victories. One retired coach quips that the only safe place to head up a kids' sports team is at an orphanage. In Minnesota, the turnover rate for coaches is so high that Darien DeRocher, the executive director of the Minnesota State High School Coaches Association, fears for the survival of scholastic sports in the state.

DeRocher's fear may be exaggerated. America's love affair with sports is deep and longstanding, and youth sports have played a key role in the romance for decades. It is hard to imagine them disappearing from the landscape of Minnesota, or any other state. They offer excitement to millions of kids and adults and, of course, provide the training ground for the superstars of the future. But that training ground is a harsher place today than ever before, and if parents, coaches, and kids continue to ride the waves of selfishness and cold-blooded ambition, De Rocher's fear may be more real than we care to admit. As Art Taylor of the Center for the Study of Sport in Society has reminded us, we need to solve the problem of poor sportsmanship (White 1997: 1). A good first step is to remember that the fundamentals of the game begin with fun.

CODE OF ETHICS FOR PARENTS

In their book *Parenting Your Superstar*, Robert J. Rotella and Linda K. Bunker provide a "Code of Ethics for Parents" involved in youth sports. Author and sports doctor Lyle J. Micheli has written that he would like to see the code "blown up giant size and put on a billboard that looms above every baseball diamond, gymnasium, football field, and wherever else sports are played" (Micheli 1990: 51–52):

I will help my child learn to enjoy sports and develop the skills that he or she is capable of performing.

I will learn the strengths and weaknesses of my child so that I may place the young athlete in situations where he or she has a maximum opportunity for success.

I will become thoroughly familiar with the techniques and rules of the sport my child chooses.

I will do my best to learn the fundamental teaching skills and strategies related to my child's sport.

I will practice and help my child so that he or she will have an opportunity for skill improvement through active participation.

I will communicate with my child the rights and responsibilities of others who are involved in sport.

I will protect the health and safety of my child by insisting that all of the activities under my control are conducted in accord with his or her psychological and physiological welfare.

I will treat each player, opposing coach, official, parent, and administrator with respect and dignity.

I will uphold the authority of officials and coaches who are working with my child. I will assist them when possible and use good judgment if I disagree with them.

I will become familiar with the objectives of the sports programs with which my child is affiliated.

I will strive to help select activities that uphold our family values.

I will help my child develop good sportsmanship and a desire to strive for success.

TOPICS FOR DISCUSSION

1. Most experts who study the lives of young people say that parents and coaches bear most of the blame for the decline of sportsmanship in youth sports leagues and high schools. Do you think the experts' view is accurate? Or are there other people who contribute to poor sportsmanship? If so, who are they?

2. Tennis legend Chris Evert does not want her three sons to grow up to be professional athletes. She says she would like to see them make their mark in the world with their brains, not their bodies. Why is Evert so reluctant to have her children enter the professional sports world? Is her reluctance justified, or is it an overreaction?

3. If you participated in sports in youth leagues, middle school, or high school, was your experience positive or negative? Did you feel undue pressure from parents or coaches to win at any cost? Did you learn valuable lessons about yourself and your teammates? Was the experience a fun one?

4. After high school football player Mike Cito was caught with a razor-sharp buckle on his helmet during a game, he was dismissed from his team and forced to apologize to the players on the opposing team. Was this punishment too lenient, too severe, or appropriate? Explain your answer.

5. Research indicates that nearly three-quarters of the boys and girls who participate in youth sports leagues quit by the time they reach age fifteen. What steps, if any, could be taken to lower the dropout rate and encourage a longer period of participation?

REFERENCES AND RESOURCES

Books

LeBlanc, Janet, and Louis Dickson. *Straight Talk about Children and Sport.* Kansas City, Kans.: Midpoint Trade Books, 1998.
   A practical reference guide concerning children's participation in organized sports.
Micheli, Lyle J., with Mark Jenkins. *Sportswise: An Essential Guide for Young Athletes, Parents, and Coaches.* Boston: Houghton Mifflin, 1990.
   One of the leading medical experts on children's sports discusses injuries, nutrition, academics, and coaches.
Poretta, Vicki, and Deb Crisfield. *Mom's Guide to Sports.* New York: Macmillan, 1997.
   One of the Mom's Guide series, the book is designed to create a more active role in sports for mothers of children ages eight to fourteen.

Rotella, Robert J., and Linda K. Bunker. *Parenting Your Superstar*. Chicago: Triumph Books, 1998.
Advice to parents on how to mentor young athletes in their families.

Wolff, Rick. *Good Sports*. New York: Dell, 1993.
A top sports psychologist discusses the roles of parents, children, and coaches in sports.

Woods, Earl. *Training a Tiger*. New York: HarperCollins, 1997.
The father of the golf superstar recounts their life together.

Magazines and Newspapers

Associated Press. "Player Booted after Helmet Cuts Players." *Columbus Dispatch*, October 21, 1996: 1D.
A report on the football helmet incident in New Mexico in 1996.

Dash, Judi. "Unsportsmanlike Behavior: Is Your Child's Coach a Tyrant?" *Family Circle*, April 23, 1996: 94–95, 123.
Lists the ten warning signs of a bad coach.

Dorman, Larry. "A Prodigy's Journey through Fame and Pain." *New York Times*, April 18, 1997: C22.
A profile of Beverly Klass, a one-time golfer who was physically abused by her father.

Executive Educator. "Sports Handshake Falls Victim to Violence." May 1994: 15.
A note on the end of the postgame handshake in a southern California football conference.

Harris, Maryls. "A New All-or-Nothing Philosophy Is Forcing Your Children to Compete against Today's Trophy Kids." *Money*, March 1997: 102–110.
Debunks the notion that children who live highly structured lives will succeed as adults.

Heilbroner, David. "The Ugly Truth about Sportsmanship." *Cosmopolitan*, October 1996: 242–46.
Attributes the increase in poor sportsmanship to lack of respect for others and parental pressure.

Kantrowitz, Barbara. "Don't Just Do It for Daddy." *Newsweek*, December 9, 1996: 56–57.
The author says young athletes achieve more when they develop their own drive for excellence.

Kelly, Katy. "Tara's Next Move." *USA Today*, April 13, 1998: D1.
Examines the life of Tara Lipinski after her gold medal performance in the 1998 Olympics.

Lemke, Jay. "Time Out!" *Minneapolis-St. Paul Magazine*. April 1997: 54–63.
A revealing profile of scholastic sports in the Twin Cities, where high turnover rates for coaches have become a serious problem.

Nelson, Jill. "The New First Family of Tennis." *USA Weekend*, April 10–12, 1998: 4–5.
A look at teenage tennis star Venus Williams and her family.

Rathbun, Mickey. "Foul Play! Parents and Coaches Can Save Good Sportsmanship from Extinction." *Sports Illustrated for Kids*, June 1997: 14–17.
Describes a program for improving behavior on the playing fields.

Reilly, Rick."The Lipinski Who Was Left Behind." *Sports Illustrated,* March 2, 1998: 128.

Portrays the lonely life of Jack Lipinski, father of the Olympic figure skater.

Ryan, Joan. "Role Models and Cautionary Tales." *Sporting News,* July 21, 1997: 8.

The noted sports columnist issues a warning to pressuring parents.

Smith, Doug. "Daughters Follow Wisdom of Father Williams." *USA Today,* April 3, 1998: 13C.

Profiles the bond between tennis players Venus and Serena Williams and their father.

Smith, Pohla, Tess Reisgies, and Jenny Kellner. "How Do They Do It?" *Sports Illustrated for Kids,* September 1995: 16–20.

A look at the lives of Jack and Pat Lipinski, the parents of figure skater Tara Lipinski.

White, Kerry A. "Officials Blow the Whistle on Athlete's Antics." *Education Week,* February 5, 1997: 1.

A roundup of ugly incidents involving young athletes.

Organizations to Contact

Coaching Youth Sports
Internet Web Site: www.chre.vt.edu
Coaching Youth Sports is an electronic newsletter created and maintained by the Health and Physical Education Department at Virginia Tech University. It emphasizes information for athletes ages six to sixteen and their parents and coaches.

Little League Baseball, Inc.
P.O. Box 3485
Williamsport, PA 17701
Phone: 717–326–1921
Fax: 717–326–1074
E-mail: llbmail@pennet.net
Internet Web Site: www.littleleague.com
Founded in 1939, Little League Baseball is now the largest youth sports organization in the world, with nearly 3 million participants.

National Federation of State High School Associations (NFSHA)
11724 Northwest Plaza Circle
P.O. Box 20626
Kansas City, MO 64195–0626
Phone: 816–464–5400
Fax: 816–464–5571
Internet Web Site: www.nfsha.org
The federation includes the state high school associations from all fifty states, the

District of Columbia, and eleven Canadian provinces. Among its standing committees are those dealing with spirit and sportsmanship in athletic contests.

National Youth Sport Coaches' Association
2050 Vista Parkway
West Palm Beach, FL 33411–2718
Phone: 407–684–1142
Fax: 407–684–2546
Internet Web Site: www.nays.org
This group is dedicated to improving youth sports by promoting injury prevention and improving standards and education requirements for coaches.

5

Player Power

In the early days of sports, players were virtual slaves who could be bought and sold by team owners like property. Today, in an era of strikes, free agency, agents, and skyrocketing television revenue, the players on the field, especially in baseball, wield much more power. Has the rise of player power helped or hurt the game?

The numbers get bigger every year, defying logic and common sense as they catapult from the roof to the sky and into the stratosphere, miles above the hard earth where the average wage earners of the planet live and work. As sports fans see the skyrocketing numbers on television, newspapers, magazines, and computer screens, they ask the same question time and again: How high can the salaries of professional athletes go? Is there any limit to what the owners of baseball, basketball, football, and hockey teams are able and willing to pay for the services of the 3,300 men who have earned places on their rosters? The logic of economics says that what goes up must eventually come down. But the world of professional sports seems to operate with a logic all its own that says something completely different: What goes up must go up even higher.

The wages are princely indeed. In 1998, the average player's salary in Major League Baseball (MLB) was $1.44 million. In all, 317 players earned $1 million or more. A public school teacher earning $36,000 annually would have to work over forty years to make the MLB annual average, assuming he or she received no raises. The minimum salary for an MLB player in 1998 was $170,000, and the total player payroll for all teams stood at $1.2 billion, an all-time high (Bodley 1998: C1). A large portion of the money—too much, critics say—is guaranteed, meaning that it is paid to players even if their on-field performance deteriorates or if they suffer serious injuries and cannot play at all.

In 1997, the New York Yankees had eighteen players on their roster earning $1 million or more, the highest number of any team. The highest-paid player was Chicago White Sox outfielder Albert Belle, who took in $10 million. He joined Robin Yount, Ryne Sandberg, Will Clark, Bobby Bonilla, Daryl Strawberry, and Cecil Fielder in the elite circle of players who spent time in the 1990s at the pinnacle of the pay scale. In 1998, the spot at the top was taken by pitcher Pedro Martinez, who signed a six-year contract with the Boston Red Sox that paid him roughly $12.5 million each season (Beaton 1997: 1C). A convenience store clerk working full time at seven dollars an hour could match Martinez's annual pay. It would take the clerk a bit longer: 857 years longer.

In the National Basketball Association (NBA), the numbers soar even higher. The average salary in the league for the 1996–1997 season was $2.2 million, with Michael Jordan snaring the top spot for his $30.14 million, one-year deal with the Chicago Bulls. Observers who thought a ceiling had been reached in 1996 when center Shaquille O'Neal signed a seven-year, $120 million pact with the Los Angeles Lakers turned out to be mistaken. The next year, the Minnesota Timberwolves agreed to pay twenty-one-year-old Kevin Garnett $125 million over six years, the richest payout in sports history. The sum was $35 million more than owner Glen Taylor paid for the entire Minnesota franchise in 1995. Is the stunning figure justified? The Timberwolves think so. Team vice president Kevin McHale describes Garnett as a "future elite player" whom he expects to excel on the level of Jordan and O'Neal (Strauss, Valdmanis, and Horowitz 1997: 1B, 2B). The riches showered on today's top performers will surely serve as benchmarks for the stars of the future. Those riches have a direct effect on fans as well. Actor and loyal Lakers fan Jack Nicholson now pays $600 a game for his courtside seat at the Los Angeles Forum, and the working folks in the rafters saw the price of the cheapest ticket jump from $9.50 to $21.00 the year after O'Neal signed his megadeal.

Performers in the National Football League (NFL) and the National Hockey League (NHL) lag slightly behind their baseball and basketball brethren. The average wage in the NFL in 1996 was $795,000; in the NHL it was $892,000. In 1987, twelve NFL players earned $1 million or more. By 1996, that number had swelled to 360, about 25 percent of the player workforce. Virtually every NFL player may someday command the same figure. When the league signed a new four-network television contract worth $17.6 billion from 1998 through 2005, salaries bolted skyward. As recently as 1980, the average salary in the league was $79,000 (Brady and Moore 1997: 1A, 2A). The situation has become so mind-boggling that *Sports Illustrated* writer Leigh Montville has proposed the creation of a new form of currency, which he christened the "athlodollar," to help fans cope with salary shock. The athlodollar would have just 10 percent of the value of real currency, and "it will be the only money teams will be allowed to pay players in and the only money players will be allowed to earn—unless they also find a real job for real money" (Montville 1997: 14).

Montville's satirical plea plucks a delicate nerve deep in the hearts of many fans. There are those who call today's players greedy and say that their greed has forever altered the nature of major league sports. The critics say the players' new gospel of dollars and cents has replaced the old gospel of joy, camaraderie, and loyalty to teammates, fans, and the game itself. They look back wistfully to the days before satellite television and trash talk and before owners offered $125 million to twenty-one-year-olds. In those days, the stadiums were named for fallen war heroes instead of corporations, the hot dogs cost twenty-five cents instead of three dollars, and the greatest thrill a player could have was slipping a championship ring on his finger, not signing a contract that made him the richest player on his team.

The players tell another story. They say that the simpler times never really existed in the way that nostalgic fans like to remember them. Money was as much on the minds of players then as it is now; the numbers were simply smaller. The players also contend that too much attention is paid to the salaries of the superstars at the top of the pay scale and too little to the athletes who toil at the bottom. They may play for only two or three seasons before leaving the game forever. The point is valid, but it is hard to fault fans for focusing on the stars. Magnificent, charismatic performers are the lifeblood of the sports world. Red Grange, the celebrated running back known as the Galloping Ghost, gave instant credibility to the struggling sport of professional football in 1925 when he headlined a barnstorming tour with the Chicago Bears. Joe Namath, the New York Jets quarterback who guided his team to victory in Super Bowl III in 1969, did the same for the fledgling American Football League (AFL) before it merged with the NFL. New York Yankees owner Jacob Ruppert bought Babe Ruth from the Boston Red Sox in 1919 because he understood Ruth's unique power to attract fans to the ballpark in droves. When Yankee Stadium opened on April 19, 1923, a packed house of 60,000 saw Ruth deliver a three-run homer to beat his former team. The Los Angeles Kings of the NHL acquired Wayne Gretzky from the Edmonton Oilers in 1988 for the same reason the Yankees snared Ruth. The Great One did not disappoint his new employer. In the first season Gretzky played with the Kings, the number of sellouts rose from five to twenty-two, the average per-game attendance increased by 3,360, and the number of Kings games appearing on local television jumped from thirty-seven to sixty (Gorman and Calhoun 1994: 168). The stars will always attract the largest piece of the spotlight, be it for their on-field heroics or the size of their paychecks.

The players also say that they deserve any amount of money that the traffic can bear, a philosophy that makes them no different from workers in any other segment of the economy. That is an argument that resonates more strongly with the public. If major league sports are viewed as a form of entertainment, there is no reason that superior talents on the field should be paid any less than talents like Tom Cruise, Jerry Seinfeld, Mel Gibson, and Oprah Winfrey, who earn millions from television shows and movies.

Most important, players insist that they have learned everything they know about greed from team owners, who have a long tradition of doing whatever is necessary to preserve their bottom line. For decades, preserving the bottom line meant keeping players' salaries as low as possible. Only since the 1970s and 1980s, which saw the rise of free agency in baseball, basketball, football, and hockey, have players been compensated at a level approaching their true market value. In free agency, an athlete who does not have a contractual obligation to perform for a team has the right to offer his services freely to any willing bidder. A team has an equal right to bid or not to bid for his services. It is a system that is taken for granted in other arenas of commerce. In the sports world, it became a reality only after decades of struggle.

"The owners have been screwing the players for one hundred years," baseball player Ken Singleton once told columnist George Will. "The players have only been screwing the owners for five. We got another ninety-five years coming" (Dudley 1994: 109).

PIECES OF PROPERTY

Singleton's bitter comment starkly highlights the precarious alliance between players and owners. It is an alliance based on strong mutual need. Without players, owners would have no product to sell to fans, corporate sponsors, and television and radio networks. Their stadiums, arenas, and ballparks would soon sit empty, as would their bank accounts. Without owners, players would find it difficult to find wealthy individuals ready to compensate them for their skills and assume the financial risks of operating a major league team. In spite of their mutual dependence, players and owners remain grudging partners at best. Their bond has endured long periods of suspicion, animosity, and, in the darkest days of labor-management strife, utter contempt.

The sport with the longest record of strained relations is baseball. As a business proposition, the game has always been rocky. The Cincinnati Red Stockings, the game's first openly professional team, earned $29,000 in revenue on their eight-month tour of the East and Midwest in 1869. Unfortunately, the cost of the team's salaries was $9,000 and the additional expenses of operation came to well over $20,000. The Red Stockings folded after one season and were later reborn as the Cincinnati Reds (Dolan 1996: 54).

As the game matured, the great expenses of running a team—building and maintaining a playing facility, operating a farm system in which to develop talent, and paying players and other personnel—continued to make ownership a daunting prospect. How did baseball owners manage to survive financially? Until the landscape of baseball underwent a marked transformation in the 1970s, they benefited enormously from the unique status that the game is granted under the nation's antitrust laws. The Sherman Antitrust Act, passed by Congress in 1890, authorized the federal government to stop large business entities from using monopolistic practices to weaken and eliminate competitors. The Clayton Act of 1914 extended the right to challenge monopolistic practices to individuals. The laws were passed primarily to curb the abuses of railroads and oil companies by subjecting them to strong oversight and regulation. They have been used in more recent times to challenge the business practices of Microsoft, the giant computer software enterprise.

Major league baseball possesses many of the features of a business monopoly. The American League (AL) and the National League (NL) are the only enterprises offering the game to consumers, and they have threatened, intimidated, and sued those who have attempted to compete with them. In spite of this, the U.S. Supreme Court granted MLB an exemption from the antitrust laws in three separate cases in 1922, 1953, and 1972. The legal rationale for the exemption has been that baseball is an "amusement" carried on in "localities" and not a business engaged in interstate commerce. Therefore, it is not subject to regulation by the federal courts. That reasoning is flimsy at best, given the vast commercial scope of the game and the fact that the Supreme Court has a long history of defining virtually all business enterprises as being engaged in interstate commerce. The more likely reason for the exemption is that the justices have been unwilling to tamper with tradition and, like much of the rest of the nation, cling to a romanticized image of the game and its heroes. That posture was expressed lucidly in the opinion written for the Court by Justice Harry A. Blackmun in 1972:

> Then there are the many names, celebrated for one reason or another, that have sparked the diamond and its environs and that have provided tinder for recaptured thrills, for reminiscence and comparisons, and for conversation and anticipation in-season and off-season: Ty Cobb, Babe Ruth, Tris Speaker, Lou Gehrig, Grover Cleveland Alexander, Rube Marquand, Wahoo Sam Crawford, Wee Willie Keeler, Three-finger Brown, Smokey Joe Wood, Dizzy Dean . . . the list seems endless. (*Flood v. Kuhn*, 407 U.S. 258 [1971]).

How has baseball's exemption from the antitrust laws affected players and fans? For fans, it means that the owners of the AL and NL are the only players on the major league map. They, and they alone, decide who may join their exclusive club. An ambitious entrepreneur with millions of dollars to invest is not free to create an MLB team in the same manner that he or she could create a computer software company, a shopping mall, or an airline. The number of new MLB franchises is rigidly controlled by the owners in order to maintain and increase the value of the franchises that already exist. The owners also determine where any new teams will be placed geographically. For fans who live in a city or region that has a team, the arrangement is suitable enough. Those who live elsewhere and yearn for a hometown team of their own to root for can only hope. The owners also decide how much each new team must pay for the privilege of entering the major leagues. The price tag is huge. The Tampa Bay Devil Rays and the Arizona Diamondbacks, which began play in 1998, each paid an entry fee of $130 million. The money was divided in equal shares among the existing owners.

For the players who competed in the major leagues until the mid-1970s, the antitrust exemption had an overwhelming impact in one area: the amount of money they were paid. Because the AL and NL owners were free to run their enterprise without fear of government intervention, they were able to control the biggest expense they faced. Like other professional sports, baseball conducted a draft in which players leaving high school or college were selected by participating teams. Once players were drafted, they were required to negotiate contracts only with the teams that had selected them, unless those teams released them from their obligations. In other words, the players were not free to sell their services to the highest bidder. That restriction distinguished them from millions of other workers who possess the freedom to switch jobs if they are offered higher salaries, more challenging work responsibilities, or better working conditions.

The arrangement was called the reserve system, because the team that owned a player "reserved" the right to control that player's ability to bid his services. If a player's contract expired and he refused to sign a new one, the team had the right to renew the contract that had expired, under the same terms and conditions, and force the player to adhere to it. The reserve system proved effective in keeping a lid on the salaries of even the game's best performers. In 1956, Yankees center fielder Mickey Mantle won the coveted Triple Crown by leading the AL in home runs, batting average, and runs batted in. That feat, which has been accomplished only four times in MLB since 1945, earned him a raise from $60,000 to $65,000 for 1957. When Mantle's production slumped slightly, the Yankee management proposed cutting his salary by $5,000, even though he won the AL's Most Valuable Player Award (MVP) for the second straight year. Mantle finally wrangled a salary of $75,000 for 1958 (Gorman and Calhoun 1994: 7).

What rationale did the owners offer for maintaining the reserve system? The owners believed that if players were allowed to negotiate freely, they would change teams constantly in search of better pay. Without the reserve system, the wealthiest owners would be able to buy the services of the most talented players and win more games. That would destroy the competitive balance among teams that was essential to promoting fan interest and long-term stability.

The owners had a point. In the pioneer days of professional sports in the nineteenth century, players did change teams frequently, often many times in a single season, when they were offered more money. That serious operational flaw led to the rise of organized leagues, in which members were barred from raiding the rosters of their competitors. In forming leagues, the owners recognized that the business of baseball was fundamentally different from other businesses because the teams needed each other to survive. General Motors certainly would be a more profitable automobile company if Ford, Chrysler, Toyota, Honda and the rest of its competitors went out of business. On the contrary, the New York Yankees would be a less profitable baseball team if all of their major league rivals closed up shop. Put simply, in baseball, as in other sports, you have to play somebody. And the someone you play cannot be just anyone. A contest between the Yankees and the gang from the Acme Pizzeria of Anytown, USA, would not generate much interest. Teams that play each other on a regular basis, and share a roughly equal level of talent, are vital to success.

The consensus, then, was that a return to the bad old days was impossible. The leagues as collective entities had to survive, even if that meant limiting the power of individual teams within the leagues to bid for talent. But the big questions remained unanswered. Would free agency destroy the game? Would it upset the competitive balance that the owners believed was necessary for baseball's success? Would it be possible for a single wealthy owner simply to buy a championship team? The events of the 1970s provided some answers.

THE RISE OF FREE AGENCY

Discontent with the reserve system grew as baseball entered the television age and owners tapped a plentiful supply of new revenue in the form of broadcast rights. As the cash flowed in, players' salaries remained low. In 1970, St. Louis Cardinals center fielder Curt Flood challenged the baseball hierarchy after the Cardinals traded him to the Philadelphia Phillies. Flood's complaint was that he did not necessarily want to play for the Phillies. He wanted to consider offers from other clubs before making his decision. "I do not feel that I am a piece of property to be bought and sold irrespective of my wishes," Flood wrote in a letter to baseball commissioner Bowie Kuhn. "I believe that any system which produces that result violates my basic rights as a citizen and is inconsistent with the laws of the United States" (Flood 1970: 94).

The Supreme Court disagreed with Flood's claim and upheld the validity of the reserve system through Justice Blackmun's opinion. It was clear that the Court had no great love for the way baseball handled its players. But it left any change in the hands of Congress, and the lawmakers in Washington also were reluctant to force the matter. Although Flood lost his lawsuit, he had challenged the established order head-on and taken his argument to the highest court of the land. The days of the reserve system, which had existed for nearly a century, were numbered.

In 1975, pitchers Dave McNally of the Montreal Expos and Andy Messersmith of the Los Angeles Dodgers refused to sign contracts with their teams for the upcoming season. The clubs then exercised their right to renew the contracts for one additional year without the players' approval. McNally and Messersmith played the 1975 season under their old contracts and then proclaimed freedom and asserted their right to negotiate freely with other teams. Their action was based on a strict reading of the reserve clause, and this time the courts supported them. The two pitchers thus became baseball's first free agents. In the new collective bargaining agreement between owners and players that was signed in 1976, free agency was granted to players with six or more years of major league experience. The floodgate opened. In 1977, 281 major leaguers signed multiyear contracts as owners rushed to prevent their best players from switching teams. The average player's salary nearly tripled between 1976 and 1980 (Zimbalist 1992: 21).

The owners had capitulated on the issue of free agency because they realized they were facing a strong, united workforce that was more than willing to flex its muscle to gain and retain economic opportunity. As early as 1885, baseball players had banded together to demand better pay and working conditions. The first formal attempt to organize players under the nation's labor laws came in 1946 when Robert Murphy, a graduate of Harvard Law School, formed the American Baseball Guild. The guild demanded that owners adopt a pension plan and provide funds to defray players' expenses during spring training. Murphy's effort to form a union failed, but the two demands ultimately were met. Today, the stipend that players receive during spring training is still known as "Murphy money" (Flood 1970: 145–47). In 1966, the players organized the Major League Baseball Players Association (MLBPA) and hired Marvin Miller, an official with the United Steelworkers Union, to serve as executive director. Under Miller's leadership, the union won several important victories, including increased health insurance and pension payments and the right to submit salary disputes to neutral arbitrators.

The resolution of the free agency issue in 1976 was a compromise. The players did not earn total freedom. There was still a draft, and players were barred from negotiating freely during the first years of their careers, when their value often is highest. The door was left open for further refinements in the system. In 1979, the owners sought to change the rules by proposing that teams losing players through free agency be compensated for their losses through the addition of other players. Yes, the owners were saying, you may take Bobby Bonilla from my team, but you must give me Mark McGwire in return. To the players, the proposal was nothing more than an attempt to render free agency meaningless. The inability to resolve the issue led to the 1981 players' strike, which forced the cancellation of 713 games between June 12 and August 1.

The owners were down but not out. From 1985 to 1987, in yet another effort to hold down salaries, they banded together and refused to bid for players entering the free agent market. Players labeled their action "collusion." The word means "acting together in concert," and it has been expressly prohibited in MLB since 1966. The courts sided with the players, and the legal settlement cost the owners $280 million. The relationship between players and owners reached its lowest point in the catastrophic strike of 1994. Owners proposed a salary cap that would limit the total amount that each team could spend on players' compensation. Just as in the past, players viewed the proposal as another attempt to weaken their right to bargain.

Most observers thought the strike would be short, no longer than the fifty-day work stoppage in 1981. There seemed to be too much at stake for both sides as ballparks sat empty and television screens offered old movies and highlights from past seasons. But negotiations reached a stalemate, and the strike lingered. Players and owners suffered massive financial losses, as did thousands of other people who earned their livelihood from baseball as restaurateurs, parking lot attendants, merchandisers, ushers, and concessionaires. There were 450 layoffs at Fenway Park in Boston and 1,200 at the Astrodome in Houston (Dolan 1996: 48). Another casualty was the World Series. The fall classic has been played through two world wars, the Depression, and an earthquake in 1989 that rocked Candlestick Park in San Francisco an hour before the start of a game between the Giants and the Oakland Athletics. The series was not played in 1994.

By the time the strike ended after 232 days on April 1, 1995, neither side had won much. There was no salary cap in place for the owners and no new avenues of bargaining opportunity for the players. The biggest loser was the game of baseball itself. Embittered by the strike, fans turned their backs. In the AL, the average per-game attendance dropped

The Major League Baseball (MLB) players' strike of 1994 embittered millions of fans when it forced the cancellation of 232 days of baseball and the World Series. Since the strike, salaries for baseball players—and players in other sports—have continued to rise dramatically, and no slowdown is in sight. For every MLB player earning the minimum salary of $170,000 in 1998, there were five who made $1 million or more. The Baltimore Orioles and the Cleveland Indians each had seventeen millionaires on their roster. For many team owners, the price of talent becomes too high too quickly. Only four MLB from 30,662 in 1994 to 24,224 in 1995; in the NL the figure went from 28,775 to 23,624. The 1995 All-Star Game had the lowest Nielsen television ratings of any other game since 1969. When the Reds and the Braves opened the 1995 NL Championship Series, there were 10,000 empty seats in Riverfront Stadium in Cincinnati (Dolan 1996: 115–117). Attendance and television ratings have improved, but the sorry spectacle of the strike left a bitter aftertaste. Both players and owners saw their reputations damaged. Fans once again felt victimized by greed and powerless to influence the bickering factions that needed to make peace before the games could go on.

BUYING A CHAMPION

As baseball struggles to regain the preeminent place it held for decades in the sports world, the ultimate effect of free agency remains a subject of dispute. It has clearly raised the salaries of players, and, contrary to the exaggerated claims of owners, it has not destroyed the game. But does it give an advantage to wealthy teams and damage competitive balance? On that question, the evidence is much less clear.

In the first decade of free agency, each of the twelve NL teams won at least one division title, as did eleven of the fourteen AL teams. When the 1994 season was ended by the players' strike, the Montreal Expos, with a comparatively meager player payroll of $20 million, held first place in the Eastern Division of the NL. These performances support the conclusion that success on the field bears little relation to the amount of money players are paid. There are other, more intangible factors—desire, competitiveness, hard work, team unity—that fuel the will to win.

Another argument can be made that money does indeed make a difference. It is not a guarantee of success; it simply increases the odds of performing well. The New York Yankees of 1976 to 1978 were a wealthy team with a wealthy owner that brimmed with high-priced talent. They won three consecutive AL pennants and two World Series. There is also the example of the 1997 season, when the five teams with the highest payrolls—the New York Yankees, Baltimore Orioles, Cleveland Indians, Florida Marlins, and Atlanta Braves—all made the playoffs. In 1996, the top four money teams qualified, and the top three—the Yankees, Orioles, and Braves—played in their league championship series. "It's getting to the point where all you have to do is look at payroll to see who is first and second," says Terry Ryan, general manager of the Minnesota Twins (Dodd 1997: C1, C2).

Ryan's concern is shared by many others. It prompted MLB to begin a revenue-sharing program that is designed to reduce the advantage that wealthy teams now have in the hunt for top talent. Teams with the most expensive payrolls must pay a "luxury tax" to assist teams at the bottom end of the scale. In 1997, five teams paid a total of $12 million into MLB's revenue-sharing pool. No one knows if the program will prove effective in leveling the playing field. But the fact that wealthier teams have agreed to hand over millions of dollars to their competitors shows how serious the concern has become. If the gap between the rich and the not-so-rich continues to widen, MLB may find itself with five or six dominating superteams and twenty-five also-rans trying desperately to catch up. If that happens, more fans than ever are likely to disappear, and the pot of gold for players and owners alike may melt away to nothing.

TOPICS FOR DISCUSSION

1. Do you think that professional athletes make too much money? Why or why not? Explain your answer.

2. Do you think that the owners of professional sports teams make too much money? Why or why not? Explain your answer.

3. Athletes react to criticisms that they make too much money by saying they are entitled to receive whatever amount the team owners are willing to pay them. Do you agree with that point of view? Why or why not?

4. Critics of high salaries for athletes often object that many of their contracts are guaranteed, that is, they require players to be paid even if they are injured or fail to perform well on the playing field. Would athletes perform better if their contracts were not guaranteed? Why or why not?

5. Some observers of the baseball scene say that money can buy a championship team, and they point to the high payrolls of strong teams like the Atlanta Braves and the Cleveland Indians to prove their point. Do you think that money can buy a winning team, or are there factors other than high salaries that contribute to success on the diamond?

REFERENCES AND RESOURCES

Books

Dolan, Edward F. *In Sports, Money Talks*. New York: Holt, 1996.
   An excellent introduction to the world of money and sports for young adults.
Dudley, William, ed. *Sports in America: Opposing Viewpoints*. San Diego: Greenhaven Press, 1994.
   Chapter 3 discusses greed, business management, and antitrust law in baseball and other professional sports.
Flood, Curt, with Richard Carter. *The Way It Is*. New York: Trident Press, 1970.

The autobiography of the National League outfielder who challenged baseball's reserve system.

Gorman, Jerry, and Kirk Calhoun. *The Name of the Game: The Business of Sports.* New York: Wiley, 1994.

Chapter 1 examines the business of baseball. Chapter 11 discusses players' salaries.

Miller, Marvin. *A Whole Different Ball Game: The Sport and Business of Baseball.* New York: Carol Publishing, 1991.

The first executive director of the Major League Baseball Players Association shares the dramatic changes he has seen in the game.

Sands, Jack, and Peter Gammons. *Coming Apart at the Seams.* New York: Macmillan, 1993.

An insightful look at baseball's struggle to remain fiscally healthy in the era of free agency.

Weiss, Ann E. *Money Games: The Business of Sports.* Boston: Houghton Mifflin, 1993.

Chapter 4 discusses escalating players' salaries.

Will, George F. *Men at Work: The Craft of Baseball.* New York: Macmillan, 1990.

In the conclusion to his book, the noted columnist and baseball fan discusses owners, players, and money in the game.

Zimbalist, Andrew. *Baseball and Billions.* New York: HarperCollins, 1992.

A professor of economics at Smith College chronicles the evolution of the baseball business from the Civil War to the 1990s.

Magazines and Newspapers

Associated Press. "Owners' Losses Total $185 Million." *Columbus Dispatch,* July 25, 1997: 1D.

Figures on baseball's revenue losses from 1993 to 1996.

Beaton, Rod. "Martinez: Red Sox Offer Record $75M." *USA Today,* December 11, 1997: 1C.

The Red Sox hurler becomes baseball's highest-paid player.

Bodley, Hal. "Baseball Puts 317 Millionaires to Work." *USA Today,* April 2, 1998: 1C.

A report on escalating baseball salaries.

Brady, Erik, and David Leon Moore. "Big Sports, Bigger Bucks: Just How High Can Players' Salaries Go?" *USA Today,* April 3, 1997: 1A.

Discusses skyrocketing compensation in baseball, basketball, football, and hockey.

Clemons, Veronica. "Are Sports Superstars Worth the Millions They Are Paid?" *Jet,* August 5, 1996: 51–54.

Several star athletes answer the question posed with a resounding yes.

Dodd, Mike. "Playoff Teams Playing the Price." *USA Today,* October 1, 1997: C1, C2.

Studies the link between the payrolls of baseball teams and their performance on the field.

Hammonds, Keith H. "O.K. Baseball, You've Got One Last Chance." *Business*

Week, April 1, 1996: 34.
A fan's perspective on the game's recent turmoil.
Hille, Bob. "What's the Deal?" *Sporting News*, November 18, 1996: 32.
A report on the 1996 negotiations stalemate between players and owners.
Howerton, Daryl. "Show Leigh the Money." *Sport*, September 1997: 69–71.
A profile of sports agent Leigh Steinberg.
Montville, Leigh. "Funny Money." *Sports Illustrated*, October 13, 1997: 134.
Humorous commentary on the salaries of professional athletes.
Ozanian, Michael, and Stephen Taub. "Adam Smith Faces Off against Karl Marx." *Financial World*, February 14, 1995: 32–35.
An explanation of how major league sports teams strive both to make money as capitalists and share money as socialists.
Strauss, Gary, Thor Valdmanis, and Bruce Horowitz. "Optimism Reflected in Dazzling Deals." *USA Today*, October 7, 1997: 1B, 2B.
The writers detail basketball player Kevin Garnett's megadeal with the Minnesota Timberwolves.
Will, George. "Purists vs. Impurists." *Newsweek*, September 29, 1997: 88.
Thoughts on baseball's present and future from the noted conservative columnist.
Wulf, Steve. "Baseball's Blue Sale." *Time*, January 20, 1997: 64.
An account of the sale of the Los Angeles Dodgers to media tycoon Rupert Murdoch.

Organizations to Contact

Major League Baseball Players Association
12 East 49th Street, 24th Floor
New York, NY 10017–1028
Phone: 212–826–0808
Fax: 212–752–3649
Internet Web Site: www.bigleaguers.com
The association represents major league baseball players in collective bargaining negotiations with team owners. Its Web Site is the only place on the Internet where browsers can access the personal sites of active players.

Major League Baseball Players Relations Committee
350 Park Avenue, 17th Floor
New York, NY 10022
Phone: 212–339–7400
The committee, which is part of the Office of the Commissioner, is responsible for negotiating major league baseball's collective bargaining agreement with players.

6

The Man in the Mirror

In a society that celebrates sports and fame, athletes have become role models for America's youth. At the same time, many of those athletes engage in violent and illegal behavior on and off the field. Are sports stars obligated to lead exemplary lives for the benefit of young fans?

It had been a bad practice for Latrell Sprewell, another exercise in drudgery in a young season that showed every promise of being a miserable one. With just one victory in their first fifteen games, the Golden State Warriors were struggling to stay above water in the Pacific Division of the National Basketball Association (NBA). As the team's leading scorer, Sprewell, a twenty-seven-year-old All-Star guard out of the University of Alabama, was feeling the heat, pushing him to produce.

Warriors coach P. J. Carlesimo was not pleased with his team's stagger out of the starting gate. But then he never seemed pleased about much of anything that happened on the basketball court. Being a happy camper wasn't Carlesimo's thing. He constantly demanded more from his players. At each stage of his coaching career, he had practiced a craft laced with profanity and confrontation. Verbal insults were a major element of his coaching style. Just a month earlier, he had gotten into Sprewell's face during a game with the Los Angeles Lakers. "Don't talk to me like that," Sprewell told him. "If you have to talk to me, talk to me like a man" (Stein 1997: 33). Now, as the coach harangued his star one more time about his lazy passing, the rage inside Sprewell exploded and before anyone in the gym could stop him, he stepped up to Carlesimo and wrapped his hands around the coach's throat. "Bitch!" Sprewell thundered, using the word that is the ultimate insult in playground slang.

"You're gonna trade me or I'm gonna kill you!" (Starr and Samuels 1997: 33).

Sprewell's teammates and assistant coaches dragged him off Carlesimo, and the player went to the locker room to shower and try to cool off. He didn't. Fifteen minutes later, Sprewell emerged and went after Carlesimo's neck a second time, committing what NBA commissioner David Stern labeled "a clearly premeditated assault." By the time the dust settled a few days later, the flamboyant guard had been hit with penalties unprecedented in their swiftness and severity. The NBA suspended Sprewell for a full year, eliminating his ability to seek work with another team in the league during that time. The Warriors voided the remaining three years of his four-year contract, which would have paid Sprewell about $25 million. In making the move, the team cited the provision in the NBA's Uniform Player Contract known as the morals clause. The clause requires all players to "conform to the standards of good citizenship and good moral character." Converse, the athletic footwear company, cancelled Sprewell's endorsement contract, believed to be worth between $300,000 and $600,000 annually. Finally, Sprewell faced a torrent of angry criticism from commentators across America.

In the midst of the condemnation, there were a few who questioned the harshness of the punishment. Sprewell's agent, Arn Tellem, called the lengthy suspension an abuse of the commissioner's powers and "totally out of line." In the only other coach-bashing incident on record, Lenny Randle of baseball's Texas Rangers earned a thirty-day suspension and a $10,000 fine in 1977 for punching manager Frank Luchesi three times before an exhibition game. Billy Hunter, the executive director of the National Basketball Players Association, said the league's action unreasonably stripped Sprewell of his ability to pursue his livelihood for a full year. He vowed to seek relief for Sprewell through the arbitration process. In March 1998, Sprewell's punishment was reduced by an arbitrator. His suspension was cut from one year to seven months, and the final two years of his voided contract were reinstated, a move that saved him over $16 million. Despite the arbitrator's action, Sprewell still lost $6.4 million and endured the longest suspension in the league's history not related to drug use.

The arbitrator's decision was widely criticized, and Tellem and Hunter were greatly outnumbered by those who supported the actions taken by the Warriors, the NBA, and Converse. "How am I going to support him?" asked Dikembe Mutombo, a vice president of the players' association. "It's like my child going to class and beating up the teacher. . . . The coaches are our teachers. He crossed the line. The last line. I think he stepped on a mine." Chuck Raasch of the Gannett News Service wrote that the incident pushed major league sports one more step down the road toward achieving the impossible: "outdoing political campaigns as

Latrell Sprewell of the Golden State Warriors throws a slam dunk in a game against the Sacramento Kings in 1996. Sprewell shocked the sports world in 1997 when he attacked his coach P. J. Carlesimo, during a Warriors practice session. When he returned to the National Basketball Association (NBA) after serving only a seven-month suspension, many, including NBA commissioner David Stern, thought the punishment was far too light. "You cannot strike your boss and still hold your job—unless you play in the NBA," Stern said after an arbitrator ruled that the Warriors' voiding of Sprewell's contract was unacceptably harsh. To many fans the arbitrator's decision seemed to be a perfect example of how professional athletes are able to engage in violent and illegal behavior without suffering consequences. (AP/WIDE WORLD PHOTOS)

the most despised public activity in America" (*Columbus Dispatch* 1997: 4F). Walt Frazier, the basketball Hall of Famer who starred for the New York Knicks from 1967 to 1976, sounded a wistful note: "I long for a return to the time when players were revered as much for their character as for their jump shots. If the sports world does not soon recover its values an incident like this may soon be repeated" (*USA Today* 1997: 15A).

Sprewell's temper tantrum came at a delicate moment for the NBA. Through the 1980s and 1990s, the league had ascended to the summit of the sports world. Featuring the talents of superstars like Larry Bird, Michael Jordan, and Magic Johnson and an aggressive, physical version of the game, the league attracted hugely lucrative television contracts, record attendance, and worldwide devotion. But in 1997, the league was enduring a seemingly endless string of violent and illegal behavior on the part of its players. During the year, nearly twenty of them were charged by police with a variety of offenses. The roundup of arrests included Tim Hardaway of the Miami Heat, cited for drag racing; Allen Iverson of the Philadelphia 76ers for carrying a concealed weapon; Rod Strickland of the Portland Trail Blazers for driving while intoxicated; and Strickland's teammates Isaiah Rider for illegal possession of a cell phone and Jermaine O'Neal for verbally abusing police officers. The troubling year also featured the latest antics of Charles Barkley of the Houston Rockets and Dennis Rodman of the Chicago Bulls. Barkley stood accused of hurling a man through a plate glass window in a Florida bar; Rodman flung insults at Mormons and female referees and also earned a suspension for head-butting a referee during an on-court argument (Starr and Samuels 1997: 28–29). Even one of the league's most prominent broadcasters faced criminal charges. Marv Albert, the voice of the New York Knicks who called his first game in 1963 at age twenty, was convicted of sexually assaulting a woman during a tryst in a Virginia hotel room. Albert's legion of fans and friends could scarcely believe the lurid allegations that surfaced at his trial. They cried, "Say it ain't so Marv!" but sadly, it was so. Albert lost his job at the National Broadcasting Company (NBC).

The long parade of woes was more than enough to scruff up the league's carefully crafted image as a wholesome entertainment product fit for consumption by children and adults. The crowning blow, however, came in the form of an exposé published in the *New York Times* in October. After interviewing more than two dozen players, former players, agents, and team officials, the newspaper reported that marijuana use was rampant in the NBA, with as many as 60 to 70 percent of the league's 350 players smoking the substance regularly. "It's scary, because you don't know when guys are using it," said Derek Harper of the Orlando Magic. "You don't know if guys are under the influence while they're playing or what the case is" (Roberts 1997: 7).

Team officials blame the problem on the league's ineffective drug testing policy, which prohibits any use or sale of cocaine and heroin but not the use or sale of marijuana. Marijuana users can be disciplined only if their use results in a criminal conviction. The NBA is committed to re-examining its policy and is trying to convince the players association to agree to add marijuana to the list of banned substances. Some characterize the lax stance as a matter of economic survival, a conscious choice to live with the lesser of two evils. "If they tested for pot, there would be no league," explains Richard Dumas, a former player who was banned from the NBA for drug and alcohol use. "Weed is something guys grow up doing, and there's no reason for them to stop. Because almost everyone does it, no one wants to test for it. They're afraid to" (Roberts 1997: 1).

The picture that the NBA presented to the world at the end of 1997 was not a pretty one. Things got uglier the next year when *Sports Illustrated* reported in detail on the huge number of out-of-wedlock children fathered by NBA players. One top agent told the magazine that he thinks there are more out-of-wedlock kids fathered by NBA players than there are players in the league. The agent said he spends more time handling paternity claims filed against his clients by pregnant women than he does negotiating their contracts. Nor is the problem limited to the NBA. Athletes in many other sports have been subjected to paternity suits and are paying support for children born out of wedlock. Gloria Allred, a Los Angeles attorney who has represented dozens of mothers in paternity suits against athletes, says that the public is not even aware of the huge number of claims because most are settled quietly before they are reported by the media (Wahl and Wertheim 1998: 64).

With each new revelation, the questions become more frequent and more difficult to answer. What effects do the misdeeds of the players have on the millions of young people who have embraced NBA hoops as their spectator sport of choice? Do athletes have a responsibility above and beyond other people to conduct their lives in a manner that promotes integrity, fair play, and respect for authority? Or is the concept of the athlete as role model an outdated relic from the nation's past, irrelevant in a modern world where the only important questions seem to be, How much does it cost? and What's in it for me?

"I AM NOT A ROLE MODEL!"

Sports history is filled with great performers who gained notoriety for bad behavior. An investigation into the membership of any athletic hall of fame would uncover very few saints. Baseball slugger Babe Ruth was reputed to be a compulsive adulterer and heavy drinker who frequently offended fans, the press, and fellow players with his foul manners. Heavyweight boxing champion Mike Tyson served three years in an Indiana prison after being convicted of rape. Magic Johnson and Wilt Chamberlain boasted that they indulged in literally thousands of flings during their careers in the NBA, and Johnson left the game after testing positive for HIV. The list of athletes who have been accused of domestic violence is depressingly long; the names include golfer John Daly, football running back Lawrence Phillips, baseball players José Canseco and Bobby Bonds, and NBA All-Star Scottie Pippen. In the 1990s, the legal troubles of the Super Bowl champion Dallas Cowboys were so numerous that owner Jerry Jones hired former Cowboy Calvin Hill to lead a campaign to improve the team's public image. Just a few months later, coach Barry Switzer was arrested at the Dallas airport when a loaded .38-caliber pistol was discovered in his carry-on bag. "If this is America's team," lamented *Sports Illustrated*, "then woe is America." Even Michael Jordan, widely viewed as a paragon of upright living, was tainted by the accusation that he accumulated large gambling debts during his basketball career.

No one knows for sure how youngsters have reacted to all the bad news. The literature of the social sciences contains little concrete evidence that young people actually change their behavior to conform to the behavior of athletes they admire or idolize. They may change their shirts, pants, hairstyles, or sneakers, but they aren't likely to turn themselves into fighters, gamblers, drug users, or reckless drivers. Indeed, it may well be parents and adults, instead of children and teenagers, who react more strongly to negative media reports about sports stars (Gelman 1993: 56–57).

The inability of social scientists to confirm the phenomenon has not convinced many people that it doesn't exist. Much of the rest of the world seems to believe that the scientists are missing something. "Don't tell me kids don't emulate!" cries Joe Garagiola, the baseball catcher turned sportscaster. Since his retirement, Garagiola has spearheaded a campaign to educate baseball players and young fans about the dangerous effects of chewing tobacco. He convinced Philadelphia Phillies outfielder Lenny Dykstra to tape a public service announcement aimed at curbing the practice. "Copy my hustle. Copy my desire. But please, don't copy my tobacco use," he pleads. Dykstra himself started chewing tobacco to emulate his own hero, seven-time American League batting champion Rod Carew. Donald Fehr, the executive director of the Professional Baseball Players' Association, agrees with Garagiola. He calls athletes "foolish" if they fail to recognize that kids and older people pay serious attention to their words and deeds—on and off the playing field (Berlow 1994: 32).

Athletes earn that attention by occupying a special place in the pantheon of celebrities. At any given point in time, a dozen or so of the most prominent sports figures can be counted as residents of what author Jib Fowles has christened Star Village, the "mythic community composed of the different types of people whom the American public wants to observe" (Fowles 1992: 67). Today, those residents include Michael Jordan, golfer Tiger Woods, figure skater Tara Lipinski, hockey star Wayne Gretzky, football quarterbacks Brett Favre and Steve Young, and retired legends like baseball player Joe DiMaggio and golfers Jack Nicklaus and Arnold Palmer. Along with the most well-known actors, comedians, musicians, and television personalities, the athletes in Star Village occupy a huge piece of territory on the nation's grand media stage. Unlike the others, however, athletes earn their place on the stage through sheer ability. In the sports world, unlike Hollywood, achievements are measured objectively. That imbues the sports stars with a kind of purity that the other celebrities lack. Actor Paul Newman, who has competed as an auto racer for thirty years, understands the difference well. In Hollywood, he says, there are many "imponderables" that affect an actor's level of achievement. There are no such imponderables in sports. "That's one of the nice, clean things about racing," Newman says. "You got there first, end of discussion, you won" (Oldenburg 1998: 2D).

The small and elite group of sports celebrities who reside in Star Village are far from the only ones who can thrill millions with their athletic displays. That opportunity presents itself to any athlete who achieves success in one of the popular spectator sports. But are those athletes obligated to do anything more than compete to the best of their ability? The NBA's Charles Barkley says no—emphatically no. Barkley rarely has expressed regret or contrition about his antics on or off the court, and he has no desire to serve as a model for young people. "Just because I can dunk a basketball doesn't mean I should raise your kids," he tells parents. Barkley wants fans to admire and respect his accomplishments on the hardwood—and leave it at that (Gelman 1993: 56). All of the troubling behavior of Latrell Sprewell and the rest of Barkley's NBA colleagues should have no effect on how we judge them as basketball players, he says. Barkley's unapologetic stance rings true to a number of observers, including writer Matthew Goodman, who finds a paradox in society's clamoring for athletes to assume the role of good citizen:

The very qualities a society tends to seek in its heroes—selflessness, social consciousness, and the like—are precisely the *opposite* of those needed to transform a talented but otherwise unremarkable neighborhood kid into a Michael Jordan or a Joe Montana. Becoming a star athlete requires a profound and long-term kind of self-absorption, a single-minded attention to the development of a few rather odd physical skills, and an overarching competitive outlook. These qualities may well make a great athlete, but they don't necessarily make a great person. On top of this, our society reinforces these traits by the system it has created to produce athletes—a system characterized by limited responsibility and enormous privilege. (Dudley 1994: 47)

In short, Goodman believes it is unfair to ask athletes to serve as role models. Because they live their lives in a kind of moral vacuum, created by years of pampered treatment from parents, friends, fans, coaches, team officials, and agents, they are ill prepared for the task. Society stands guilty of worshipping the false god of athletic talent. That talent can become so captivating that it becomes the base on which much nobler characteristics—humility, courage, wisdom, concern for others—are mounted. Even the fabled sportswriter Red Smith confessed to "godding up the players" during his long career at the *New York Times*, that is, granting them character traits that they did not possess in order to make them appear to be better people than they really were (Berkow 1994: 15).

Some of Smith's colleagues in the media today seem intent on doing precisely the opposite. Instead of creating gods out of sports heroes, they create devils. Any unintentional act or casual utterance of a star player, especially one that is in any way controversial, stands a good chance of making its way into print, television, radio, or cyberspace. Sports sociologist Harry Edwards believes that this threat has put today's athletes on guard. Those who take their obligation to serve as role models seriously therefore alter their behavior to avoid offending *anyone*, and by doing so they actually become less admirable people (Edwards 1994: 32). The ultimate irony in Edwards's view is that Charles Barkley, by loudly disclaiming the role model assignment, has in fact become a role model himself by igniting a public debate on the question of whether athletes should be role models.

SETTING AN EXAMPLE

Barkley's point of view on the subject of role models has been countered most vocally by Karl Malone, an NBA forward with the Utah Jazz. Malone says athletes don't choose to become role models. Instead, they are chosen. By virtue of their wealth, status, and fame, they become a focus of the world's attention, whether they seek it or not. The only choice an athlete has is to be a good role model or a bad one. "I don't think we can accept all the glory and money that comes with being a famous athlete and not accept the responsibility of being a role model, of knowing that kids and even some adults are watching us and looking for us to set an example," says Malone. He doesn't, however, recommend that parents go to extremes, like the ones in Utah who proudly tell him that his picture is hanging in their living room, next to the picture of Jesus Christ. "Is it any wonder some athletes don't want to be role models?" he asks (Dudley 1994: 43–44).

Malone would prefer that parents be the primary role models for their children. Few can argue with that. He believes it is a role they should assume. But merely asserting that parents should take the lead does not end the debate about the place of athletes. Unfortunately, there are some parents in the world who should not be role models for their children. Among the rest there are many who are either unwilling or unable to assume the responsibility. "Kids need someone to idolize in order to become better themselves," says Doctor Robert Burton, a Northwestern University psychiatrist. "Without that, there's not much hope for them" (Gelman 1993: 56).

Sports agent Steve Woods is among those trying to keep hope alive. Like many others who work with the NBA, Woods laments the league's image problems and would like to see them addressed. He believes that the network of people who surround today's players—family members, agents, friends, and team officials—cannot realistically challenge their behavior because they are too dependent on the players' money. "Money is not corrupting players as much as money is corrupting support systems around the players," Woods says (Nance 1997: 21C). In a document he titled the NBA Manifesto, Woods offered a number of suggestions for change to league commissioner David Stern. They include organizing a mentor program that would link incoming NBA players with retired ones; creating family inclusion programs that would help wives, parents, children, and siblings of players to understand their roles better; and banning alcohol from team airplane flights and locker rooms.

The National Football League also has launched a campaign to counter the flood of negative publicity caused by the actions of many of its players. In 1998, league commissioner Paul Tagliabue announced a policy that will require any player or other employee of the league who is charged with a violent crime such as domestic violence or possession of a weapon to be subjected to immediate evaluation and counseling, if necessary. Any player or employee who is convicted of or pleads guilty to a violent crime will be subjected to a fine and a suspension without pay. A second conviction will carry a longer suspension or banishment from the league.

Cincinnati Bengals head coach Bruce Coslet, like his colleagues, welcomes the policy. Coslet understands that violent crimes such as domestic violence, weapons possession, and assault often receive less publicity than crimes related to drug or alcohol use. Violent crimes, however, may occur with even greater frequency. "It shouldn't be tolerated," Coslet says. "When you play or coach in the National Football League, you accept a certain amount of responsibility. We want to put forth the image the league wants to put forth. We want to be tough and efficient on the field, but you've got to leave it on the field" (Ridenour 1998: 15E).

There also is a need to step back from the negativity and see the bigger picture. In the sports world, true heroism is reserved for the very few, such as Jackie Robinson, who risked death when he broke major league baseball's color barrier, and Roberto Clemente, the Pittsburgh Pirates batting champion who died in a plane crash while leading a mercy mission to deliver food and supplies to earthquake victims in Nicaragua. Another candidate would be Mickey Mantle. During his career, Mantle was a spirited rabblerouser who was reputed to spend many nights closing the bars of Manhattan with his New York Yankee teammates. But in the last months of his life, shriveled by liver cancer brought on by decades of heavy drinking, he made a compassionate plea for people to make organ donations. When he did, pledges from prospective donors rose dramatically. Nor did Mantle hide from his past sins. He stood before the cameras one last time to warn young people about the dangers of alcohol and tell them, "Don't do what I did" (*Los Angeles Times* 1995: B8).

Robinson, Clemente, and Mantle may be among the few true heroes, but there are many other athletes who live their lives as model citizens and inspire respect with their words and deeds. In the NBA, Jerry Stackhouse of the Philadelphia 76ers is at work sponsoring a sports leadership program in Morehead City, North Carolina, that trains young athletes in their roles and responsibilities. Grant Hill of the Detroit Pistons is vice chairman of the tenth Special Olympics, held in the summer of 1999 in North Carolina. Hill first became involved with the games for people with mental retardation as a high school senior, and the Special Olympics has been a central part of his life ever since. And former NBA superstar Earvin Magic Johnson is strongly committed to promoting economic development in the inner cities of Los Angeles and his hometown of Lansing, Michigan. Stackhouse, Hill, and Johnson certainly fit the description of role models for their community activism.

So does David Robinson, the six-foot, eleven-inch center of the San Antonio Spurs. With his wife, Valerie, Robinson has donated $5 million to build a prep school in a poverty-stricken neighborhood on San Antonio's East Side. The school's curriculum focuses on character, moral development, and personal responsibility. The project is part of Robinson's campaign to look beyond the basketball court and involve himself with the homeless, education, and children's charities. Says Robinson's teammate Avery Johnson: "If you see the phrase 'role model' in the dictionary, his picture is going to be there" (Jerome and Harnes 1997:

100–102). In today's world, it is easy to forget that the pictures of many other athletes can be found there, too.

TOPICS FOR DISCUSSION

1. Basketball stars Karl Malone and Charles Barkley disagree on the question of whether professional athletes are obligated to serve as role models: Malone says yes; Barkley says no. With whom do you agree? Why?

2. Reflect for a moment about the athletes you admired in your younger days, and about the ones you admire today. Do you imitate their behavior on or off the playing fields? Do you try to live your life the way they live their lives? Or do you simply enjoy watching them perform?

3. The large number of players who allegedly smoke marijuana in the National Basketball Association (NBA) has prompted the league to propose adding pot to its list of banned substances. The players' association would like to maintain the status quo, which prohibits the use or sale of cocaine and heroin but not marijuana. Would you add marijuana to the NBA's list of banned substances? Why or why not?

4. Writer Matthew Goodman believes that star athletes are ill-equipped to serve as role models because they grow up with special privileges that can warp their sense of responsibility. Do you agree with Goodman's point of view? Why or why not?

5. In 1998, the National Football League (NFL) instituted a policy that allows the league to require evaluation and counseling of any player charged with a violent crime. Any player convicted of a violent crime would be subject to a fine and suspension without pay. What do you think about the NFL's new policy? Is it too lenient, too harsh, or appropriate? Explain your answer.

REFERENCES AND RESOURCES

Books

Benedict, Jeff. *Public Heroes, Private Felons: Athletes and Crimes against Women.* Boston: Northeastern University Press, 1997.
   Chronicles and criticizes the many acts of violence committed by athletes against their girlfriends and wives.
Berlow, Lawrence H. *Sports Ethics.* Santa Barbara, Calif.: ABC-CLIO, 1994.
   An excellent analysis of the role model issue in the book's introduction.
Dudley, William, ed. *Sports in America: Opposing Viewpoints.* San Diego: Greenhaven Press, 1994.

The question of whether athletes should be considered role models is debated in Chapter 1.

Fowles, Jib. *Starstruck: Celebrity Performers and the American Public*. Washington, D.C.: Smithsonian Institution Press, 1992.

Includes prominent sports stars in an examination of society's relationship with celebrities.

Ungerleider, Steven, Ph.D. *Quest for Success: Exploring the Inner Drive of Great Olympic Athletes*. Waco, Tex.: WRS Group, 1995.

Chapter 11, "Giving Something Back to the Community," discusses the positive activities of several Olympic medal winners.

Magazines and Newspapers

Araton, Harvey. "Barkley Is a Role Model after All." *New York Times*, January 30, 1995: C10.

A commentary on the on- and off-court behavior of the NBA's Charles Barkley.

Berkow, Ira. "The Worship of False Athletic Gods." *New York Times*, June 25, 1994: 15.

Comments on the role model issue in connection with the O. J. Simpson case.

Callahan, Gerry. "The Worst Kind of Coward." *Sports Illustrated*, July 31, 1995: 76.

A commentary on Boston Celtics center Robert Parish and his history of violence against women.

Cohen, Richard. "At 14, She's Not a 'Woman' and She's Not a Role Model." *Washington Post*, March 25, 1997: A17.

Considers the rising fame and fortune of Olympic gold medalist Tara Lipinski.

Columbus Dispatch. "What They're Saying." December 7, 1997: 4F.

A collection of comments on the Latrell Sprewell case.

Duffy, Mary. "Center of Attention." *Women's Sports and Fitness*, March 1996: 68–71.

A profile of basketball player Rebecca Lobo, considered to be an exemplary role model.

Edwards, Harry. "The Athlete as Role Model: Relic of America's Past." *Sport*, November 1994: 32.

Reflects on the changing role of athletes in American society.

Gelman, David. "I'm Not a Role Model." *Newsweek*, June 28, 1993: 56–57.

Concludes that children are less affected by the misdeeds of sport stars than many adults suspect.

Jerome, Richard, and Joseph Harnes. "Hoop Dreamer." *People*, December 1, 1997: 100–102.

A report on the many good works performed by NBA center David Robinson.

Los Angeles Times. "And, Yes, a Role Model at the End." August 15, 1995: B8.

An editorial comment on the last months of the life of baseball legend Mickey Mantle.

Nack, William, and Lester Munson. "Sports' Dirty Secret." *Sports Illustrated*, July 31, 1995: 63–74.

An in-depth report on the epidemic of domestic violence among professional athletes.

Nance, Roscoe. "Agent: Support System Key to Stemming Arrests." *USA Today*, September 5, 1997: 21C.

Sports agent Steve Woods calls for stronger support from family members and team officials in curbing the misbehavior of NBA players.

Oldenburg, Ann. "Newman's Own Perspective." *USA Today*, March 4, 1998: 1D, 2D.

Actor Paul Newman compares the experiences of auto racing and acting.

Ridenour, Marcia. "NFL Details Policy on Crime, Players." *Columbus Dispatch*, March 29, 1998: 15E.

A story on the policy on violent crimes committed by NFL players implemented by the National Football League in 1998.

Roberts, Selena. "N.B.A.'s Uncontrolled Substance." *New York Times*, October 26, 1997: Section 8: 1, 7.

A detailed report on marijuana and alcohol use by NBA players.

Starr, Mark. "Cowboys Will Be Boys." *Newsweek*, January 13, 1997: 56–59.

Discussed the off-field troubles of the NFL's Dallas Cowboys.

Starr, Mark, and Alison Samuels. "Hoop Nightmare." *Newsweek*, December 15, 1997: 26–29.

Latrell Sprewell's suspension for choking his coach is seen as evidence of a widening gulf between players and coaches in the NBA.

Stein, Joel. "Tall Men Behaving Badly." *Time*, December 15, 1997: 91–92.

Reports on the Latrell Sprewell choking incident.

USA Today. "Opinionline." December 12, 1997: 15A.

A roundup of comments on the Latrell Sprewell incident.

Vescey, George. "No Message. No Statement. The Right Thing on Sprewell." *New York Times*, December 5, 1997: C27.

Applauds the stern, swift action taken by authorities against Latrell Sprewell.

Wahl, Grant, and L. Jon Wertheim. "Paternity Ward." *Sports Illustrated*, May 5, 1998: 62–71.

A comprehensive look at the legal, financial, and emotional consequences that occur when professional athletes father out-of-wedlock children.

Wise, Mike. "Player Suspended for Year by N.B.A." *New York Times*, December 5, 1997: A1, C29.

A news report on the suspension of the NBA's Latrell Sprewell for attacking his coach.

Wulf, Steve. "Sportscasters Behaving Badly." *Time*, June 2, 1997: 88–89.

Highlights the troubles of sportscasters Marv Albert and Frank Gifford.

Organizations to Contact

National Basketball Association (NBA)
645 Fifth Avenue, 10th Floor

New York, NY 10022
Phone: 212–826–7000
Fax: 212–826–0579
Internet Web Site: www.nba.com
The NBA recently launched the Sportsmanship Athlete Program in conjunction with the National Federation of State High School Associations. The program's goal is to showcase coaches, students, and fans in the nation's high school athletic programs that make good sportsmanship possible.

NBA Players Association (NBAPA)
1700 Broadway, Suite 1400
New York, NY 10019
Phone: 212–333–7510
Fax: 212–956–5687
The association represents the interests of NBA players in labor negotiations and arbitration. It also sponsors educational programs and career counseling for players.

7

Gender Games

The passage of Title IX in 1972 created a new world for female athletes, and the growth of girls' and women's sports programs has been spectacular. In the midst of that growth, female athletes still face sexual harassment, low salaries, and resistance to their presence on the playing fields. What does the future hold for women's sports?

As a girl growing up in southern California in the 1950s, Billie Jean Moffitt fell in love with baseball at the age of eight or nine, when her father, a rabid sports fan who loved to play and watch all kinds of games, took her to see a minor league contest between the Los Angeles Angels and the Hollywood Stars. "Right away, I loved it," she writes in her autobiography, "but it was unfair for me to love it, because there was no place for an American girl to go in the national pastime" (King 1982: 12).

Baseball was far from the only sport that offered no future for young women in the 1950s. The landscape of the sports world was markedly different from the one that exists today. To say that that landscape was dominated by males would be an understatement. Of course, there were games for girls and women to play, just as there had been since the days of ancient Greece, when females, barred from the Olympic Games, competed in their own sports festival in honor of Hera, the Greek goddess of women and the earth. In the nineteenth century, women in the United States participated in large numbers in croquet, swimming, field hockey, and "pedestrianism," a forerunner of modern race walking. In 1876, Mary Marshall challenged a male pedestrian named Peter L. Van Ness to a three-day series of races in New York City. In perhaps the first Battle of the Sexes in American athletics, Marshall outwalked Van Ness and collected the $500 first prize (Greenberg 1997: 24).

The world of women's sports expanded in the twentieth century to include Olympic competition, softball, golf, and tennis. But any young woman like Billie Jean Moffitt who made a commitment to excel in athletics was considered strange, and most people in the world still clung to the belief that females were physically, emotionally, and mentally unsuited for the rigors of baseball, ice hockey, long-distance running, and other demanding sports. "Girls' " basketball was a feeble imitation of the male game, played on only half the court, with players allowed only two dribbles before being required to pass the ball to a teammate. As in other sports, an emphasis was placed on ladylike dress and decorum at all times. As late as 1979, the members of the California Dreams of the professional Women's Basketball League, who had graduated to the male version of the game, were required to attend charm school for instruction in cultivating "beauty and feminine self-presentation" (Nelson 1991: 7).

Instead of playing baseball, Billie Jean Moffitt took up tennis, one of the sports in which females could compete without appearing too unladylike. Even on the tennis court she felt out of place because her father was a fireman, and tennis was a game still played primarily in country clubs by bankers, lawyers, doctors, and their families. During the Southern California Junior Championships, she was forbidden to pose for a group photograph because she was competing in a pair of homemade shorts instead of a proper tennis dress. When she was sixteen, a male coach told her she had an excellent chance to become a world-class tennis player because she had a special reason to do well. What was that special reason? "You'll be good because you're ugly," he told her. The aspiring champion said she was "devastated" by the comment (King 1982: 13, 191). She also suffered from weight problems, poor vision, sinus infections that hampered her breathing, and battered knees that eventually would require several operations.

She overcame all of those obstacles to become perhaps the greatest woman ever to play the game and, to millions of fans, the personification of women's tennis under her married name, Billie Jean King. Coached by tennis legend Alice Marble as a teenager, Billie Jean was so focused on the game that Marble had to lock her in her bedroom to make sure she did her homework. In 1961, at age seventeen, she won her first Wimbledon title in England, teaming with Karen Hantze to win the women's doubles. The next year, she upset top-seeded Margaret Smith in the first round of the singles competition and earned the rapt attention of the tennis world. In 1966, she won her first Wimbledon singles title. She would win five more there, as well as five U.S. Open titles, one Australian Open title, and one French Open title. In 1973 at the Houston Astrodome, before the largest crowd ever to see a tennis match, King defeated male rival Bobby Riggs in her own Battle of the Sexes and

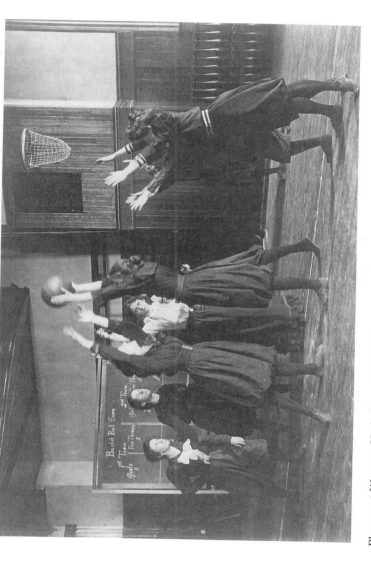

Players at Western High School in Washington, D.C., in 1899 scrap for the basketball as their teacher (in white blouse) looks on. The first basketball game for females was played between teams from the University of California at Berkeley and Stanford University in 1896, just five years after the game was invented by James Naismith. Today, women's basketball is one of the most popular participant sports. It shows every sign of becoming the professional team game that tennis legend Billie Jean King says is needed to place women in the front rank of the sports world. (Reproduced from the Collection of the Library of Congress)

struck a resounding blow against male chauvinism in sports. After the ballyhooed event, watched by 40 million television viewers, she told the media that tennis had always been reserved for males and "I've always been pledged to change all that."

Changing "all that" is an apt description of what has transpired in American sports since the heyday of Billie Jean King's tennis career. If she were growing up today instead of in the 1950s, she might well have had the chance to compete and excel in the sport that was her first love as a child. In the years since she humbled Bobby Riggs and his male fans in the Astrodome, the growth of girls' and women's sports has been phenomenal. While the number of young males participating in high school sports has remained at about 3.6 million since 1972, females are now playing games in record numbers. In 1972, less than 8 percent of the athletes playing high school sports were female. By 1996, that percentage had swelled to nearly 40 percent (Kiernan 1997: H9). The percentage of female collegiate athletes has increased from 15 in 1972 to 34 in 1996 (*Issues and Controversies* 1997: 298). In 1972, only $100,000 in scholarship money was awarded to female athletes playing at the colleges and universities in the National Collegiate Athletic Association (NCAA). By 1996, women were receiving $180 million in scholarship money, about half the amount awarded to men (Lee 1997: 39).

The primary force behind the rise of women's sports has been the federal law known as Title IX, which was passed by Congress and signed by President Richard Nixon in 1972. By entering the courts to enforce the statutory mandates of Title IX, girls and women are mounting an energetic campaign against the old boys' network that long has dominated sports in America.

THE FEDERAL MANDATE

Formally known as Title IX of the Education Amendments of 1972, the federal law passed by Congress states that "no person in the United States shall, on the basis of sex, be excluded from participation in, be denied the benefit of, or be subjected to discrimination under any education program or activity receiving federal financial assistance." Any institution found to be in violation of Title IX can have its federal funding terminated.

The law and the administrative regulations that were written after the law's passage do not mention girls or women. Instead, they refer to "the underrepresented sex," that is, the sex that is excluded to a greater degree than the other from any education activity or program, such as athletics. In theory, males could be the underrepresented sex, but in practice it nearly always refers to females. The language of the law applies not only to colleges and universities, but also to public elementary schools, middle schools, and high schools, nearly all of which receive some form of fiscal aid from the U.S. government. Nor does the mandate against sexual discrimination apply only to athletic programs at schools, colleges, and universities. Since its passage, Title IX has come to be strongly identified in the public eye with women's sports, but it also has been pivotal to the advancement of women in endeavors far removed from the sports world. In 1997, female artists used Title IX as a basis for a complaint against three art museums in New York City. They claimed that females were underrepresented in the museums' displays.

What must an institution and its athletic department do to demonstrate that they are in compliance with the mandate of Title IX? The Office of Civil Rights in the U.S. Department of Education, charged with enforcing the law, generally asks three questions to make that determination. First, does the school's athletic program meet the test of "substantial proportionality"? This means that if 50 percent of the students enrolled in an institution are female, then roughly 50 percent of the athletes who participate in interscholastic sports there must be female. Second, can the school show that it has expanded its sports programs for women on a regular basis? Even if the school has a disproportionately large number of male athletes, it can demonstrate compliance by adding women's teams consistently over a period of time. Finally, is the school "effectively accommodating" the interests of its women athletes in some manner other than equal participation or program expansion? For example, a school could show that the presence of a club or intramural team for women in a particular sport, as opposed to an interscholastic team, is sufficient to meet their demand for athletic participation. Or, in a more improbable example, it could demonstrate that its female students have no interest at all in pursuing any athletic opportunities beyond those currently offered.

If a school can answer yes to any one of the three questions posed, it is deemed to be in compliance with Title IX. However, as with any other law that is passed, the standards set forth on paper are often general and ambiguous. And even if the standards themselves are clarified through court decisions or administrative guidelines, there is often a vast difference between what the mandate requires on the page and what actually is enforced.

Since the passage of Title IX in 1972, the Office of Civil Rights has not withheld federal funding from any institution for any act of sexual discrimination in athletics (*Issues and Controversies* 1997: 298). Nor has it ever established a definite date by which all schools must be in compliance. At the same time, a survey conducted by the *Chronicle of Higher Education* in 1997 found that only 28 of the 303 institutions in Division I of the NCAA had achieved "substantial proportionality" in the 1995–1996 school year under the most common interpretation of that mandate. That interpretation deems an institution to be in compliance when the number of female athletes is no more than 5 percent less than the percentage of female undergraduates enrolled (Naughton 1997: A39).

The ever-changing numbers with regard to participation opportunities, scholarship money, and the number of women's teams at all levels of the education system make it difficult to determine how much progress is being made at any point in time toward complete compliance with the Title IX mandate. The most accurate assessment probably comes from Donna Lopiano, executive director of the Women's Sports Foundation. "The glass is half empty and half full," she says. "We are about halfway there" (Naughton 1997: A39).

THE UNLEVEL PLAYING FIELD

Getting the glass halfway full has been a long battle for advocates of women's sports. Their fight has been waged primarily in the courtrooms of America, where individual female athletes, backed by their parents and organizations such as the Women's Sports Foundation, Trial Lawyers for Public Justice, and the National Women's Law Center, have filed lawsuits against educational institutions to gain their fair share of resources, participation opportunities, and scholarship awards.

To date, most of the lawsuits have been filed against colleges and universities instead of high schools, because in higher education the spotlight on women's sports is brighter, the violations of Title IX are clearer, and the data needed to establish the validity of claims in court are more readily available. Many universities with high-profile athletic programs, including Colgate, Auburn, Texas, Colorado State, and Washington State, have been defendants in Title IX lawsuits. Colorado State reinstated its women's softball program in 1993 after former team members filed suit. Female athletes at Texas settled their class action lawsuit that challenged the school's failure to provide an equal number of participation opportunities for women. At the time the suit was filed in 1992, 47 percent of the undergraduates enrolled were female, but they had access to only 23 percent of the slots on interscholastic athletic teams. Other schools and universities, facing the prospect of possible legal action and adverse publicity, have improved their women's sports programs on their own.

A series of lawsuits filed by parents in four Nebraska school districts in 1995 offers a detailed picture of the many differences that can exist between male and female sports programs. In those lawsuits, the parents claimed that girls received inferior equipment, supplies, uniforms, and locker rooms. The parents also asserted that the boys' basketball teams had a schedule advantage because they played on weekends, while the girls' teams played in midweek, which made studying more difficult. The parents claimed that the boys' teams had the benefit of cheerleaders, band performances, and publicity and that the salaries of boys' coaches were higher than those for girls' coaches (Salter 1996: 27–28). In their efforts to settle the lawsuits, the schools agreed to create equitable schedules for boys' and girls' teams and to upgrade the equipment and locker rooms used by girls.

In the course of her research on gender equity, Susan True of the National Federation of State High School Associations has discovered many other situations similar to those found in the Nebraska school districts. "We were absolutely appalled to hear some of the situations that existed," she says. "At one high school, for instance, the boys' teams were receiving new uniforms every two years, while the girls' teams hadn't had new uniforms in seven years. There were girls' basketball teams that were practicing with plywood placed in a parking lot because they were not allowed in the gymnasium. I don't know if people realize that is all part of equity" (Salter 1996: 30).

The U.S. Supreme Court has played a pivotal role in the battle for gender equity under Title IX. In 1984, in the case of *Grove City v. Bell*, the Court ruled that the law applied only to the specific program within an institution that received federal funding instead of to all the programs of the institution. The ruling virtually eliminated Title IX as a vehicle for achieving gender equity in sports because no school, college, or university athletic departments receive direct federal aid for their programs. This meant that they were free, under the Supreme Court's interpretation of the law, to continue to discriminate against female athletes without fear of losing federal financial aid for their parent institutions. In 1988, Congress overruled the Supreme Court's decision in *Grove City v. Bell* by passing the Civil Rights Restoration Act over the veto of President Ronald Reagan. The act declares that Title IX applies to any athletic department with a parent institution that receives federal funds, regardless of whether the athletic department itself receives funding (Salter 1996: 56).

In 1997, the Supreme Court provided a vital boost to Title IX enforcement when it refused to hear the case of *Cohen v. Brown University*. By allowing the ruling of the lower court in favor of the female athletes to remain in effect, the Court gave its blessing to the three-question test that has been used to measure gender equity in athletic programs. The case arose from a decision by Brown University in Rhode Island to eliminate four sports, including two men's teams, women's gymnastics, and women's volleyball. Brown gymnast Amy Cohen and the other female athletes who brought the case said that the loss of those participation opportunities, even with the elimination of the men's teams, meant that Brown had failed the test of substantial proportionality, which requires the percentage of female athletes to be roughly equivalent to the percentage of females enrolled at the school. The university maintained that it was meeting the athletic needs of its female students and was therefore in compliance with the law. More than sixty other colleges and universities supported Brown's position (*Issues and Controversies* 1997: 79).

"The impact [of the decision] is as much psychological as anything else," says Donna Lopiano of the Women's Sports Foundation. "A lot of people—football coaches especially—were absolutely convinced that some rich school would go to court and salvation would be at hand and Title IX would be overturned. That was their dream. We hope now they realize there is no way out, that we can move forward and do what we were supposed to do 25 years ago" (Wulf 1997: 79).

WHAT ABOUT THE MEN?

Lopiano's comments on the Brown University case illuminate the emotional controversy that has surrounded Title IX since its passage: opponents vehemently contend that the law hurts boys' and men's sports programs by requiring a shifting of funds and resources to girls' and women's programs and by forcing the outright elimination of many male teams. There also are many who believe that Title IX has been used to force the sexual integration of the playing fields, to the detriment of males. "Over my dead body will girls ever play Little League baseball," fumed one male coach in the 1970s, before Congress revised the terms of the organization's federal charter and forced it to include females. "If one of them ever struck out a boy, he would be psychologically scarred for life" (Lipsyte 1997: H9). And despite the vast cultural changes that have occurred in the last quarter-century, there are still many who believe that it is inappropriate for women to be involved in athletics to as great a degree as men in any capacity—be it player, coach, referee, trainer, administrator, or even fan. "Young men today are swimming in a different sea," says Don Sabo, a former football player who is now a sports sociologist as D'Youville College in New York. "But I still have to tiptoe when I speak to male high school and college athletes . . . because when you start talking about gender issues, young men start feeling very put upon" (Lipsyte 1997: H9).

For many years, opponents of Title IX had a powerful ally in the NCAA. As an organization largely controlled by athletic directors and men's football and basketball coaches at the nation's major universities, the NCAA strongly supported a proposed amendment in 1974 that would have exempted college athletics from the law's requirements. Later the NCAA initiated a lawsuit that sought to render the law's administrative regulations invalid. Only after those two maneuvers failed did the NCAA soften its opposition and move toward compliance. It was not until 1991, ten years after it became the governing body for women's college athletics, that the NCAA's members formally adopted gender equity in athletics as a basic principle of the organization (Tarkan

1995: 26). Executive director Cedric Dempsey admits that progress has been slow. "We are trying to change a culture," he says. "It is more difficult than it might appear" (Chambers 1997: C10).

Concerns raised by Title IX opponents about reductions in men's programs are valid. In 1995, Congressman Dennis Hastert of Illinois chaired hearings in Washington on the issue of how Title IX affects opportunities for male athletes. The evidence shows that many men's programs in colleges and universities for sports other than basketball or football were discontinued between 1982 and 1996: thirty-two in gymnastics, twenty-seven in swimming, and forty-eight in wrestling (Wieberg 1997: 11C). Like many others, Hastert believes that the interest level of each gender should be considered when participation opportunities and resources are allocated. They maintain that males are more interested in playing sports than females and therefore should be given more chances to participate. In their view, it is ludicrous to enforce a law that compels females to participate in athletics as a matter of decree. Maureen Mahoney, one of the attorneys who represented Brown University in the *Cohen* case, shares those sentiments: "Are there substantially more men than women who have the desire and ability to compete on the varsity level? Because if there are, accomplished male athletes should not have to duke it out among themselves to get the slots that are left after all the women have been accommodated" (Mahoney 1997: 78).

The law's supporters counter those arguments with two points. First, they reject the notion that women are by their nature less interested in athletic competition than men. When Title IX passed in 1972, only 7 percent of the interscholastic athletes in high school were female. By 1992, that number had risen to 37 percent (Tarkan 1995: 26). To the law's supporters that does not indicate lack of interest. It indicates precisely the opposite. Once the doors of opportunity were opened and females were offered a chance to play, they did so by the millions.

Supporters also dismiss the claim that enforcement of Title IX necessarily leads to the elimination of men's programs. They contend that the true heart of the controversy is football, a sport played only by males and one that requires a huge allocation of resources for uniforms, equipment, liability insurance, field maintenance, travel expenses, and large coaching staffs. With Division I-A schools in the NCAA offering eighty-five football scholarships and often fielding teams with as many as 120 members, it is extremely difficult to achieve gender parity in terms of participation or financial aid. No single women's sport in the NCAA is allocated more than twenty scholarships (Wieberg 1997: 11C). If football expenses could be pared and the number of participants reduced, there would be considerably less need to eliminate smaller men's sports such as gymnastics, wrestling, and swimming.

Football supporters point to the fact that scholarship grants in the sport have been reduced steadily over the years and that other expenses have been cut significantly. Some question the second claim, especially when they read of the huge sums spent by a university to attract a coach. The same difficulty can arise when they read of the equally huge sum spent to buy out of the contract of the coach who has been fired because he could not produce the winning teams needed to keep the football program prominent and financially healthy.

On many campuses, football remains a virtually untouchable enterprise immune to significant change, backed by influential supporters, a century of rich tradition, and millions of vocal fans. Along with men's basketball, it also generates millions of dollars in revenue through the sale of game tickets and television broadcast rights. Only rarely does a school actually make the drastic move of discontinuing football, as Boston University did in 1997. It is one of only three Division I schools to drop the sport since 1992. In the words of David F. Salter, "College football's hierarchy has attacked gender equity with the tenacity of a blitzing linebacker facing fourth down at the one yard line" (Salter 1996: 49). Instead of confronting that linebacker, universities have chosen, in the view of Title IX advocates, to take the less painful course of eliminating other men's sports in order to level the playing field for women.

ONWARD AND UPWARD

In spite of the cultural and financial obstacles in their path, advocates of gender equity in sports can point to three decades of progress since the passage of Title IX. It is true that the executive directors of the major sports organizations remain overwhelmingly male, as do the vast majority of university athletic directors, sports journalists, agents, and team owners. Female coaches also are in short supply. Fewer than half of the women's college teams are coached by females; in high schools the percentage is below 40 (Collins 1997: 19). But those percentages will increase over time, as many of the female athletes who were given their first chances to play under Title IX become available to fill coaching positions. The disparity in coaching salaries for men's and women's coaches remains large. Sixty percent of all coaching pay at the college level still goes to men's team coaches, with the highest wages earned by those who coach football and basketball teams. The NCAA's 1997 Gender Equity Study revealed that the average salary for women's basketball coaches at the nation's 300 largest universities was $60,603. The average for men's basketball coaches was $99,283 (*USA Today* 1997: 16A).

It is on the playing fields themselves that real progress is evident. Women's team sports have assumed a more prominent place on the sports stage. In the 1996–1997 school year, the total number of female participants at the college level as reported by the NCAA stood at

128,209. Men's participation for that year stood at 200,627. The more critical numbers are the increased rates for participation. Female participation increased by 3.4 percent from the previous year, a rate over six times greater than the male increase of 0.54 percent. Of the 248 new college teams created in 1996–1997, 227 were for women. More than 800 teams for women were created at the college level from 1992 to 1996 (Tarkan 1995: 26). Women's basketball now has 966 teams, more than any other men's or women's sport.

Women's professional sports teams also have assumed a more prominent place on the stage, bolstered by the gold medal performances at the 1996 Olympics by America's basketball, softball, and soccer teams. The triumph of Team USA in Atlanta paved the way for the Women's National Basketball Association (WNBA), which debuted in 1997 backed by corporate powerhouses Nike, Coca-Cola, and American Express. The American Basketball League (ABL), a second league for women, also began play in 1997. The Women's Professional Fastpitch League for softball debuted in 1997. The six-team league drew 200,000 fans in its inaugural season. In 1998, the National Soccer Alliance, a professional league for women, opened play with eight franchises. The group has set its standards high: operating budgets of at least $1 million for each team, with a minimum of $400,000 for players' salaries, and stadiums with seating capacities of at least 5,000. In a society long used to seeing its most prominent female athletes excel as teenage prodigies in individual sports like tennis, figure skating, and gymnastics, the emergence of so many women's teams at the same time signals a new era.

Women also are entering sports that always have been considered male domains. The most recent example is ice hockey. USA Hockey, the sport's national governing body, reports that female participation in American amateur hockey has increased nearly fivefold since 1990. That year, only 5,000 females played the game. By 1997, the number had jumped to nearly 24,000. In 1998, five years after goalie Erin Whitten made history by becoming the first woman to record a victory in a men's professional hockey game, women's hockey debuted in the Olympics, with the United States winning the gold medal in a six-team event in Nagano, Japan. It will become a full-medal sport, with participation by many more teams, at the Winter Games in Salt Lake City, Utah, in 2002. The success of the American women in Nagano has spawned an effort to create a women's professional league. "The sport has wonderful role models," says Dianne Antos, who is working to land a franchise in Bridgeport, Connecticut. "They're articulate, college-educated females. I would like the young girls of this country exposed to them" (Raboin 1997b: 14C).

The ultimate goal of gender equity advocates is to increase playing opportunities for young females of all talent levels, regardless of whether

New York Liberty center Rebecca Lobo (50) cleans the glass as her teammate Theresa Weatherspoon (11) and Linda Burgess (42) of the Los Angeles Sparks look on. The Women's National Basketball Association (WNBA) was one of two new professional roundball leagues for women that began play in 1997 after the gold medal triumph of the American team at the 1996 Olympics in Atlanta. Owned and operated by the National Basketball Association (NBA), the WNBA benefits from the NBA's sophisticated marketing and merchandising operations. With ticket prices averaging just $15, the WNBA attracted an average of 9,000 fans per game during its first season. (AP/WIDE WORLD PHOTOS)

they ever win a gold medal, set a world record, or play on a professional team. The key concern is increasing opportunities at an early age. Most athletic programs for children in elementary schools are sponsored by private groups that do not fall under the jurisdiction of Title IX because they receive no fiscal aid from the federal government. They operate with scant resources and volunteer coaches that make it difficult to sustain boys' programs as well. But parents are demanding athletic parity for their daughters because they realize that the long-term benefits for girls who play sports are identical to the benefits for boys. "The things they learn when they are working with their team and creating goals are things they will use later in life," says Summer Sanders, who won four medals as a swimmer in the 1992 Olympic Games. "Girls need to realize that they don't have to be afraid of failure. They have to realize they can take risks" (Salter 1996: 39).

Millions of girls are taking those risks now. There is every reason to believe that millions more will do so in the future.

TOPICS FOR DISCUSSION

1. The central criticism of the anti-discrimination law known as Title IX is that it hurts boys' and men's sports programs by shifting resources away from them and into girls' and women's programs. Do you believe that criticism is justified? Why or why not?

2. Reflect on the sports programs for boys and girls in your own middle school and high school. Do the girls have equal access to locker rooms, practice fields, and equipment? Are there as many opportunities for girls to participate in sports as boys? Would you say that girls are subject to discrimination? If so, how could that discrimination be remedied?

3. Title IX advocates contend that the true cause of discrimination against females is football, a sport played only by males that requires huge operating expenses, large rosters, and costly facilities. Is there a way to level the playing field for females and males without abolishing football or reducing the amount of resources devoted to it? Or must football be abolished to create true gender parity?

4. The growth of professional team sports for women has been remarkable in the 1990s, with leagues being created for basketball, softball, hockey, and soccer. Do you follow these professional leagues as a fan? Do they arouse the same level of interest in you as the established male leagues? Why or why not?

5. The Office of Civil Rights in the U.S. Department of Education has been criticized for lax enforcement of the Title IX law. Do you believe

that the criticism is justified? Why or why not? Could the office be doing more to ensure equal athletic opportunities for females? If so, what?

REFERENCES AND RESOURCES

Books

Chambers, Marcia. *The Unplayable Lie: The Untold Story of Women and Discrimination in American Golf.* New York: Pocket Books, 1995.
Unveils the hidden history of discrimination against women in many of the nation's private golf courses and country clubs.

Greenberg, Judith E. *Getting into the Game: Women and Sports.* New York: Grolier, 1997.
An excellent one-volume history of women in sports, from the ancient Olympic Games to the Title IX era.

King, Billie Jean, with Frank Deford. *Billie Jean.* New York: Viking Press, 1982.
The autobiography of the tennis superstar and promoter of women's sports.

Markel, Robert, Susan Waggoner, and Marcella Smith. *The Women's Sports Encyclopedia.* New York: Henry Holt and Company, 1997.
A comprehensive guide to female sports, athletes, and records.

Nelson, Mariah Burton. *Are We Winning Yet? How Women Are Changing Sports and Sports Are Changing Women.* New York: Random House, 1991.
Profiles several female champions and raises provocative questions about femininity, sexual orientation, and athletic competition.

Powe-Allred, Alexandra, and Michelle Powe. *The Quiet Storm: A Celebration of Women in Sport.* Indianapolis: Masters Press, 1997.
Offers inspirational stories of women who have faced obstacles in the sports world.

Salter, David F. *Crashing the Old Boys' Networks: The Tragedies and Triumphs of Girls and Women in Sports.* Westport, Conn.: Praeger, 1996.
A balanced discussion of the intense and often hostile debate about the effects of Title IX.

Magazines and Newspapers

Brady, Erik. "Suit Winner Dislikes 'Hero' Acclamation." *USA Today*, June 20, 1997: 1C, 2C.
A profile of Amy Cohen, the Brown University gymnast who sued her school to win athletic opportunities for young women.

Brown, Debbie. "Title IX Opened Doors for My Career." *USA Today*, June 23, 1997: 13A.
The head volleyball coach at the University of Notre Dame describes how Title IX helped her advance in her playing and coaching career.

Chambers, Marcia. "For Women, 25 Years of Title IX Has Not Leveled the Playing Field." *New York Times*, June 16, 1997: A1, C10.

An overview of the history and current status of Title IX.

Collins, Mary. "And the Men Shall Lead Them." *Women's Sports and Fitness*, April 1997: 19–20.

A report on the acute shortage of female coaches in high school and college sports.

Issues and Controversies on File. "Title IX." July 18, 1997: 298–304.

An excellent discussion of Title IX that includes a chronology of key dates.

Kiernan, Denise. "Word May Be Out, But Schoolgirls Need to Get Message." *New York Times*, June 22, 1997: H9.

Discusses the benefits of sports participation for girls and young women.

Lee, Janet. "Fair Game." *Women's Sports and Fitness*, June 1997: 37–40.

A retrospective on the first twenty-five years of Title IX.

Lipsyte, Robert. "In the Gender Game, New Rules to Play By." *New York Times*, June 22, 1997: H9.

Reflects on the changes facing young male athletes in the new world created by Title IX.

Mahoney, Maureen. "The Numbers Don't Add Up." *Sports Illustrated*, May 5, 1997: 78.

An attorney defends the position of Brown University and other schools that have fought against implementation of Title IX.

Moran, Malcolm. "At UConn, Winning Does Not Add Up." *New York Times*, June 22, 1997: H9.

Contrasts the great success of the University of Connecticut's women's basketball team with the school's struggle to achieve gender equity under Title IX.

Naughton, Jim. "Women in Division I Sports Programs: 'The Glass Is Half Empty and Half Full.' " *Chronicle of Higher Education*, April 11, 1997: A39–40.

Presents the publication's extensive survey on gender equity in college sports programs.

Raboin, Sharon. "Pro League Organizer Signs 16 Women, Talks with 3 Hockey Sites." *USA Today*, October 7, 1997b: 14C.

A report on efforts to start a professional league for women.

Raboin, Sharon. "Women Try to Make Cut." *USA Today*, August 22, 1997a: 3C.

A report on the tryouts in Lake Placid, New York, for the first U.S. Olympic women's hockey team.

Tarkan, Laurie. "Unequal Opportunity." *Women's Sports and Fitness*, September 1995: 25–27.

Discusses efforts by opponents to dismantle Title IX.

USA Today. "Why Pay Women Less?" November 17, 1997: 16A.

Editorializes in favor of equal pay for coaches of women's team sports.

Wieberg, Steve. "NCAA Finds Too Little Progress." *USA Today*, June 20, 1997: 11C.

A detailed progress report on Title IX, published on the twenty-fifth anniversary of the law's passage.

Wulf, Steve. "A Level Playing Field for Women." *Time*, May 5, 1997: 79–80.

A report on the victory of Title IX supporters in the case of *Cohen v. Brown University*.

Organizations to Contact

National Association for Girls and Women in Sports (NAGWS)
1900 Association Drive
Reston, VA 20191
Phone: 703–476–3450
Fax: 703–476–9527
NAGWS serves the needs of administrators, teachers, students, and parents involved in sports programs for girls and women.

National Women's Law Center
11 DuPont Circle, N.W., Suite 800
Washington, D.C. 20036
Telephone: 202–588–5180
Fax: 202–588–5185
The center works to guarantee equality for women under the law and to seek advancement and protection of their legal rights. In 1997, the center filed a complaint with the U.S. Department of Education against twenty-five universities it believes have discriminated against women athletes in scholarship funding.

Women's Intercollegiate Athletics
340 Carver-Hawkeye Arena
University of Iowa
Iowa City, IA 52242
Phone: 319–335–9247
E-mail: mary-curtis@uiowa.edu
Internet Web Site: www.lib.uiowa.edu/proj/ge
This Internet Web Site, maintained by Mary C. Curtis and Christine H. B. Grant, is dedicated exclusively to issues concerning gender equity in sports. The pamphlet entitled *Gender Equity: Judicial Actions and Related Information* is available for $6.

Women's Sports Foundation
Eisenhower Park
East Meadows, NY 11554
Phone: 516–542–4700
Toll-free phone: 800–227–3988
Fax: 516–542–4716
E-mail: wosport@aol.com
Internet Web Site: www.lifetimetv.com
Established in 1974 by Billie Jean King, the foundation is dedicated to increasing opportunities for women in sports through education, advocacy, recognition, and grants. It publishes *Women's Sports and Fitness* magazine.

8

In the Name of God

In the 1990s, more athletes than ever are expressing their religious faith openly, often to the dismay of fans, commentators, and their teammates. Are the arenas of sport an appropriate place to proclaim the glory of God?

They can be found in nearly every part of the sports world, from the energized boxing rings of Las Vegas and Atlantic City to the sprawling stock car tracks of the South, from the boisterous stadiums of football to the lush, green fairways of professional golf. In the 1990s, more athletes than ever before have begun openly expressing their religious faith in front of opponents, teammates, fans, and television cameras. They kneel. They pray. They shout. They exult and point their fingers to the sky, offering thanks to the Christian God and his son, Jesus Christ, who they say have given them the courage and strength to compete and win in their chosen sports. And when their workday is done and their season is over, they continue to spread the word in the world beyond sports, using their status and celebrity to draw young and old alike into camps, leagues, programs, and organizations whose purpose is to serve the Lord just like they do.

Their actions make many people uncomfortable. The "God Squadders," as they sometimes are derisively called, have been tagged as hypocrites, showboats, and bullies who try to force their religious faith on others. They have been instructed to keep their religion to themselves. They have been informed, in the manner of a wise elder instructing a dim-witted child, that God has no interest in whether they win or lose their contests and that it is wrong to pray for victory because praying for victory means praying for other human beings to suffer defeat. None of the negative comments seem to deter the God Squadders from joyously proclaiming their faith. If anything, they have precisely the opposite effect. The God they know has nothing to do with hypocrisy, showboating, or intimidation. Instead, God is a deeply personal presence, a force that guides them as they work to survive and prosper in a career full of physical risk and uncertainty. They want to share that personal presence with other people, on and off the playing field.

Hundreds of athletes have accepted Jesus Christ as their personal Lord and Savior. At one time, athletes who professed their religious beliefs openly were considered sissies. That time has passed. Journalist Chris Smith reported in 1997 that Christian athletes seemed to be approaching a majority in several professional sports, especially golf, football, and baseball (Smith 1997: 27). Humorist Roy Blount, Jr., says that so many Christians have invaded professional sports that when he set out to "select an 'All-Religious Team' and an 'All-Heathen Team' to compete in an imaginary 'Christian v. Lions Bowl' he couldn't find enough heathens to fill a squad" (Higgs 1995: 13).

On the Professional Golfers' Association (PGA) Tour, Tom Lehman, Steve Jones, Paul Azinger, and Corey Pavin are among those bearing the torch for Christ. Pavin's devotion so impressed fellow Christian and basketball star David Robinson that Robinson named his son Corey. In major league baseball (MLB), the most overtly Christian team is the Texas Rangers, led by their born-again manager Johnny Oates. Pregame chapel services at the Ballpark in Arlington regularly draw two dozen or more team members. Defensive end Reggie White of the National Football League's (NFL) Green Bay Packers is perhaps the most vocal Christian in sports. The All-Pro "Minister of Defense" is an ordained preacher who heads a fundamentalist congregation in his hometown of Knoxville, Tennessee. He also has emerged as an influential leader and spokesman in the African-American community. White is not afraid to speak his mind. In a speech before Wisconsin state lawmakers in 1998, he condemned homosexuality as a sin and chastised political leaders for allowing it to be practiced openly in society. Quarterback Steve Young of the San Francisco 49ers follows a quieter but no less devout path. As the great-great-great grandson of Brigham Young, the nineteenth-century leader of the Mormon church, Young is one of the NFL's most active participants in church, school, and community activities. Young's fellow quarterback Mark Brunell also is deeply religious, as are nearly thirty of his teammates. "We have a lot of guys on this team who love the Lord," Brunell says (Hubbard 1998: 71–72). That love may help account for the Jaguars' rapid rise from expansion team to Super Bowl contender in less than half a decade of existence.

Even the most flamboyant and fun-loving stars of the gridiron have turned to religion. Deion Sanders of the Dallas Cowboys, perhaps the most flamboyant of all, now draws hundreds of people to "Prime Time

University of Kentucky quarterback Tim Couch offers thanks to heaven as he watches a teammate catch his pass and scurry into the end zone in a 1997 game against the University of Louisville. Couch is one of thousands of athletes who view God as the ultimate role model and use their visibility to proclaim God's righteousness. (AP/WIDE WORLD PHOTOS)

Tuesdays," his weekly Bible study class at a church in Plano, Texas. The crowd includes rich and poor, black and white, young and old, male and female. On the stage in front of them, microphone in hand, they see a person who in many ways seems identical to the trash-talking, showboating, flashy defensive back and punt returner who is known to the sports world as Neon Deion. But there is one important difference: Sanders has embraced the Lord. He says his religious transformation occurred in 1997 when he suffered through a profound depression and lurched dangerously close to taking his own life. All the glory, fame, and riches of his athletic career could not erase the deep emptiness he felt inside himself. "People doubt he's a real Christian and then they come here and see he's a real, true Christian," says teammate Emmitt Smith (Associated Press 1998: 14E). Today, Sanders feels the call to reach out to others in distress, and in church he offers his shoulder to those who feel a need to cry and a hug to those who need a warm embrace.

In the boxing ring, heavyweight champion Evander Holyfield fights with Jesus Christ firmly embedded in body and soul. Holyfield vocalized his faith in 1996, when he knocked out Mike Tyson in the first of their title bouts. "You can't choose against my God!" Holyfield bellowed at Tyson. "My God is the only true God!" His words were a reference to Tyson's embrace of the Muslim God Allah while he was serving a prison term in Indiana after being convicted of rape (Bayless 1996: 7). George Foreman, another heavyweight champion, retired in 1977 because he believed the violent nature of the sport conflicted with his Christian beliefs. He changed his mind a decade later and returned to the ring to recapture the heavyweight crown by knocking out Michael Moorer. Now an ordained minister, Foreman continues to preach the word of God.

Religion also has a strong presence in the world of the National Association of Stock Car Auto Racing (NASCAR). Jeff Gordon, the circuit's top driver, prays every day with his wife and says his relationship with Christ has guided him through the stressful experiences of sudden success and overwhelming wealth. Driver Ernie Irvan believes that his faith saved his life after he slammed into a concrete wall at 180 miles per hour during a practice run at Michigan International Speedway in 1994. He suffered massive injuries to his heart, head, and lungs. Doctors gave him a 10 percent chance of survival and said that even if he did survive, he would never race again. Irvan was back on the track fifteen months later. "I knew if God healed my body I would be able to compete again," he said. "I guess God still has some things for me to do" (Plummer 1995: 154).

Not all of the devoutly religious competitors in the sports world are Christians. Islam has over 1 billion adherents throughout the world, including 5½ million in North America. Muslims, those who practice the Islamic religion, are the second most visible religious group in sports.

Other than Tyson, the most famous is Hakeem Olajuwon, the dominating center for the Houston Rockets of the National Basketball Association (NBA). He adheres faithfully to the tenets of Islam and has made two *hajs*, or pilgrimages, to the holy city of Mecca. He says the trips, which symbolized his decision to become a serious Muslim, taught him patience and tolerance and changed his state of mind on the basketball court. He no longer belittles his opponents or explodes in anger as he had in his days at the University of Houston. But Olajuwon did not lose his competitiveness when he underwent his religious conversion:

> But even in my new tolerance I was not going to be rolled over. Christianity teaches you to turn the other cheek, and when people found I had made my pilgrimage and was more serious than ever about my religion they thought it might make me soft on the court. There was no chance of that. In Islam you can be as aggressive as you want as long as you play fair. You can never be the aggressor, you can't trip or elbow people, but I never played like that anyhow. I rely on hard work, skills, and competition. I wouldn't curse or use foul language anymore, that was out, but Islam is different from what people think. In Islam if someone slaps you, you have two choices: you can slap back as hard, but not harder, than you were slapped, or you can—and this is recommended—leave it for Allah to consider. (Olajuwon 1996: 214–215)

Olajuwon also fasts during the daylight hours in the holy month of Ramadan, which begins in late January, during the middle of the NBA season. Islamic law excuses from the fasting mandate those who, like Olajuwon, must travel on their jobs. But he fasts anyway and says it improves his game: "I feel much better. I feel lighter, faster, much more mentally focused. . . . Your whole body goes through a change. It's like a rebirth" (Hubbard 1998: 51).

Another Muslim in the NBA spawned a controversy in 1996 when he refused to stand for the national anthem at the beginning of games. Mahmoud Abdul-Rauf, who played at Louisiana State University (LSU) as Chris Jackson, said standing would violate his Muslim beliefs, which forbid bowing to any nationalistic ideology. Abdul-Rauf was labeled a traitor by many fans, and the NBA suspended him. The suspension was lifted when he said he was willing to stand during the anthem if he could pray to Allah (Hubbard 1998: 52).

Nor are all of the religious competitors in the sports world famous household names. Thousands of athletes at all levels of competition call themselves Christians. One of those is Sister Marion Irvine of Santa Rosa, California, who produced a sterling time of 2:51:01 to win her age group title at the 1993 Los Angeles Marathon. The sixty-three-year-old member of the Dominican order was one of over one hundred nuns in the race. Like her more high-profile counterparts, she says her relationship with God is the foundation of her athletic talent. And like them, she sees no contradiction between her twin passions for hard sweat and holy water. When asked whether it was appropriate for a nun to run twenty-six miles dressed in nothing but a racing singlet and running shorts, she laughed and replied, "Nobody ever suggested that I run in a habit" (Yesko 1995: 34).

SANCTIFIED SWEAT

Because athletes have become so open and vocal about their faith in recent years, the fusion of religion and sports may seem like a new phenomenon. In fact, the two share a long and entwined history. The Olympic Games in ancient Greece were staged every four years in honor of Zeus, the supreme god and ultimate symbol of power and law. The "muscular Christians" of nineteenth-century England believed that the physical condition of the human body had religious significance and that the body could be used as an instrument of good works—that is, a way of spreading the gospel of Jesus (Coakley 1994: 429). Indeed, the pulpit that sports provides for the religiously inclined always has been a magnificent one, with a steady stream of popular events and a large, ready-made audience that always includes a large number of young people. The muscular Christians spoke eloquently from that pulpit, infusing their games with a knightly tradition that featured a dedication to skill, a sense of honor, and a belief in physical force as a solution to conflict (Higgs 1995: 32).

That knightly tradition became a major feature of sports in the United States as well. Although the Puritans who founded the nation strictly condemned any frivolous activity, they did not include sports on their list of taboos. What the Puritans forbade was mere idle play, which served no larger purpose and was practiced by the lazy and unambitious. Sporting contests, on the other hand, were seen as ways to serve and glorify God. The Puritans embraced swordsmanship, wrestling, and horsemanship, and those who excelled at them were hailed as among the greatest achievers in society (Higgs 1995: 23).

In the nineteenth century, the foundation of modern American athletics was laid with the emergence of private athletic clubs and intercollegiate sports. Both possessed a strong religious component. The Young Men's Christian Association (YMCA), the most popular private club of the era, was founded in 1844 in England and transplanted to America a short time later. It was dedicated to promoting the spiritual, social, and physical well-being of its members. The Young Women's Christian Association (YWCA), founded in 1877, aspired to the same goals. Sports pioneers James Naismith and Amos Alonzo Stagg both launched their careers with the YMCA. Naismith invented basketball at the YMCA International Training School in Springfield, Massachusetts, in 1891. Stagg joined the organization as a sophomore at Yale University and abandoned a planned career in the ministry to become a football coach. He saw coaching as a way to pursue his true love of football and serve God at the same time.

Like virtually all other prominent American colleges, Yale was founded by a religious sect for the purpose of training ministers. As the popularity of college sports grew, the teams of Yale and the others were strongly linked to the missions of their sponsoring institutions. Those links survive most strongly today at the University of Notre Dame, which is identified with the Roman Catholic church, and Brigham Young University, the leading institution of the Mormon church. Liberty University in Lynchburg, Virginia, founded by fundamentalist leader Jerry Falwell, aspires to expand the religious tradition. Falwell wants to build a sports program at Liberty that rivals the excellent ones at Notre Dame and Brigham Young. He also wants his program to enjoy the same firm religious footing. Falwell filed a lawsuit in 1995 against the National Collegiate Athletic Association (NCAA) to ensure the right of Liberty's football players to kneel in prayer after a touchdown without being penalized (*Fortune* 1995: 246).

Harvard, Princeton, and Yale—known as the Big Three—thoroughly dominated college football in its early decades, from 1880 to 1930, and their teams included many members who, like Stagg, had first intended to pursue careers in the church. Stagg himself went on to become the sport's first great coach. He joined Naismith at the Springfield YMCA and headed the school's first football team, known as "Stagg's stubby Christians." Naismith was one of his players. In 1892, Stagg moved to the University of Chicago, where he molded a powerhouse and invented the T formation, the onside kick, the quarterback option play, numbers on jerseys, and padded uniforms. Stagg also began a tradition that flourishes today at thousands of sports events filled with young amateurs, student-athletes, and professionals alike—the pregame prayer. He also led his teams in the singing of the Doxology after the games were over as a way to give thanks to God for guiding the players through the contest without injury.

Generally athletes turn to God and the church for the same reasons as other people: to find comfort and support from a community of like-minded people, to seek ethical and moral guidance, and to gather the courage needed to face mortality and the fear of death. Many of today's high-profile athletes also see religion as a way to counteract the special pressures they feel in the professional sports world. As they climb the ladder of success, they discover how precarious their situation really is.

Age erodes their physical skills, and there are younger, stronger performers ready to replace them. Holding their roster spots and starting positions can become a supreme mental and physical challenge. Injuries can end their careers forever at any moment. The temptations of drugs, alcohol, and sex are always with them. And the large salaries that they earn can bring guilt, anxiety, and a renewed sense of responsibility to help others. Religion can become both a refuge from the sports world and a way to live within it.

Does their religious faith make them better athletes? The athletes themselves answer with a resounding yes, and it is hard to argue with their claim. Many coaches, managers, and team officials view Christian athletes as better performers and better financial investments. They work harder, keep themselves in better physical and mental condition, and offer a more positive image to the team's fans and community. George W. Bush, the managing partner of MLB's Texas Rangers before being elected governor of Texas in 1994, believes that faith makes a difference. "The question we asked was 'Does character matter?' We said it does. Then we made decisions based on that" (Smith 1997: 29).

HAVE SPORTS BECOME A RELIGION?

Some academics and commentators contend that modern sports are not only influenced by religion, but that they have become, for fans and participants, a form of religion itself. In his book *Sport in Society: Issues and Controversies*, Jay J. Coakley (1994) offers several similarities between sports and the Judeo-Christian religious system.

- Both have places and buildings for communal events. Sports have stadiums, ballparks, and arenas. Religions have churches and temples.
- Both are controlled through structured organizations and hierarchical systems of authority. Sports have commissioners, athletic directors, and coaches. Religions have bishops, ministers, rabbis, and priests.
- Both have heroes and designations of honor for those heroes with the greatest level of skill and accomplishment. Sports have halls of fame. Religions have saints.
- Both designate certain days and times of the year as special. Sports have Super Bowl Sunday, New Year's Day, March Madness, and Derby Day. Religions have Easter, Lent, Passover, Yom Kippur, and sabbath days.
- Both place high value on discipline, self-denial, and the devel-

opment of character. Coaches and clergy alike support the philosophy of "no pain, no gain."

DOES GOD CARE WHO WINS?

Not everyone agrees with the Rangers' management philosophy that equates strong performance on the field with strong character and religious faith. *New York Times* sportswriter Skip Bayless, himself a Bible-reading Christian, says nothing inspires more cynicism among his colleagues than an athlete finding God (Bayless 1996: 7). Many of the cynics in the press and elsewhere simply have seen too much false faith. In the sports world, as in all the other arenas of life, there are many professed Christians who talk the talk but do not walk the walk, and they place their well-meaning brethren in a bad light. As with many of the churchgoers in Texas who flock to see Deion Sanders lead his Bible study class, there is a degree of skepticism. The only way to know truly whether athletes live by the word of God is to view them in their daily lives, away from the media, fans, teammates—and from the church. New York Yankees pitcher David Cone wonders about the motives of the devout athletes. "Is the objective the so-called spreading of the word of God," Cone asks, "or is it to make yourself look better, or to try to conform and fit in?" (Smith 1997: 27). Cone sees a measure of intolerance for agnostics, atheists, and those of non-Christian faiths in all of the prayer and worship before, during, and after games.

Nor do the dissenters agree with the notion that faithful Christian athletes are rewarded by God with victories. For them, the purpose of religious faith is to ask and seek to resolve the most important questions of human existence. It has nothing whatsoever to do with the outcome of athletic contests. "Isn't it demeaning," asks journalist Robert Scheer, "to sell religion like sneakers, claiming that it provides the winning edge?" (Scheer 1997: B7). Richard J. Wood, a Quaker minister who is dean of the Yale Divinity School, describes the notion of God's taking sides in a game as a heresy. "It doesn't seem to me odd that God would know in detail what happens in football games," Wood told William Nack of *Sports Illustrated.* "What seems to me odd is that God would care." Even many conservative, fundamentalist Christians are bothered by the claim. "I think it's very dangerous for us to identify the will of God with a specific win," says Richard Mouw, president of the Fuller Theological Seminary in Pasadena, California. "God isn't a Michigan or Notre Dame fan." Reggie White shrugs off the claims of the naysayers. "How do they know?" he asks. "They're not God" (Nack 1998: 47–48).

White's comment strikes squarely at the heart of the matter. The naysayers are not God. But neither are the religious athletes who glorify God and give him credit for their triumphs. No one can claim to know with absolute certainty what role, if any, God plays in the everyday affairs of humankind. The miracle of religious faith is that it moves people to live their lives with courage, conviction, and compassion even when that sense of certainty is missing. In the sports world and in society at large, the gulf that separates true believers and religious skeptics seems almost impossible to bridge. And so it seems likely that the God Squadders who have become so common on the playing fields will continue to express their faith. Like the devout athletes of the past, they have a story to tell and an audience waiting to hear it.

TOPICS FOR DISCUSSION

1. How do you personally react when you see an athlete praying on the field during a game? Does it strike you as a sincere gesture by a true believer or does it seem forced and phony? Does it make you uncomfortable to see such an open expression of religious faith?

2. Mahmoud Abdul-Rauf, a Muslim who plays in the National Basketball Association (NBA), was suspended in 1996 for failing to stand during the national anthem before a game. Do you think his suspension was justified? Why or why not?

3. The Texas Rangers of Major League Baseball (MLB) have been openly partial to Christians when deciding which players to include on their roster. The team's management believes that Christians have better character, and that better character makes better players. Do you agree with that point of view? Or are the Rangers going too far?

4. Many prominent ministers and theologians believe it is wrong to pray for victory in an athletic contest. Do you agree with them? Why or why not? Explain your answer.

5. Have you ever personally displayed your religious beliefs during an athletic contest? How did it make you feel? What was the reaction of your coaches, teammates, and opponents?

REFERENCES AND RESOURCES

Books

Coakley, Jay J. *Sport in Society: Issues and Controversies*. 5th ed. Madison, Wis.: Brown and Benchmark, 1994.
Chapter 16 is entitled "Sports and Religion: Is It a Promising Combination?"
Higgs, Robert J. *God in the Stadium: Sports and Religion in America*. Lexington: University of Kentucky Press, 1995.

A thorough look at the ways sports and religion have been intertwined through history.

Hoffman, Shirl J., ed. *Sport and Religion*. Champaign, Ill.: Human Kinetics Books, 1992.

A collection of essays from popular and scholarly publications on the relationship between sports and religion.

Holyfield, Evander, and Bernard Holyfield. *The Humble Warrior*. New York: Thomas Nelson, 1994.

The heavyweight boxing champion writes about his Christian faith and his up-and-down playing career.

Hubbard, Steve. *Faith in Sports*. New York: Doubleday, 1998.

An award-winning sportswriter examines contemporary athletes and their religion, on and off the field.

Olajuwon, Hakeem, with Peter Knobler. *Living the Dream*. Boston: Little, Brown, 1996.

The star NBA center discusses his childhood and youth in Nigeria and his Islamic faith.

Books and Magazines

Associated Press. "Faith Goes 'Prime Time.' " *Columbus Dispatch*, May 9, 1998: 14E.

The reporter visits football star Deion Sanders at his Bible study class at a Texas church.

Baker, Ken. "True Believers." *Women's Sports and Fitness*, March 1998: 67–69.

Profiles female athletes who express their faith on the playing field.

Bayless, Skip. "God's Playbook." *New York Times*, December 1, 1996: sec. 8, p. 7.

The veteran sportswriter, a Bible-reading Christian, criticizes public prayer by athletes.

Copp, Jay. "God Works Out." *U.S. Catholic*, January 1998: 27–31.

Copp praises the spiritual values found in physical activity.

Fortune. "Only in America." October 16, 1995: 246.

A brief note on Jerry Falwell's fight against an NCAA rule that prohibited prayer on the football field.

Kelly, Jason. "Keep God Out of the Big Leagues." *U.S. Catholic*, April 1997: 22–27.

The author pleads for religious restraint in the sports world.

Nack, William. "Does God Care Who Wins the Super Bowl?" *Sports Illustrated*, January 26, 1998: 46–48.

Discusses the activities of Christians in the NFL with several prominent theologians and ministers.

Plummer, William, Rochelle Jones, and Gail Wescott. "Back on the Fast Track." *People*, November 27, 1995: 151–54.

An account of the severe accident and miraculous recovery of NASCAR driver Ernie Irvan.

Scheer, Robert. "God Wants Me to Make a First Down." *Los Angeles Times*, December 30, 1997: B7.

A humorous look at prayer in sports.

Smith, Chris. "God Is an .800 Hitter." *New York Times Magazine*, July 27, 1997: 26.
   Profiles the Texas Rangers, major league baseball's most openly religious team.
Yesko, Jill. "A Leap of Faith." *Women's Sports and Fitness*, May–June 1995: 34.
   A brief article on Muslims and Orthodox Jews in sports.

Organizations to Contact

Athletes in Action (AIA)
Internet Web Site: www.aiasports.org/aia.
Founded in 1966, Athletes in Action is one of forty ministries within Campus Crusade for Christ, International. Its mission is to develop athletes, coaches, and others in the sports world into Christ-centered athletes. AIA maintains staff on university campuses in thirty-three states. A listing of individual campus ministries is available on the group's Internet Web Site. AIA sponsors an annual Super Bowl breakfast at which it presents the Bart Starr Award, given to the NFL player who best exemplifies the character and leadership qualities of the Hall of Fame quarterback who starred for the Green Bay Packers.

Campus Crusade for Christ, International (CCCI)
100 Sunport Lane
Orlando, FL 32809
Phone: 407–826–2000
Internet Web Site: www.ccci.org
Founded in 1951, CCCI has 144,000 Christian activists in colleges and universities in the United States and over twenty foreign countries. One of CCCI's forty ministries is Athletes in Action.

Fellowship of Christian Athletes (FCA)
8701 Leeds Road
Kansas City, MO 64129
Phone: 816–921–0909
Fax: 816–921–8755
E-mail: fca@fca.org
Internet Web Site: www.fca.org
Founded in 1954, the FCA's mission is to present athletes with the challenge of receiving Jesus Christ into their lives. It maintains over 5,000 "huddles" or chapters nationwide and sponsors summer sports camps at over thirty sites.

9

Pumping Up

Many athletes play for keeps, even if it means using steroids and other unauthorized drugs to fight injuries and maintain their competitive edge. The use of performance-enhancing drugs often is tacitly condoned by coaches, doctors, team owners, and corporate sponsors. Will drugs always be a part of the sports world?

The lonely figure on the running track in Indianapolis was a sad sight to behold. In front of a crowd of media representatives and a cluster of microphones and cameras, Mary Slaney, America's finest female distance runner, stood bewildered, angry, and on the verge of tears. She was suspected of using unauthorized performance-enhancing drugs one year earlier at the trials to select the members of the 1996 U.S. Olympic team.

With her grim-faced husband, Richard Slaney, at her side, she bitterly denounced the drug-testing procedure that had revealed in her urine sample an unacceptably high level of testosterone, the male sex hormone that is the major ingredient in steroids, the chemical compounds that promote endurance and physical strength in those who ingest them. USA Track & Field, the governing body for the sport in the United States, suspended Slaney indefinitely from competition after waiting over a year to finalize results and implement the presuspension hearing process. Slaney also was suspended by the International Amateur Athletic Federation (IAAF), track and field's worldwide governing body.

Slaney steadfastly denied using banned substances before the 1996 Olympic trials or at any other time. "This is an attack on my integrity," the thirty-eight-year-old runner told the *Eugene (Oregon) Register-Guard.* "It is an attack on everything that I believe to be good in the sport. . . . If someone were to ask me how I feel about USA Track & Field right now, I would say I hope it burns in hell" (*USA Today* 1997: 3C).

The suspension occurred as Slaney was attempting yet another comeback in a storied career. She was christened Little Mary Decker as a four-foot, eight-inch, eighty-six-pound fifteen-year-old who rocked international track and field by winning the 800-meter run at the United States–Soviet Union dual meet in 1973. The cute nickname was a bit misleading. She was young and physically small, but the hard-bitten baby boomer with the instincts of a pit bull was a different kind of heroine for American sports fans, who had long preferred their female sports stars to be polite, graceful, and decidedly demure. Mary Decker was none of those. Like her great contemporary Steve Prefontaine, she ran fiercely, possessed by a blunt arrogance that both awed and repelled her competitors.

Blessed with what Olympic marathon champion Frank Shorter called "a remarkable combination of form and strength," Decker added six inches and twenty-five pounds and proceeded to dominate women's distance running in the United States for the next two decades. By 1974, she held world records at three distances. In 1982, she won the Sullivan Award as the nation's outstanding amateur athlete. The next year, she ran brilliantly in the first track and field world championships, capturing both the 1,500- and 3,000-meter runs. A long string of physical ailments hampered her running for many years but did nothing to quell her fierce competitiveness. She competed in the Olympic Games in 1984, 1988, and 1996 and is almost certainly the finest runner in history never to win a medal. By 1997, twenty-four years after her first major competition, she still held American records for the 800-meter, 1,500-meter, 2,000-meter, and 3,000-meter runs. Overall, she set seventeen world and thirty-six American records.

Slaney vowed to appeal her suspension, first to an arbitration panel and then to the courts if necessary. She decried the testing program for testosterone as discriminatory because in women, unlike in men, the amount of that hormone varies so widely that it is virtually impossible to determine acceptable and unacceptable levels. Slaney's representatives also maintained that three circumstances easily could have distorted the urine sample she provided at the Olympic trials: she was in the midst of her menstrual period, she was taking birth control pills, and she drank a large amount of liquid immediately before she was tested. "I have never taken anything that's banned," she said in a tearful television interview. "That's absurd. I haven't done what I've been accused of doing" (USA Today 1997: 3C).

Despite her vehement denials, Slaney's reputation as a champion will be tainted for the rest of her life. She will be remembered not only for her great courage and phenomenal longevity, but also as an athlete who was once reported to have "tested positive." Such is the force of a mere accusation that an athlete has used testosterone or other substances to improve his or her performance. Like many before her, she stood for a long moment in the public eye accused of being, in simplest terms, a cheater—an athlete who violated the rules of her sport to gain an advantage over her opponents.

Enwrapped in a web of anger, mistrust, and recrimination, she is at the heart of a controversy that leaves the typical sports fan in a daze of confusion. The technical and scientific aspects of drugs and drug testing programs are complex, truly understood only by experts. The bureaucratic grab bag of organizations that govern track and field often seem like warring fiefdoms, intent on their rivalries with each other but indistinguishable to those beyond the walls. The legal process used to resolve disputes is lengthy and shielded from public view. Slaney's case seems particularly confusing because at first she was not even told which substance she was accused of taking. "I've never seen anything like this," said her attorney Jim Coleman. "It's like they're charging her with a crime, but they're not telling her what it is" (Associated Press 1997: 4F). In September 1997, three months after her angry press conference, Slaney suddenly was exonerated of the drug charges by a three-woman arbitration panel in a USA Track & Field hearing. The public never learned any more about the details of her alleged drug use.

The case of Mary Slaney in particular and the controversy of performance-enhancing drugs in general raise difficult questions: What drugs, if any, did Mary Slaney actually take? Did those drugs improve her running? Are athletes who test positive for banned substances the only ones who use drugs, or are they simply the ones who are unfortunate enough to get caught? Because the world of performance-enhancing drugs has been shrouded in secrecy for decades, it is difficult to obtain information about the extent of their use. But the weight of the available evidence clearly indicates that a large number of athletes throughout the world have used and continue to use a wide and growing variety of them. Politicians, track and field meet promoters, sports organization officials, and many athletes themselves rail against the evils of what is commonly known as "doping." Yet the practice appears to be flourishing. If so many people disapprove, why does doping continue? And if the ultimate goal for athletes is to do their absolute best in competition, then why is it wrong for them to take drugs that help them achieve that goal?

BIGGER, FASTER, AND STRONGER

The practice of doping has a long and infamous history in the sports world. Gladiators fortified themselves with stimulants before they battled each other in the Colosseum in ancient Rome (Rogak 1992: 35). The first documented drug-related death in sports occurred in 1886, when a

Because of the exhausting training regimen, distance running is a sport in which performers are constantly tempted by the allure of performance-enhancing drugs. When distance runner Mary Slaney (1277, at left) faced accusations of unauthorized drug use in 1997, she fought back and denounced the testing procedures used by track and field officials as arbitrary, unfair, and ineffective. When the accusations against Slaney were later dropped, her description seemed uncannily accurate, and track and field officials were forced to ask once again how, and if, they can control the use of performance-enhancing drugs in their sport. (AP/WIDE WORLD PHOTOS)

long-distance cyclist in Europe collapsed during a race after swallowing a "speedball," a mixture of cocaine and heroin intended to boost strength and endurance. Tom Hicks, the American who won the marathon at the Olympic Games in St. Louis in 1904, freely admitted to sipping brandy and tiny amounts of strychnine during the twenty-six-mile race to maintain his stamina. He collapsed shortly after finishing but survived (Dolan 1992: 17–18).

In the twentieth century, doping increased as sports became more popular, competition became more intense, and medical science created more powerful substances. Anabolic steroids were first developed in the 1930s for medical use. These compounds, which may be either natural or synthetically produced by humans, are made up of body substances called hormones. They may be taken in pill, powder, or liquid form. Many athletes inject liquid steroids with syringes. Testosterone, the hormone that increases a user's male characteristics, promotes muscle growth by increasing the amount of protein delivered to muscle cells. This infusion of protein greatly aids the rebuilding and recovery process that follows a strenuous workout. It enables an athlete to regain strength quickly and tackle his or her next workout sooner and in much better condition. When the cycle is repeated many times, a steroid user can develop incredible levels of strength and endurance.

Anabolic steroids containing testosterone became the substance of choice for many athletes of both sexes, particularly those who participated in track and field and swimming, which require months of intense and exhausting training. Athletes in the Soviet Union and other communist nations used steroids with great frequency in the 1950s and 1960s. At that time, neither the Olympic Games nor other international competitions had drug-testing programs. Their record-breaking performances startled observers and gave rise to one of the enduring stereotypes of the cold war era: communist athletes as joyless, muscle-bound automatons who won medals simply as if they were putting in a day's work in a factory, doing their patriotic duty to demonstrate the superiority of their economic system over capitalism (Dolan 1992: 57).

At the Summer Olympic Games in 1976, the East German women's swimming team performed so relentlessly that two American swimmers, Shirley Babashoff and Wendy Boglioli, voiced their suspicions about steroid use to the press. At the time, they were dismissed as whiners and poor losers. In 1991, after the fall of the communist regime in East Germany, the swimming team coaches admitted that every female who won a medal in 1976 was ingesting a banned substance. They were aided by a government-financed program that determined exactly when a substance would leave a swimmer's system, making it undetectable in a drug test (Ewald 1996: 30). The Stasi, the East German secret police organization, is believed to have played a role in the intricate web of deceit, which involved as many as 10,000 athletes. Many of the female athletes who took drugs became infertile. Four coaches faced criminal indictment in 1997 for their role in the doping.

The most notorious of all doping incidents occurred in 1988 at the Summer Olympics in Seoul, South Korea. Canadian runner Ben Johnson unleashed a thunderous display of raw power in the 100-meter finals, winning the gold medal with ease against the world's best sprinters, including American Carl Lewis, who finished second. Despite slowing down near the finish line, Johnson set a world record of 9.79 seconds. His drug test revealed the presence of stanozolol, a synthetic form of testosterone frequently used because it leaves the body more quickly than other forms. Johnson's manager claimed that the sprinter had been given a bottle of Gatorade spiked with steroids during the competition. Olympic officials rejected that flimsy explanation, saying that the test clearly indicated long-term use (Nuwer 1994: 60–62). Johnson lost his gold medal, his world record, and the respect of millions of fans. After his suspension and reinstatement, he tested positive for steroid use again in 1993. He remains ineligible for competition in 1998.

The specter of steroid use has widened since the Ben Johnson incident. In 1992, American sprinter Gwen Torrance accused three of her Olympic opponents of using them (Nuwer 1994: 63). Since 1991, nearly thirty Chinese athletes in Olympic sports have been suspended from international competition for drug use (*Sports Illustrated* 1997: 23). A cloud of suspicion hovers over Irish swimmer Michelle Smith, who won three gold medals and one bronze at the Olympic Games in Atlanta in 1996. At five feet, three inches, with small hands and feet, she is by her own admission at a physical disadvantage in her sport. She performed poorly at the 1992 Olympic Games. But by 1996, she had lowered her personal best times in several events under the guidance of her new coach and husband, Erik de Bruin, a one-time discus thrower who had no previous experience as a swimming coach and who once was suspended from track and field competition for four years for an offense involving testosterone. She attained peak condition at the age of twenty-six, a time when nearly all female swimmers are in physical decline.

Smith passed four drug tests in Atlanta, but in the months before the Olympics she competed in events where no drug testing took place. In 1998, Smith faced another doping inquiry. She was investigated for possibly tampering with a urine sample that she provided at a swimming meet in Ireland. Like Mary Slaney, she angrily denied the charges and vowed to do whatever it takes to defend herself, her coach and husband, and her reputation. Some are inclined to take Smith at her word when she says she is drug free. Others assume, based on the mass of circumstantial evidence, that she took anabolic steroids (Bamberger 1997: 80–85). That assumption seemed accurate when Smith was banned from swimming for four years in 1998, after she was accused of tampering with a urine sample during another testing procedure.

That same assumption seems to arise whenever an athlete delivers an outstanding time on the track, in the swimming pool, or in any other competition where strength and endurance are at a premium. Author Edward F. Dolan believes that the controversy surrounding performance-enhancing drugs "has done physical and psychological damage to athletes of both sexes, of all nationalities, and at all levels of competition—from the highly paid professional to the beginning amateur. . . . It has damaged the very nature of sports, twisting many of the world's best-loved games and events into anything but the healthful, exciting and fair contests of skill and prowess that they were intended to be" (Dolan 1992: 15).

DYING TO WIN

The negative effects of steroid use are well-documented in the medical community. Selling steroids in the United States without a medical prescription is illegal. Use of steroids above authorized amounts also is banned by nearly every major athletic organization, including the National Football League (NFL), the National Collegiate Athletic Association (NCAA) and the U.S. Olympic Committee (USOC). Despite these sanctions, athletes can obtain steroids readily by mail order and from coaches, trainers, friends, and family members eager to provide them. In 1997, the Federal Bureau of Investigation (FBI) launched a probe of steroid sales via the Internet. Steroids also can be obtained from unethical doctors who are willing to write prescriptions for the drugs even when they are not used for legitimate medical purposes, such as the treatment of cancer (Rogak 1992: 26–27). Professional athletes are not the only ones who use steroids. High school students and even middle school students, the large majority of them male, use them to improve athletic performance. Other students who do not participate in athletics also use steroids simply to make their bodies more muscular and attractive. A growing number of users are female. The American Medical Association reported in 1997 that the number of girls in grades nine through twelve using steroids had doubled in six years. Another study released by the University of Massachusetts in 1998 found steroid use among middle-school females to be virtually the same as use by middle-school males (Associated Press 1998: 8A).

Medical experts disagree on the question of whether steroids are physically addictive. They do agree, however, that they easily can become psychologically addictive. They can create in users an urgent compulsion to ingest the drug to maintain a sense of well-being. Among the possible negative effects of steroid use are high blood pressure, hair loss on the head, increased or lowered sexual drive, impotence, insomnia, and liver malfunction. Diseases such as AIDS and hepatitis B may be contracted by steroid users who share syringes to inject the liquid form of the drug into their bodies.

Women who increase their testosterone level by using steroids may experience growth of facial hair, deepened voices, shrunken breasts, and interruption or cessation of their menstrual cycles. These changes, like most of the other effects, are usually irreversible; they do not disappear when use stops (Dolan 1992: 39–40). Heidi Kreiger, a shot putter who was one of the thousands of East German females who used steroids during the communist regime, took on so many male characteristics that she decided to undergo a sex change operation. She is now Andreas Kreiger (*Sports Illustrated* 1998: 22).

The most-publicized effect of steroid use is increased hostility and aggression, a condition known as "roid rage." Dozens of steroid users have been involved in arsons, rapes, traffic altercations, assaults, bar fights, and incidents of domestic violence. Roid rage is particularly common among the many athletes who take steroids without medical supervision. Lacking knowledge of the consequences of their actions, they believe that "more is better" and flood their bodies with many varieties of the drug (Dolan 1992: 42–45).

Steroids are far from the only drugs that athletes use to improve their performances. Amphetamines and painkillers have been popular with athletes, particularly football players, for decades. Amphetamines are known by a number of nicknames, such as *speed, dexies, bennies, poppers, joy juice,* and *black beauties.* They are stimulants that lower sensitivity to pain and provide an immediate and powerful surge of energy that can be used to great advantage on any playing field. In the 1980s and 1990s, cocaine, which possesses many of the same qualities, became a popular drug among athletes and in society. Painkillers are used to deaden the effects of the brutal physical punishment that football players endure during their season (Dolan 1992: 68–70, 89–90).

Green Bay Packers quarterback Brett Favre is among the players in the NFL who have suffered from addiction to painkillers. He revealed his dependency on the narcotic Vicodin at a press conference in May 1996, when he announced that he had voluntarily entered the league's substance abuse program. The wakeup call came when he suffered a violent seizure as a result of painkiller use during a visit to a Green Bay hospital for ankle surgery. With the support of his family and the Packers organization, Favre has ended his dependency.

Diuretics, which promote urination and weight loss, are used by jockeys, wrestlers, and boxers who must maintain low weights in order to compete in certain weight classes. Beta-blockers reduce the heartbeat rate and lower blood pressure. They are used by archers, riflers, pool players, and golfers to calm their fingers and hands and improve their aim. Many young female gymnasts and figure skaters, who compete in sports where physical appearance is vital, are attracted to brake drugs, which suppress ovulation and inhibit the normal development of hips and breasts at puberty (Rogak 1992: 36). The latest drug of choice in the National Hockey League (NHL) is Sudafed. Players ingest the legal substance before a game not to clear stuffy noses but to gain a surge of energy on the ice. And athletes in all sports are increasingly attracted to creatine, a legal substance that promotes strength and endurance in much the same manner as steroids without, according to its supporters, the negative side effects.

Newer and stronger drugs are developed on a regular basis to meet the demands of competitive athletes. Perhaps the most highly coveted new drug is human growth hormone (hGH). It is similar in its effects to steroids but cannot be detected in the drug testing programs now used in most sports competitions. Also similar to steroids is erythropoietin (EPO), used by long-distance runners, swimmers, and cross-country skiers and also undetectable in urine samples. At the Olympic Games in Atlanta in 1996, Russian and East German athletes tested positive for a substance called bromantan, which is virtually unknown in the medical community and therefore not on the list of banned substances. It has long been used by Russian soldiers to maintain alertness and promote quick adaption of the body to heat and cold (Bamberger and Yaeger 1997: 60–70).

The primary motivation of athletes to take performance-enhancing drugs is the will to win. Most elite athletes are said by psychologists to have compulsive personalities. Their entire sense of self-worth hinges on achieving great success in their chosen sports. They are markedly different from the millions of people who play sports to stay physically fit or simply to enjoy themselves and who have achieved some measure of success in other aspects of their lives (Dolan 1992: 47). These driven competitors use steroids and other drugs even if they are aware of their dangers, even if using violates their sense of fair play, and even if they do not want to use drugs. The drugs give them a boost toward success and an edge that cannot be achieved any other way. Often that edge is nothing more than the chance to compete effectively against other athletes who are using the same drug, or something even more effective. "If you are especially gifted, you may win once," physician Michael Karsten told *Sports Illustrated*, "but from my experience you can't continue to win without drugs. The field is just too filled with drug users" (Bamberger and Yaeger 1997: 62).

WHAT ABOUT DRUG TESTING?

Drug testing programs are used on a regular basis in most sports to detect the presence of steroids and other substances in levels above those deemed to be acceptable. Drug testing in the Olympic Games began in 1968, but for the first fifteen years it was ineffective because of undependable technology (Voy 1991: 77). In the early years of the testing program, many athletes who had not used banned substances tested positive, and many who did use banned substances tested negative.

In 1983, drug testing improved greatly with the development of a process that uses gas chromatography and mass spectrometry. This process can identify banned substances in urine samples in extremely minute quantities. At the 1983 Pan-American Games in Caracas, Venezuela, American athletes were informed of the new process and given a chance to provide urine samples before the competition began rather than risk disqualification. Upon receiving their precompetition test results, ten male track and field athletes left Caracas and returned to the United States. Jeff Micheals, a heavyweight weight lifter, chose to compete and won three gold medals. He later tested positive for the presence of anabolic steroids and was stripped of his medals (Voy 1991: 83–86).

At the 1984 Summer Olympics in Los Angeles, an all-time high of twelve athletes tested positive for performance-enhancing drugs. Four years later in Barcelona, Spain, the number of positives was five. In 1996 in Atlanta, 2,000 of the 11,000 athletes were tested, and the number of positives was two. New and advanced equipment was used that can detect the presence of steroids taken up to three months before competition. In 1998, a German scientist claimed to have devised the first effective test for EPO. The International Olympic Committee is considering using the test in future competitions.

The declining number of positive tests appears to indicate that drug testing is working and that more and more Olympic athletes are competing drug free. In fact, according to many doctors, trainers, and athletes involved in international athletics, precisely the opposite is true. Doctor Robert Voy, a staunch opponent of performance-enhancing drugs who directed the drug testing program for the USOC in 1984 and 1988, has a simple explanation: the athletes and their supporters who want to use drugs are smarter and more strongly motivated than the people who do the testing. Their will to win is so strong and the rewards of success are so great that they find a way to do whatever is necessary to avoid detection. "They know how to get in under the radar," Voy says (Bamberger and Yaeger 1997: 62).

Voy has exposed many weaknesses in the testing program used in the Olympic Games. First, the dates of most tests are announced weeks or even months in advance, giving athletes time to clear banned substances from their systems. The announcement of testing dates allows athletes to test themselves before competition to determine precisely how much of a substance they can take—and when—to avoid detection. Second, the International Olympic Committee (IOC) allows the use of many performance-enhancing drugs at surprisingly high levels. For example, a typical male athlete could ingest 200 milligrams of testosterone three times a week and still test negative under current guidelines. Third, and most important, well-trained chemists, known as "gurus" in the sports world, are able to concoct substances that cannot be detected by even the most sophisticated testing equipment. And only a testing program that analyzes blood can accurately detect the presence of human growth hormone and EPO, the new drugs of choice for many world-class athletes. Indeed, blood analysis is by far the most reliable method of detecting substances in the human body. But blood testing is widely viewed as intrusive and nearly unworkable in track and field and swimming competitions. The International Cycling Union is the only major sporting body that performs blood testing (Bamberger and Yaeger 1997: 62–67).

Drug testing also faces obstacles that have nothing to do with driven athletes, wizardly gurus, or faulty testing techniques. The central one may simply be the lack of will to eradicate performance-enhancing drugs from international sports. There are many powerful factions within the current system, and most of them would be hurt badly by the exposure of widespread drug use: the corporate sponsors of the Olympic Games and other competitions that would lose the participation of many disqualified world-class athletes, the athletes themselves, past and present, who would face shame and denigration for their tainted accomplishments, the enforcement bodies that would appear to have failed for so many years in their drug control efforts, and the doctors, trainers, coaches, and manufacturers who profit from the sale and use of performance-enhancing drugs. Furthermore, no single faction within the international sports world has the power to eradicate drugs, even if the will to do so existed. This lack of will and power has created "a massive holding action against reform" and an implicit, if unstated, agreement to carry on business as usual—that is, to denounce the use of drugs as unacceptable publicly but silently condone their use (Hoberman 1992: 101, 238).

The agreement to carry on business as usual is fueled by the profound ambivalence that exists in society toward athletic performance. On the one hand is a strong demand that sports competition be pure and clean and free of any artificial aids or enhancements. At the same time is an equally strong demand that athletes extend themselves to the most extreme limits that their bodies can endure. The demand to go to extremes has been taken to heart by many of the world's most talented athletes.

And today, more than ever before, going to extremes means using performance-enhancing drugs.

SHOULD STEROIDS BE LEGALIZED?

A small group within the athletic community supports legalizing the use of steroids and other banned substances. The group's most prominent member is Norman Fost, a professor of pediatrics and director of the medical ethics program at the University of Wisconsin at Madison. Fost makes four arguments in favor of permitting performance-enhancing drugs in sports. First, he believes that athletes are fully entitled to seek competitive advantages over their opponents. They have done so since the beginning of sports competition through the use of better equipment, better coaches, better diets, and better training programs. Although he admits that no athlete should have an unfair advantage, Fost believes that steroids and other drugs are not unfair when all athletes have the chance to use them if they wish. Second, Fost claims that the medical harms of steroids have been exaggerated and that more extensive studies are needed to determine their true dangers. He also believes that even if steroids are proved to be dangerous, mentally competent adults should not be prohibited from using them. Nor does Fost believe that any athlete is forced to use steroids simply because his or her competitors use them. In his view, all athletes have the choice to use or not to use. Finally, he rejects the notion that steroids should be banned because they confer an "unnatural" advantage on those who use them. They are no more unnatural than many other performance aids, including weight machines, computerized exercise programs, biomagnetic therapy, and greased swimsuits that increase a swimmer's speed by reducing friction between the suit and the water (Dudley 1994: 226–33).

Few in the sports world support Fost's view. But there are indications that steroids and other drugs are gaining more official acceptance. In 1997, the IAAF reduced its penalty for athletes who test positive for banned substances from a four-year ban on competition to a two-year ban. The IAAF claims it made the change to maintain consistency with its member nations, many of which impose two-year bans. To some, however, the change was a signal that performance-enhancing drugs are now more acceptable in track and field. It drew disapproval from Linford Christie, the sprinter who earned an Olympic gold medal in the 100-meter race in 1992. Christie believes that an eight-year ban or even a lifetime ban would be more appropriate. "If we're going to eradicate drugs from the sport, the deterrent has to be strong," he says (Associated Press 1997: 8E).

Most people in the sports world would say that Christie's goal is very far from being accomplished—probably as far as it ever has been. As long as the rewards of winning are great and as long as medical science is able to create new and improved substances that can enhance athletic performance and remain undetected by tests, many of the world's most driven athletes will compete under their influence.

TOPICS FOR DISCUSSION

1. Author John Hoberman says that society has come to tolerate performance-enhancing drugs in sports because millions of people like to watch the highest possible level of performance on the playing fields. He maintains that if athletes did not use drugs, their performances—and the interest level of the fans—would deteriorate. Do you agree with his view? Is society at large partly responsible for the use of drugs by athletes?

2. Do you know anyone personally who has suffered the negative effects of steroid use? How did they behave? Did the steroid use affect their relationships with friends and family? Did it affect their ability to maintain grades in school? Did it lead to violence?

3. Athletes who use performance-enhancing drugs often justify their actions by saying that nearly all of their competitors do the same thing, and that they themselves would be at a disadvantage if they did not use drugs. What do you think of that reasoning? Is the use of unauthorized drugs justified simply because other athletes use them?

4. Doctor Norman Fost of the University of Wisconsin is part of a small group that believes steroid use for athletes should be legalized. Is his point of view persuasive? What would be the consequences of allowing athletes to use steroids legally?

5. Have you ever personally admired a star athlete who was punished for unauthorized use of drugs, such as runner Ben Johnson? How did your feelings about that athlete change, if at all, after the drug use was exposed?

REFERENCES AND RESOURCES

Books

Dolan, Edward F. *Drugs in Sports*. Rev. ed. New York: Franklin Watts, 1992.
    A fine overview of the uses and effects of steroids, amphetamines, cocaine, marijuana, and other drugs used by athletes.
Dudley, William, ed. *Sports in America: Opposing Viewpoints*. San Diego: Greenhaven Press, 1994.
    Presents divergent perspectives on steroid use and other contemporary sports issues.

Favre, Brett, with Chris Havel. *Favre: For the Record*. New York: Doubleday, 1997.
The star quarterback of the NFL's Green Bay Packers discusses his addiction to painkillers and alcohol and his recovery efforts.

Galas, Judith. *Drugs and Sports*. San Diego: Lucent Books, 1997.
Examines drug testing, the social use of drugs by athletes, and ethics and education programs.

Goldman, Bob, and Ronald Klatz. *Death in the Locker Room II: Drugs and Sports*. Chicago: Elite Sports Medicine Publications, 1992.
Goldman and Klatz, noted sports physicians, update the book that first documented the epidemic of steroid drug abuse.

Hoberman, John. *Mortal Engines: The Science of Performance and the Dehumanization of Sport*. New York: Free Press, 1992.
A fascinating and complex analysis of the origins and history of "doping" in sports, written by a professor at the University of Texas at Austin. For advanced readers.

Nuwer, Hank. *Sports Scandals*. New York: Franklin Watts, 1994.
Contains one chapter on the use of performance-enhancing drugs. An excellent introduction to the topic for high school readers.

Rogak, Lisa Angowski. *Steroids: Dangerous Game*. Minneapolis: Lerner, 1992.
Rogak gears her discussion specifically to younger readers.

Voy, Robert, M.D., with Kirk D. Deeter. *Drugs, Sport and Politics*. Champaign, Ill.: Leisure Press, 1991.
The former chief medical officer for the U.S. Olympic Committee criticizes the cover-up of drug use in sports and offers a reform plan.

Magazines and Newspapers

Associated Press. "Confusion Hasn't Cleared Up in Slaney Case." *Columbus Dispatch*, June 13, 1997: 4F.
A report on the early developments in the drug suspension case of distance runner Mary Slaney.

Associated Press. "Kids as Young as 10 Using Steroids, Study Finds." *Columbus Dispatch*, May 5, 1998: 8A.
A report on a study of steroid use conducted by researchers at the University of Massachusetts.

Bamberger, Michael. "Under Suspicion." *Sports Illustrated*, April 14, 1997: 72–81.
Bamberger interviews Irish Olympic swimming star Michelle Smith and her coach, Erik de Bruin.

Bamberger, Michael, and Don Yaeger. "Over the Edge." *Sports Illustrated*, April 14, 1997: 60–70.
This detailed exposé contains many alarming revelations about the widespread use of drugs in international sports competitions.

CQ Researcher. "High School Sports." September 22, 1995: 825–48.
This comprehensive issue paper, prepared by the staff of *Congressional Quarterly*, examines drug testing and several other issues in interscholastic sports.

Downes, Steven. "Shouting at the Gale." *Running Times*, November 1997: 50–58.

Laments the current confused state of drug testing programs in track and field.

Ewald, Russ. "Can Athletic Wrongs Be Righted?" *Women's Sports and Fitness*, April 1996: 30.

A brief story on the use of steroids by the East German women's swimming team at the 1976 Olympic Games.

Farber, Michael. "Hockey's Little Helper." *Sports Illustrated*, January 2, 1998: 74–76.

Reports on the growing use of Sudafed as a performance-enhancing drug among players in the National Hockey League.

King, Peter. "Bitter Pill." *Sports Illustrated*, May 27, 1996: 25–30.

Documents the darkest days of Brett Favre's addiction to the painkiller Vicodin, when the Green Bay Packers quarterback nearly died in a hospital in Green Bay, Wisconsin.

Longman, Jere. "Slaney Angry over Duration of a Drug Study Taken at '96 Games." *New York Times*, May 15, 1997: C26.

Distance runner Mary Slaney lambasts the drug-testing procedures used by international sports organizations.

Marantz, Steve. "Addiction by Distraction." *Sporting News*, May 27, 1996: 10–11.

A discussion of the plights of football quarterback Brett Favre and baseball pitcher Dwight Gooden.

Nocera, Joseph. "Bitter Medicine." *Sports Illustrated*, November 6, 1995: 74–88.

Profiles the role played by team doctors in encouraging drug use by players.

Schnirring, Lisa. "Drugs and High School Athletes." *Physician and Sports Medicine*, October 1995: 25–26.

A brief note on drug testing programs for high school athletes.

Schwenk, Thomas L., M.D. "Psychoactive Drugs and Athletic Performance." *Physician and Sports Medicine*, January 1997: 32–46.

A highly technical review of the effects of several drugs on athletic performance.

Sports Illustrated. "Timing Is Everything." May 12, 1997: 23.

A note on the suspension of Chinese athletes for unauthorized drug use.

Sports Illustrated. "Wall of Silence May Crumble." March 23, 1998: 20, 22.

Reports on the trials of six East German coaches and doctors facing charges of doping athletes in the 1970s and 1980s.

USA Today. "Slaney Says Attack on Integrity Untrue." May 27, 1997: 3C.

Runner Mary Slaney responds to accusations that she took performance-enhancing drugs.

Wulf, Steve. "What's the Attraction?" *Time*, August 11, 1997: 81.

A report on the use of biomagnetic therapy by several notable professional athletes.

Organizations to Contact

American College of Sports Medicine
P.O. Box 1440

Indianapolis, IN 46206–1440
Phone: 317–637–9200
The group focuses on research, education, and the practical application of sports medicine and exercise.

International Olympic Committee (IOC)
Chateau de Vidy
CH–1007 Lausanne, Switzerland
Phone: 021 253271
Fax: 021 241552
Internet Web Site: www.olympic.org
The IOC controls and develops the Olympic Games and oversees the activities of all national Olympic committees.

United States Olympic Committee (USOC)
One Olympic Plaza
Colorado Springs, CO 80909–5760
Phone: 719–632–5551
Fax: 719–578–4654
Internet Web Site: www.olympic-usa.org
The USOC is the governing body that supports and oversees the activities of American athletes in Olympic sports. Its Online Library includes a comprehensive section on drug control.

10

Beating the Spread

Gambling and sports have been deeply entwined since the days of the Black Sox scandal, and America's love affair with sports betting shows no signs of cooling off. Gambling has blighted the careers of many star athletes, and critics say that it has violated the integrity of the games they play. Is there a way for gambling and sports to exist together?

In the summer of 1997, the 1,400 members of the National Association of Collegiate Directors of Athletics (NACDA) gathered for their annual convention. As the men and women who oversee the operation of the nation's college and university sports programs, the athletic directors spent their time at the convention talking to one another about many topics related to their profession, including academic eligibility for student-athletes, merchandising and marketing techniques, stadium and arena renovations, and Title IX and women's sports issues. The convention of the NACDA was not unlike thousands of others held each year by businesses, trade associations, and professional groups.

The only aspect of the convention that struck some people as unusual was its location. Just as they had in 1985 and 1995, the athletic directors met in 1997 in Las Vegas, the undisputed gambling capital of the nation, the city that rose from the desolate Nevada desert to become a neon mecca, drawing millions to its betting palaces, blackjack tables, slot machines, and video poker games.

Las Vegas seemed an unusual site for the convention because of the strong stance against gambling taken by the college sports establishment. The rules of the National Collegiate Athletic Association (NCAA) strictly bar student-athletes from wagering on the outcome of any college sporting event. Anyone who violates those rules can have his or her eligibility to compete revoked. The organization has a full-time staff member who works with law enforcement agencies to discourage gambling on sports. Just a few weeks before the NACDA convention in Las Vegas, the NCAA had moved to discontinue a popular tradition in rowing, the oldest of all college sports. That tradition calls for the oarsmen of a defeated crew to hand over their jerseys to the members of the winning crew after a race. The organization's rules state that there can be no offer or acceptance by players of a "tangible item" in the course of a sporting event. In the NCAA's view, jerseys are tangible items, and giving or receiving them at the end of an athletic contest is a type of gambling wager.

A few months before the Las Vegas convention, an NCAA committee made up primarily of athletic directors had tried to prevent a large number of reporters from covering the NCAA basketball tournament. The committee was unhappy because the newspapers that employed the reporters printed point spreads on college basketball games as well as advertisements for gambling experts who make their living offering advice to bettors. After the press objected to the proposed ban, the committee dropped its campaign. It was satisfied when sports editors agreed to send a letter to newspaper publishers acknowledging the problem of gambling in college sports.

That problem was on the minds of at least one of the athletic directors who went to Las Vegas. "I just think in today's world where we're concerned about sending messages, that having a meeting out here is kind of odd," Joe Castiglione of the University of Missouri told the *Dallas Morning News*. "To select this site for an industry very concerned about the intrusion of gambling . . . makes it kind of strange" (Blackistone 1997: 4D).

Castiglione's view is one that is not openly expressed often in the college sports world, or in the sports world at large. Although many players, coaches, and team and league officials may feel uneasy about the intractable bond that has developed between gambling and sports, it is a bond that has come to be accepted as inevitable and even necessary to promoting and maintaining fan interest. Since 1638, when Puritans from England passed the first antigambling law shortly after arriving in the New World, Americans have carried on a passionate romance with betting and games of chance. George Washington was an avid bettor on cockfights and horse races. State lotteries arose in the nineteenth century, but they were discontinued after numerous allegations of fraud. In the twentieth century, illegal gambling became a lucrative business for organized crime groups. After Nevada legalized gambling in 1931, the influence of organized crime, which owned and operated a number of the state's casinos, continued to be strong (Savage 1997: 17–19). In 1978, Atlantic City, New Jersey, became the gambling capital of the East when casinos were legalized there.

Today, gambling in its many forms permeates American society to a greater degree than ever before. Bingo games for charitable purposes draw thousands of bettors to church basements and school cafeterias every week. Office betting pools are hugely popular, with workers wagering on the outcome of every conceivable type of event. One group of employees in Ohio regularly bet on the delivery dates and times of co-workers' babies, the amount that each would weigh, and whether it would be a boy or a girl. In a game with a more ghoulish twist, another group placed wagers on which former U.S. president would be the next to die.

A sizable number of the millions of people who bet can be described as compulsive. They suffer from an urgent impulse or desire that is difficult to control but is capable of being diagnosed and treated. In 1998, an analysis of compulsive gambling described by experts as the most comprehensive ever was released by the Harvard University Medical School. That study found that 1.29 percent of adults in the United States and Canada had a gambling disorder in the years 1994 through 1997. The most significant aspect of the study is that it was funded by the gambling industry, which for many years had been reluctant to concede that some of its customers had become addicted.

For both serious and casual bettors, the opportunities to gamble are legion. The most distinctive feature of modern gambling is that it has the endorsement of government. It is no longer viewed as a vice but as a form of entertainment. The preferred term for the activity today is not gambling but *gaming*, and lottery games are sponsored by thirty-five states, the District of Columbia, the Virgin Islands, and Puerto Rico. Together they generate over $20 billion annually in ticket sales. In 1988, Congress passed the Indian Gambling Regulatory Act, which allows Native American tribes to operate casinos on their own land. They do so in over twenty states. In addition, Illinois, Iowa, Louisiana, Mississippi, Missouri, and Indiana offer gambling on riverboats in the Mississippi and Ohio rivers (Layden 1995: 84). The only states that do not offer any form of legal wagering are Hawaii and Utah (Crist 1998: 91).

Interest in sports betting has boomed as well. Only Delaware, Montana, Nevada, North Dakota, and Oregon permit legal betting on sports events. Nevada is the only one of the five that permits betting on individual games. The other four states allow betting on parlay cards, on which bettors pick the winners in two or more events. Sports betting centers, known as "sports books," are now a major feature of the most popular casinos in Las Vegas and Reno. Their giant television screens and vividly lighted odds boards attract bettors who eat, drink, and often play the other games that the casino offers as they monitor the events on which they have wagered money (Savage 1997: 22).

The biggest gambling boom of all has come in illegal sports betting, usually done through bookmakers, or bookies—individuals who accept bets from gamblers and earn money by taking a commission, or *vigorish*, on each losing bet. In 1983, one study estimated that $8 billion was wagered illegally on sports events in the United States. By 1997, the Council on Compulsive Gambling, a New Jersey–based group that assists problem gamblers, placed the figure at over $100 billion. The National Football League's (NFL) Super Bowl alone generates about $4 billion in illegal bets each January. Illegal sports betting accounts for about 20 percent of the $600 billion that Americans are believed to wager each year (Crist 1998: 85).

Many of the fans who bet on sports events are young, relatively affluent, and male (Layden 1995a: 70–72). They do not remember when sports gambling was illicit behavior that was frowned on and had to be concealed. For many of them, a weekend spent gambling is as normal as a weekend spent reading, hiking, going to the movies, or pursuing any other leisure activity. They view betting as a natural human instinct and believe the maxim that explains why it is so popular: the greatest thrill in life is gambling and winning. The second greatest thrill is gambling and losing.

WINNERS AND LOSERS

There are many ways to place a bet on a sporting event, but the basics of the system are relatively simple and have endured for decades. The team that is expected to win the competition is called the *favorite*; the team that is expected to lose is called the *underdog*. These teams are placed side by side on the odds board in a casino and in the betting charts that appear in most daily newspapers.

Because bookmakers earn money only when their customers lose bets, they must create a way to prevent the vast majority of bettors from placing money on the favorite. Their goal is to attract a roughly equal amount of betting money to each team. That is accomplished by creating an artificial advantage for the underdog. In football and basketball, that advantage is called the *point spread*. Point spreads are devised by experts called *oddsmakers*, most of whom work in Las Vegas. They analyze games on a full-time basis and sell their information to bookmakers across the nation.

Imagine that a game is being played in the National Basketball Association (NBA) between the Chicago Bulls and the New Jersey Nets. The Bulls are playing on their home court, with a record of thirty wins and five losses. All of their key players are injury free. The Nets are playing away from home, with a record of five wins and thirty losses. Two of their key players are injured and cannot compete. In this scenario, nearly every bettor would place money on the Bulls. If the bookmaker

Gamblers at the sports book of the Mirage Hotel in Las Vegas exchange high fives and celebrate after winning Super Bowl bets in 1996. Sports betting was a prominent feature of America's gambling explosion in the 1990s. In its legal and illegal forms, it is now believed to account for about 20 percent of the $600 billion that Americans are thought to wager each year at casinos, racetracks, riverboats, state-run lotteries and betting pools. Millions of people see sports betting as an essentially harmless form of mass entertainment; its opponents contend that it hurts individuals, families, and society and corrodes the most important value of sports competition: spontaneous, unscripted contests between two sides giving maximum effort to achieve victory. (AP/WIDE WORLD PHOTOS)

adds twenty-five points to the Nets' final score at the end of the game, bettors would have a much harder time making their choices. That twenty-five points added by the oddsmakers and the bookmakers is the point spread. If the final score of the game is Chicago 130, New Jersey 100, bettors who picked Chicago win because the Bulls won the game by more than twenty-five points. If the final score is Chicago 130, New Jersey 125, bettors who picked New Jersey win because the Bulls won the game by fewer than twenty-five points. If the Bulls were to win by exactly twenty-five points, all money would be returned to bettors under the most commonly used system, known in gambling slang as a *push*.

In baseball, tennis, boxing, and golf, a different betting method, called a *money line*, is used. As with the point spread, one competitor is the favorite and one is the underdog. As a favorite in a baseball game, the Cleveland Indians might appear on the money line next to the number −180. This means that bettors would need to wager $180 on the Indians to earn $100 if they win the game. Their opponent in the game, the Milwaukee Brewers, might appear on the money line as the underdog next to the number +170. This is the amount that a bettor would win if he or she placed $100 on the Brewers to win the game.

This simple system lures millions of bettors into the action. An added attraction is that bets initially can be placed on credit. Most bookmakers collect or dispense money only after the client's losses or winnings exceed a certain figure. This feature of illegal bookmaking adds to its allure by giving it, at least for a time, an element of make-believe. For the adventurous gambler, there is always a pot of gold at the end of the rainbow—a payoff that can be had with no effort at all, simply by placing a bet with a bookmaker.

ATHLETES WHO BET

Compulsive sports gamblers who engage in addictive behavior over an extended period of time nearly always lose significant amounts of money. Many are capable of doing whatever is necessary to obtain the funds they need to pay debts to their bookmakers—and to continue betting. Thousands of individuals and families have been damaged by the insatiable need of gamblers for quick cash and by the theft, deception, violence, and extortion they commit to get it.

Most of the world takes little notice of these desperate characters when they simply watch sports. But when they play the games, their predicaments arouse intense interest. Athletes gamble on sports for the same reasons that other people do: the thrill of the action, the excitement of the dice roll, the chance of winning something for nothing. Unlike other people who bet, however, they can inflict serious damage on their teams and sports.

The assumption in the sports world has always been that each athlete is giving maximum effort to achieve victory each time his or her team enters a stadium, arena, or ballpark. The attraction of sports events is that they are unscripted and spontaneous. No matter how superior one team or individual may be, the results of the competition are not known in advance. When athletes gamble, they give the impression that the games they play are being compromised, even if in fact they are not. If an athlete bets, there will always be those who believe that he or she is more interested in easy financial gain than in the rewards of victory on the playing field. And when players go one step further and take money from gamblers seeking to influence the outcome of games in which they actually play, the unscripted and spontaneous essence of the contest is not merely compromised but destroyed.

The most famous athlete who gambled is Pete Rose, the all-time hit king of major league baseball (MLB). In his twenty-four-year career as a player with the Cincinnati Reds, Philadelphia Phillies, and Montreal Expos, Rose was perhaps the summer game's most visible star. Lacking the natural athletic ability of his more talented peers, he played five positions and became a legend through sheer desire and tireless effort. No one who watched baseball from 1963 to 1986 can forget the enthusiasm and hustle that the stocky, crew-cutted Rose displayed every day on the diamond. He appeared in seventeen All-Star Games and six World Series and won four National League batting crowns. In 1985, he broke Ty Cobb's MLB record for base hits and finished his playing career with 4,256, a number that probably never will be surpassed. After retiring as a player, Rose managed the Reds from 1987 to 1989.

During the entire length of his career as a player and manager, Rose gambled. Indeed, he was introduced to the pastime long before he entered the major leagues. Like many other chronic bettors, Rose grew up in a flourishing gambling culture. His father took him to the horse races for the first time when he was eight years old. His uncle was an accomplished pool hustler on Cincinnati's West Side. By the time Rose became a star, he was already an experienced bettor. His favorite venue was River Downs, a racetrack near Cincinnati. During his first year with the Reds in 1963, he spent nearly every off-day there, betting whatever he could muster on his rookie's salary of $7,500 (Sokolove 1990: 21–42, 194). Later in his career he began to bet on basketball and football. "I think he loved the action," said a man who bet with Rose at a Florida greyhound track. "This guy has got more energy than any human being I've ever seen. I don't think he needed to drink, I don't think he needed food. He needed the action" (Sokolove 1990: 227).

Baseball authorities were aware of Rose's gambling long before it became public in 1989. Betting in all of its forms has generated grave concern in the game since the Black Sox scandal, the sports world's most notorious gambling incident. In 1920, eight players on the Chicago White Sox were indicted on criminal charges for taking bribes from gamblers to perform poorly against the Cincinnati Reds in the 1919 World Series. The players succeeded in throwing the Series to the Reds, who won five games to three in the experimental best-of-nine games format. Their motive was simple: they needed money. Like other major leaguers in the era before player free agency and the rise of television, the White Sox toiled for extremely low wages. Star pitcher Eddie Cicotte, a thirteen-year veteran who compiled twenty-nine wins in 1919, made less than $6,000. He was promised a $10,000 bonus if he won thirty games by the end of the season. After his twenty-ninth win, White Sox owner Charles Comiskey, who was renowned for his cheapness, ordered Cicotte benched. The sad irony of the Black Sox scandal is that the players themselves were double-crossed by the gamblers who orchestrated the fix. They received only a small fraction of the money they had been promised (Gutman 1992: 172–182).

The eight indicted players were acquitted at their trial in 1920. In fact, the jurors hoisted the players on their shoulders and paraded joyously through the courtroom after the verdict was announced. Despite the popularity of the jury's decision, baseball commissioner Kenesaw Mountain Landis banned the eight players from baseball for all time. His firm action set a precedent for the hard-line stance against gambling that exists to this day. Brooklyn Dodgers manager Leo Durocher was suspended for the 1947 season for consorting with gamblers (Gutman 1992: 91). Hall of Famers Willie Mays and Mickey Mantle were banned from the game after they began performing public relations duties for casinos in Atlantic City. In 1991, two umpires were placed on probation for placing small bets on professional sports other than baseball (Gutman 1992: 91, 196–98, 254).

The commissioner's office had conducted an ongoing, low-key investigation of Rose's activities since 1970. That investigation revealed extensive gambling and widespread associations with known gamblers, but no proof of illegal wagering. Nor did it reveal any violation of the game's own rules against gambling, which forbid only betting on baseball games (Ginsburg 1995: 243–44). The great mystery is why the authorities allowed Rose's activities to continue unabated, without even at least warning him that he was treading in dangerous waters. In all likelihood, his status as a superstar protected him. In Cincinnati, where he played most of his career, he was a hometown hero. He received adulatory coverage from the media, and on the road he attracted fans to ballparks. He also had a habit of changing bookies whenever his debts mounted, which made the extent of his gambling more difficult to grasp (Sokolove 1990: 195).

When Rose's behavior became a public scandal in 1989, he denied betting on baseball or on his own team. He continues to deny it today. The report compiled by Washington attorney John Dowd on behalf of the commissioner's office indicates otherwise. It contains evidence of fifty-two bets on the Reds in 1987 alone, when Rose was managing the team but not playing, as well as samples of his fingerprints and hand-writing on baseball betting slips. Nine people also stated to Dowd that they knew Rose bet on baseball (Ginsburg 1995: 246–49). Rose questions the authenticity of the handwriting and fingerprint analyses and the credibility of the witnesses who spoke against him (Rose and Kahn 1989: 246–47). "Does going to the racetrack make me a bad guy?" he asked a group of reporters in 1989. "I don't bet big. I bet more than you guys but I make more money than you guys. My financial statement is as long as my arm. I've never had the electricity turned off because I couldn't pay the bill. I've never wanted to kill the cab driver on the way home from the track" (Kindred 1995: 3).

Baseball commissioner Bartlett Giamatti banned Rose permanently from baseball on August 23, 1989. One year later, Rose pleaded guilty to charges of income tax evasion and was sentenced to five months in federal prison. The conviction stemmed from the actions he took to con-ceal a portion of his income in order to use more money to continue gambling. Like the fourteen other players who have received lifetime bans, Rose was granted the right to apply for reinstatement. He did so in September 1997. He hopes that reinstatement will pave the way for his entry into the Baseball Hall of Fame, where he would have been inducted long ago if not for his gambling activities. In order to be granted reinstatement, Rose probably will have to admit that he bet on baseball while he was a player and manager (Bodley 1997: 3C).

As serious as the misdeeds of Pete Rose were, there is no evidence that he ever took money to influence the outcome of a game in which he played. That crime is more difficult to commit than it was in the days of the Black Sox. Most professional athletes make too much money today to be the primary targets of gamblers seeking to fix games. And casinos and bookmakers become suspicious whenever an unusually large amount of money from an unknown person is bet on a team in a game that normally would stimulate much less interest. In many cases, they refuse to take the bets and report the activity to law enforcement au-thorities.

Despite those obstacles, the fixing of games does occur. The most vul-nerable sport is college basketball. With only five players on a team, a single athlete who plays regularly is able to influence the outcome—or, much more commonly, the point spread—of a game. Point-shaving scan-dals have occurred in the sport with great regularity since the University of Kentucky canceled its 1952–1953 season after five top players were implicated in a scheme. From 1959 to 1961, thirty-seven players at

Pete Rose gets horizontal for his patented head-first slide in a 1981 game with the Philadelphia Phillies. He displayed the same reckless abandon in the gambling world as he did on the baseball diamond. Banned from the game in 1989 after his betting habits were exposed, Rose is seeking reinstatement to the game and entry into the Baseball Hall of Fame. To gain what he seeks, Rose may have to admit that he bet on baseball games during his career as a player, an accusation he has denied repeatedly. Whatever the future may hold for Rose, the saddest part of his saga is that he could not admit to a gambling addiction and deal with it before it drove him from the game he loved—and still loves—so deeply. (AP/WIDE WORLD PHOTOS)

twenty-two schools faced accusations of point shaving. Rick Kuhn, a forward on the Boston College team in the 1978–1979 season, was convicted of conspiracy to commit sports bribery and interstate gambling. Tulane University's John (Hot Rod) Williams stood trial in 1986 for shaving points in exchange for cash and cocaine. He was acquitted and went on to play in the NBA (Layden 1995a: 51–52). In 1997, former Arizona State University players Stevin "Hedake" Smith and Isaac Burton, Jr., pleaded guilty to taking bribes for fixing four games in 1994. And in 1998, Northwestern University player Kenneth Dion Lee admitted receiving $12,000 for point shaving in three games in 1995.

SPORTS BETTING AND THE YOUNG

College athletes are not the only people on campus who are involved in gambling. The university environment is conducive to betting. Many students have access to cash, a high level of intelligence, an interest in sports, and a community of enthusiasts, usually a fraternity, that provides support and reinforcement for the activity. The first comprehensive study of gambling by college students was conducted in 1991. After surveying students at six schools in five states, researchers concluded that 23 percent of the students gambled at least once a week (Layden 1995b: 71). Arnie Wexler, a one-time addict who placed his last bet in 1971 and now runs a counseling service for compulsive gamblers, believes the practice is rampant on college campuses. "It's easier to place a bet on a college campus than it is to buy a can of beer or a package of cigarettes," he says. "You just pick up a telephone and call a bookie on campus. You don't even have to leave your room" (Kindred 1996: 7).

A major investigation conducted by *Sports Illustrated* in 1994 and 1995 confirmed Wexler's observation. The magazine's reporters uncovered significant activity at several major universities, including Clemson, Florida, Georgia, and Texas Tech. At each institution, several student bookies each had between 50 and 200 clients who bet with them on a regular basis. Other bookmaking operations have been uncovered at Northwestern University, the University of Rhode Island, and Michigan State University. In 1997, six students at Boston College were indicted on sixty-three gambling-related charges by the Middlesex County district attorney's office in Massachusetts.

Many of the bettors and bookmakers described themselves as former high school athletes who followed sports avidly. Like other gamblers, they were lured into the action after an initial period of great betting success that boosted their confidence and gave them an aura of invincibility. The regular bettors often brought friends or acquaintances into the action and became small-time bookies themselves (Layden 1995a: 68–90). Some students are unable to handle the pressure. In 1997, a nineteen-year-old college sophomore from Long Island was so distraught over losing $6,000 in the World Series that he committed "suicide by cop" by rushing two police officers with a toy revolver, forcing them to shoot him to death.

University and enforcement officials seemed largely unconcerned about the situation for many years. When Wexler wrote a letter to the *NCAA News* in 1995 offering to help its member institutions identify and treat problem gamblers, he received no expressions of interest. Concern heightened in 1998 after the Arizona State scandal and after a former captain of the Colombo crime family spoke to NCAA athletic directors. Michael Franzese, who left the mob in the late 1980s, told them that nearly every major university has a bookmaking operation on or near campus. Although the bookies themselves are students, many of the operations have links to organized crime operatives like Franzese, who try to establish relationships with unsuspecting players by plying them with drinks, favors, and adulation. "We don't all wear black shirts, white ties, and pin-striped suits," he says (Associated Press 1998: 6E). Despite its popularity, gambling on campus is not an investigative priority for law enforcement organizations. They are hesitant to launch probes of student bookmakers because the law requires a large amount of evidence for convictions, and courts usually hand down light punishments to offenders. The jurisdiction of the NCAA itself extends only to student-athletes. It has no authority over other students (Layden 1995b: 54).

The allure of gambling has attracted those even younger than the college aged. Gambling expert Harry Lesieur of Illinois State University conducted a survey of 7,000 teenagers in 1995 and found that between 10 and 14 percent of them were at risk of becoming compulsive gamblers (Harden and Swardson 1996: A8). In 1995, police in Nutley, New Jersey, arrested three high school students accused of helping older men run a bookmaking operation by recruiting young bettors and strong-arming them when they failed to pay their debts on time. The students were charged with kidnapping, theft by extortion, and making terroristic threats. In the same year, police arrested four men whose betting clients included at least fifty students from Byram Hills High School in Westchester County, New York (Layden 1995b: 52).

Several companies that produce baseball trading cards also have faced charges that the method by which they sell their product to millions of young collectors is, in fact, a form of gambling. In the early 1990s, when sales of trading cards began to wane, the industry invented "chase cards," an updated version of the bonus cards that appeared in packs in the 1950s and 1960s. The new twist is that chase cards are much more valuable, with some reported to be worth as much as $1,500 on the collectors' market. The goal is to spur sales by offering buyers only a few chase cards that will be coveted because of their supposed high resale value.

That strategy threw a complaint in 1992 from the New York City Consumer Affairs Department, which charged the industry with misleading advertising because buyers had no way of determining how often they would find a chase card in a pack. The companies agreed to begin printing the odds of finding a chase card on the front of each package. In 1996, that practice led to a lawsuit against the industry by a lawyer who claimed that all of the elements of gambling were present. The lawyer said he watched his young son feverishly stockpile cards for three months before he realized what was happening (Fatsis 1996: B1, B12). The trading card companies characterized the lawsuit as ridiculous. Others had a different opinion. One attorney involved in the case called chase cards "a clever marketing scheme to get kids addicted to gambling and make card companies rich" (Vest 1996: 59).

The most dangerous potential venue for young bettors is the Internet, where cyberspace casinos have blossomed to meet the demand for gambling at the cutting edge of technology. From the privacy of their own homes, gamblers can now bet on sports through establishments that are based outside the United States in the Caribbean, Europe, and the South Pacific in an effort to circumvent antigambling laws. Several jurisdictions have prosecuted the cyberspace casinos by using federal laws that bar the transfer of gambling information on telephone lines. Senator Jon Kyl of Arizona has introduced the Internet Gambling Prohibition Act in Congress that would ban on-line wagering completely (Crist 1998: 85). Kyl is chairman of the technology subcommittee of the Senate Judiciary Committee and he says Internet gambling is one of his top legislative priorities. Kyl's bill passed the Senate by a vote of 90–10 in 1998.

Kyl is seeking the ban because he says the practice undermines all of the values that sports represent. His effort has the support of the NCAA, the NFL, the National Hockey League (NHL), the Christian Coalition, and Ralph Nader's Public Citizen group. It is opposed by gamblers, bookmakers, civil libertarians, and the operators of cyberspace casinos, who say their venues are the wave of the future and cannot, and should not, be stopped. While Kyl's bill has succeeded in drawing attention to the vast and growing scope of Internet gambling, there is little chance that it will actually stop the advance of technology that will, in one form or another, make sports betting even easier than it is today.

SHOULD SPORTS BETTING BE LEGALIZED?

The widespread popularity of sports betting has led many people to call for its legalization everywhere, not only in Nevada and the four other states that permit it. The position of those who favor full-scale legalization is that sports betting will continue regardless of whether it is legal, and that it is better to have the practice sanctioned and controlled by government than operated by private companies and bookmakers, many with ties to organized crime. The tax revenue reaped by government-sponsored sports betting could be used to provide many of the services that citizens demand without wishing to pay for them through increases in sales, income, or property taxes.

Supporters of legalization also argue that sports betting is a "victimless" crime that brings no harm to those who do not participate. They point to data indicating that gambling is a low priority for law enforcement. In 1996, there were only 15,000 arrests for gambling in the United States—one-tenth of 1 percent of all arrests. By contrast, there were over 1 million arrests in the same year for drug-related offenses—8 percent of all arrests. Among the supporters of legalization is Brooklyn district attorney Charles Hynes in New York City. He would like to see sports betting operated by his state in the same manner in which it now operates off-track horse betting (McGraw 1997: 52–55). Supporters of legalized sports betting also pose more fundamental concerns about the role of government in controlling personal behavior. Why should government pass and enforce laws for engaging in an activity that, in their view, should be a matter of individual choice?

Oddsmaker Mort Olshan sees hypocrisy in a system that continues to make sports betting an illegal act. "To have a law that is not respected is like having no law at all," he told author Dan Moldea. "The government is making lawbreakers out of the forty million Americans who bet. England is very civilized about it. They have gambling controlled by the state, and the system works. It is integrated into their society. It adds some fun and excitement to their lives" (Moldea 1989: 433).

The notion that sports betting is a victimless crime is disputed vigorously by opponents of legalization. They do not accept the premise that betting should merely be a matter of individual choice. Instead, they see heavy costs to communities and to society at large. The Council on Compulsive Gambling claims that 5 percent of all gamblers are compulsive and that 90 percent of that group become criminals who turn to theft, embezzlement, and robbery to support their habit. They leave a long trail of lost employment, broken relationships, increased drug and alcohol abuse, and negative effects on children (McGraw 1997: 52). Opponents also say that legalization will not drive illegal bookmakers out of business because legal betting requires bettors to post money at the time they make their bets. Unlike illegal gambling, it does not offer gamblers the luxury of operating on credit, a luxury that many gamblers view as a necessity.

The staunchest foes of legalized betting are the major professional leagues, particularly the NFL. In the view of the NFL, legalization will violate the integrity of its game by increasing gambling activity and the chances that games will be fixed. Each game would no longer be a contest with a winner and a loser but merely an event through which people can make money. "You're going to introduce more people to gambling," says Jack Danahy, former head of NFL Security. "I'm not naive enough to think that a lot of people don't bet on football . . . but let's not encourage or enhance it more" (Moldea 1989: 434).

Whether it is further encouraged by government, it is a safe bet that sports gambling will continue to thrive. Most of America seems relatively at ease with an arrangement in which college athletic directors can hold their annual convention in Las Vegas and trigger only a few instances of pointed commentary. Some seers predict that the future will bring more action than ever, with walk-up windows like those at racetracks adorning every stadium, ballpark, and arena, and with millions of gamblers placing bets on their favorite teams by keyboard in front of computer screens in their living rooms.

On the other hand, there is at least one sign that the saturation point for gambling may be approaching. Casino gambling in New Orleans, trumpeted as a sure-fire bonanza in the early 1990s, has been a huge bust. Four riverboats have opened and closed in the city in less than four years, and the giant gambling enterprise Harrah's Entertainment has pulled the plug on construction of its $830 million casino near the French Quarter (Associated Press 1997: 2G). If a major game-fixing scandal erupts and the public will no longer pay to watch games whose outcomes they believe have been predetermined, sports gambling could suffer the same fate as the New Orleans casinos. If that happens, the odds boards and computer screens will go dark, the telephone lines will go dead, and all bets will be off.

TOPICS FOR DISCUSSION

1. Many individuals and organizations are working today to ban sports gambling on the Internet. Do you agree with their position? Or do you think that sports gambling on the Internet should be allowed? Why or why not?

2. Do you know anyone personally who has become addicted to sports gambling? Did their addiction have a negative effect on your relationship? Did that person suffer serious harm as a result of the addiction?

3. Many fans believe that Pete Rose should be permitted to enter the Baseball Hall of Fame even though he was banished from the game for his gambling activities. Others believe that his gambling should disqualify him from entry. What do you think?

4. Gambling supporters say that illegal sports betting is a "victimless" crime that harms no one except, in some cases, the individual who bets. Anti-gambling activists say that betting is harmful because it can have negative effects on the the bettor's spouse, children, friends, and workplace. Which point of view seems more accurate to you? Why?

5. Have you ever personally bet on a sports event or participated in a betting pool with friends? Does it seem like an activity that could get out of hand and cause you harm? Or is it simply an enjoyable diversion from daily life?

REFERENCES AND RESOURCES

Books

Ginsburg, Daniel. *The Fix Is In: A History of Baseball Gambling and Game Fixing Scandals*. Jefferson, N.C.: McFarland & Company, 1995.
   An excellent and detailed discussion of gambling in the national pastime, with chapters on Pete Rose and the Black Sox scandal.

Gutman, Dan. *Baseball Babylon*. New York: Penguin Books, 1992.
   Colorfully recounts the many gambling scandals that have rocked baseball.

Manteris, Art, with Rick Talley. *Bookie: Inside Las Vegas Sports Gambling*. Chicago: Contemporary Books, 1991.
   The director of race and sports operations at the Las Vegas Hilton describes the business of sports betting.

Moldea, Dan. *Interference: How Organized Crime Influences Professional Football*. New York: Morrow, 1989.
   One of the nation's greatest experts on organized crime details the links between gambling, football, and the mafia.

Rose, Pete, and Roger Kahn. *Pete Rose: My Story*. New York: Macmillan, 1989.
   The baseball superstar offers his version of the scandal that led to his banishment from the game.

Savage, Jeff. *A Sure Thing? Sports and Gambling*. Minneapolis, Minn.: Lerner, 1997.
   Covers all of the major issues surrounding sports betting in an attractive and easily understood format.

Sokolove, Michael Y. *Hustle: The Myth, Life and Lies of Pete Rose*. New York: Simon & Schuster, 1990.
   A baseball beat reporter who covered Pete Rose in Cincinnati and Philadelphia offers a convincing portrait of a deeply flawed individual.

Magazines and Newspapers

Associated Press. "Success for Casinos in Big Easy Not in Cards." *Columbus Dispatch*, October 4, 1997: 2G.
   A report on the woes of casino gambling in New Orleans.

Associated Press. "Colleges Warned about Gambling Problem." *Columbus Dis-*

patch, January 13, 1998: 6E.

Former mobster Michael Franzese speaks to the NCAA convention about gambling on the nation's college campuses.

Blackistone, Kevin. "If Gambling's So Evil, Why Did ADs Meet in Vegas?" *Columbus Dispatch*, June 20, 1997: 4D.

Chastises college athletic directors for holding their annual convention in Las Vegas.

Bodley, Hal. "Baseball Officials Divided on Reinstatement." *USA Today*, August 4, 1997: 3C.

A report on the controversy surrounding Pete Rose's request to be reinstated to baseball.

Callahan, Gerry. "Dark Days at BC." *Sports Illustrated*, November 16, 1996: 52–55.

Reports on the bookmaking ring that enwrapped several members of the school's football team.

Crist, Steven. "All Bets Are Off." *Sports Illustrated*, January 26, 1998: 82–92.
Assesses the rapid rise of gambling on the Internet.

Fatsis, Stefan. "Trading Cards: Wholesome Fun or Gambling?" *Wall Street Journal*, October 25, 1996: B1, B12.

A story about the controversy surrounding chase cards in trading card packs.

Golway, Terry. "Life in the 90's." *America*, November 23, 1996: 8.

A commentary on the ambivalence and hypocrisy that exist in American society with regard to sports gambling.

Harden, Blaine, and Anne Swardson. "States View Addiction as Chance They Have to Take." *Washington Post*, March 4, 1996: A8.

Discusses the growth of gambling among the nation's youth.

Kindred, Dave. "A You-Bet-Your-Life-Lesson." *Sporting News*, August 28, 1995: 3.

A comment on Pete Rose's continuing struggle to restore his reputation after being banished from baseball for gambling.

Kindred, Dave. "Ignoring Gambling Won't Make It Go Away." *Sporting News*, November 18, 1996: 7.

Criticizes the refusal of colleges and universities to face the gambling issue head on.

Klein, Frederick C. "At NCAA Time, It's Everybody into the Pool." *Wall Street Journal*, March 28, 1997: B7.

Reports on the popularity of office betting pools for sports events.

Layden, Tim. "Bettor Education." *Sports Illustrated*, April 3, 1995a: 68–90.

The first part of a comprehensive three-part series on campus gambling focuses on the lifestyle of young bettors.

Layden, Tim. "You Bet Your Life." *Sports Illustrated*, April 17, 1995b: 46–55.

The final part of a three-part series discusses the history of gambling on campus.

McGraw, Dan. "The National Bet: Laying an Illegal Wager on a Sports Game Has Never Been Easier. And More Americans Are Doing It Than Ever." *U.S. News and World Report*, April 7, 1997: 50–55.

A comprehensive look at the explosion of sports betting and the issue of legalization.

USA Today. "New Report Says Gambler Bet $1M on Ariz. State Game." August 4, 1997: 11C.

A brief note on the investigation of point shaving by members of the school's basketball team.

Vest, Jason. "Lawyers Hold All the Cards." *U.S. News and World Report*, December 2, 1996: 57–59.

Reports on the lawsuits filed against sports card companies.

Organizations to Contact

Gamblers Anonymous International Service Office
P.O. Box 17173
Los Angeles, CA 90017
Phone: 213–386–8789
Fax: 213–386–0030
E-mail: isomain@gamblersanonymous.org
Internet Web Site: www.gamblersanonymous.org
Gamblers Anonymous is a fellowship of men and women who share their experience, strength, and hope with each other so that they may solve their common problem and help others recover from a gambling problem.

National Center for Responsible Gaming
540 Pierce Avenue
Kansas City, MO 64110
Phone: 816–531–1878
Fax: 816–531–3459
E-mail: contact@ncrg.org
Internet Web Site: www.ncrg.org
Created and funded by the gaming industry, the center focuses exclusively on investigating compulsive and underage gambling.

National Council on Problem Gambling
P.O. Box 9419
Washington, D.C. 20016
Phone: 410–730–8008
National help line: 800–522–4700
Fax: 410–730–0669
E-mail: ncpg@erols.com
The group has thirty-five affiliate councils nationwide and provides help lines, educational presentations, and information services.

Dream Domes and Pleasure Palaces

With major league sports teams ready to pull up stakes and move at a moment's notice, cities across America are eager to use public money to provide them with state-of-the-art arenas, ballparks, and stadiums. What message do these extravagant structures send about society's spending priorities?

In the spring of 1997, Columbus, Ohio, was not the place to be for people weary of discussing the role of spectator sports in American society. Ohio's largest city, and one of the largest metropolitan areas in the nation without a major league baseball, football, basketball, or hockey team, spent March and April engaged in a boisterous effort to secure a National Hockey League (NHL) franchise.

For one group of people, the objective was to rally the voters of Franklin County and convince them to approve a 0.5 percent sales tax increase to fund construction of a 20,000-seat arena near the site of the old state penitentiary downtown. With a commitment to build an arena in place, the city felt it had an excellent chance to land one of the four NHL expansion franchises scheduled to begin play in 1998 and 2000. The plan also called for a 30,000-seat stadium adjacent to the arena for the Columbus Crew, the city's soccer team. But it was the arena—and the chance it offered to snare a bona-fide major league sports team—that excited the faithful. There was a consensus among the city's business and government leaders that the moment was here. Voters had rejected four previous ballot issues that would have provided public money for the construction of a sports arena. If Columbus was ever going to emerge from the shadows of its rivals Cincinnati and Cleveland, this was precisely the right time and the right way to do so.

From its headquarters near the proposed arena and stadium site, Citizens for Downtown's Future, an organization formed to work for passage of the sales tax increase, touted the benefits of the project to the public: 4,000 new jobs in the construction industry alone; hundreds more in the hotels, restaurants, and shops that would surround the complex; $100 million in new tax revenue each year that would generate additional funds for fiscally strapped local schools; dozens of entertainment events for families and children of all ages; and above all, the world's finest hockey teams playing their fast, rugged, game every year in the heart of Ohio. The *Columbus Dispatch* hailed the project as "an exceptional opportunity" for the city. "The closer you look," advocates advised the voters, "the more you'll agree."

At the same time, another organization, Voters Against Stadium Taxes, was telling the other side of the story: the project is nothing more than taxpayer-sponsored welfare for wealthy team owners and pampered players. The economic benefits of the project are grossly exaggerated. The money could be spent for any number of more worthy uses, including schools, roads, sewers, health care, mass transit, and support for the arts. The financial risks should be assumed by those who stand to benefit directly, not by the county's taxpayers. Besides, Columbus is a great town right now. Let's keep it that way. We don't need a major league hockey team and a $285 million dollar white elephant to make our city a better place to live.

The debate in Columbus was loud, long, and cantankerous. By the time citizens went to the polls in May, the issue had dominated radio talk shows, newspaper editorial columns, and barbershop discourse for over two months. It is a debate that has been staged in nearly every major city in America at some time in the past two decades. The stadium finance game never ends. Instead, it repeats itself and escalates in intensity as owners strive to secure facilities that will provide the additional revenue they need to pay top-notch players and field competitive teams. Fueling the game is the nation's long-standing love affair with spectator sports, an affair that begins for millions of fans in virtual infancy and lasts forever, providing a strong dose of escapism and fantasy that diverts attention from the less glamorous aspects of life.

As author James Michener observed, America in the decades after World War II has been living in the Age of the Stadium, an era where this particular architectural symbol, like other symbols in other times, "acquires a significance far beyond its mere utilitarian purpose." Just as in the Age of the Pyramid in ancient Egypt, the Age of the Cathedral in medieval Europe, and the Age of the Railroad Station in the nineteenth century, citizens look to their symbols with a sense of wonder and deep emotional attachment (Michener 1976: 338). For many people, sitting inside a football stadium on a Sunday afternoon surrounded by 80,000 fans rooting for the home team is something akin to a religious experience.

They may be watching a mere child's game played by overgrown boys. The stadium in which they are sitting may have been erected with millions of dollars of taxpayers' money for the benefit of a multimillionaire team owner. The team for which they are rooting may leave town next year if it can find another city willing and able to provide a better facility at a better price. None of that seems to matter. For the moment, cities and their fans seem willing to pay whatever it takes to build and maintain the dream domes and pleasure palaces of the sports world.

THE AGE OF THE STADIUM

By the year 2000, there are scheduled to be at least 120 major league baseball, football, basketball, and hockey franchises in North America: thirty in major league baseball (MLB), thirty-one in the National Football League (NFL), twenty-nine in the National Basketball Association (NBA), and thirty in the National Hockey League (NHL). Thirty-four of those franchises will be playing in stadiums, ballparks, and arenas that were built in the 1990s at a total cost of more than $4 billion (Laing 1996: 23). At least a dozen more franchises are scheduled to move into new venues early in the new century, and an additional dozen are seeking upgrades and renovations for the venues in which they currently play (Sandomir 1997: C25).

Some of the existing facilities were built with private funding, but the vast majority were constructed primarily with public funds provided by state, county, and local governments in the form of tax revenue or government-guaranteed construction bonds sold to investors. Many of the most elegant facilities, including Comiskey Park in Chicago, Arrowhead Pond in Anaheim, California, and the Alamodome in San Antonio, were almost completely financed with public funds (Wright 1997: 2A).

Until the end of World War II, nearly all sports facilities were built, owned, and operated by team owners. The legendary venues of the 1920s and 1930s—Boston Garden, Madison Square Garden and Yankee Stadium in New York City, Wrigley Field in Chicago—were not financed with taxpayers' dollars (Gorman and Calhoun 1994: 204). The first of the great publicly financed stadiums was built in the late 1950s, when Brooklyn Dodgers owner Walter O'Malley grew unhappy with his baseball team's home, fabled Ebbets Field of Flatbush. Opened in 1913, it had been the site of numerous Dodger triumphs, including nine National League pennants, the debut of Jackie Robinson in 1947 as the first African American player in MLB, and the storied team's first World Series title in 1955. But Ebbets Field contained fewer than 32,000 seats, the third-smallest capacity in the National League, and a mere 700 parking places.

O'Malley attempted to purchase land from New York City on which he could build a bigger home for the Dodgers, but negotiations proved futile. In 1957, the city of Los Angeles offered O'Malley title to 300 acres of prime real estate in Chavez Ravine, just north of the central business district. The city also pledged to provide nearly $3 million for access roads and another $18 million to pay a portion of the cost of the stadium itself. O'Malley made history, and broke the hearts of thousands of New Yorkers, when he moved his team to Los Angeles for the 1958 season. Dodger Stadium opened in 1962 with 56,000 seats and 24,000 parking spaces. As the National League's third-oldest ballpark—after Chicago's Wrigley Field and San Francisco's Candlestick Park—it remains the home of the Dodgers today. In 1978, it became the first ballpark to attract 3 million fans in a season. It has been hugely successful as a site for other entertainment events as well as baseball, and it would not have been built without the property and funding provided by the city of Los Angeles (Gorman and Calhoun 1994: 204–5).

More publicly financed facilities arose in the era of expansion that began in the 1960s, when the popularity of professional sports soared and more cities strived to play the major league game. In the 1960s and 1970s, MLB added eight new teams. During the same twenty-year span, the NBA added fourteen, the NHL fifteen, and the NFL fifteen, including ten teams from the American Football League that joined in 1970. The expansion boom fueled the creation of multiuse stadiums, which could be used by both baseball and football teams. Three Rivers Stadium in Pittsburgh, Riverfront Stadium in Cincinnati, and Veterans Stadium in Philadelphia were prized as cost-efficient even though they were criticized as sterile and dull in their design. The Astrodome, the world's first enclosed baseball and football stadium, opened in Houston in 1965. Hailed as the eighth wonder of the world in its early years, the home of the Astros baseball team seems like a quaint, outmoded relic today when compared to newer facilities. Indeed, the Houston Oilers of the NFL abandoned the Astrodome in 1997 and relocated in Nashville, Tennessee, where 76,000-seat Cumberland Stadium, built for the team with public funds at a cost of $292 million, is scheduled to open in 1999.

In the 1990s, multiuse stadiums fell out of favor as owners began to search for facilities they did not have to share with other teams. In 1992, the Baltimore Orioles left Memorial Stadium, their home for thirty-seven years, and opened the season in Oriole Park at Camden Yards, a stunning state-of-the-art structure in downtown Baltimore, built with city and state funds at a cost of $228 million. The exterior brick facade and intimate interior provide the look and spirit of an old-time ballpark and now attract sell-out crowds of more than 48,000 on a regular basis. In 1994, the Cleveland Indians left massive, decrepit Municipal Stadium on the shore of Lake Erie, which they had shared with the NFL's Browns for over four decades, and moved a mile inland to Jacobs Field, a 43,000-seat park that copies the cozy feel of Camden Yards. The city of Cleveland and the state of Ohio provided $178 million to build the facility. Other MLB teams followed the lead of the Orioles and Indians. The Seattle Mariners won funding from the Washington State legislature to leave the Kingdome and construct a baseball-only facility, and the Cincinnati Reds obtained voter approval of a plan to build a ballpark of their own on the Ohio River to replace Riverfront Stadium, which they share with the Bengals of the NFL. At the same election, voters also approved a new, separate stadium for the Bengals.

The never-ending campaigns for newer and better playing facilities often seem to diminish the importance of the games themselves and the athletes who play them. Fielding a winning team will always be a vital component of success in the sports world, for it is the factor above all others that generates fan interest. But what the stadium finance game reveals is that when it comes time to determine the bottom line—how much money a team makes each year and how much it can be sold for in the future—having a winning team is not enough.

THE BOTTOM LINE

Why is revenue generated from stadiums, ballparks, and arenas so pivotal to the financial success of sports franchises? And how do franchises generate that revenue? The answers to those questions lie in the unusual business practices that prevail in major professional sports leagues, practices that distinguish them from other moneymaking ventures.

Franchises earn money from their facilities in a variety of ways. Modern venues offer teams a chance to profit from parking fees, merchandise sales, food and drink sales, naming rights for the facilities themselves, and in-stadium advertising displays. The amount of money earned from each of those sources depends on the lease agreement that is negotiated between the team and the owner of the facility, usually a city or county or a quasi-governmental agency. In a typical arrangement in MLB, the ballpark owner receives the bulk of the parking fees, the team receives all money from merchandise sales, and food and drink revenue is split between the ballpark owner and the team (Gorman and Calhoun 1994: 206–7). Most teams also pay rent, usually a percentage of game ticket receipts.

Revenue earned from facilities is pivotal because, unlike the two other major revenue sources that a team has—national television broadcast rights and gate ticket receipts—it is not shared with other members of the team's league. Unlike other business competitors, baseball and football team owners pool a large portion of the revenue they receive and divide it among themselves. This is done to promote and stabilize the league as a whole, which is also a business entity. In the NFL, receipts

One of the most luxurious and elegant of the new baseball parks is Oriole Park at Camden Yards, opened in 1992 in downtown Baltimore. Built with public funds at a cost of $210 million, Camden Yards has become a popular attraction and huge success, prompting the city of Baltimore and the state of Maryland to ante up another $176 million for a new stadium for the Baltimore Ravens of the National Football League. The Orioles' lucrative earnings from their new home have allowed them to attract and keep many outstanding players. In 1998, the Orioles had the highest player payroll in major league baseball, at just over $70 million. The team is an excellent example of how playing venues that attract fans and create revenue can be used to create a competitive advantage on the playing field. (AP/WIDE WORLD PHOTOS)

from television broadcast rights are split evenly among the league's thirty teams. In some cases, that money can amount to more than two-thirds of a team's annual income (Gorman and Calhoun 1994: 61). Game ticket receipts also are split, with the home team receiving 60 percent and the visiting team 40 percent. In the National League, visiting baseball teams receive 10 percent of all ticket revenue; in the American League visiting teams receive 15 percent (Rosentraub 1997: 90).

The most lucrative sources of stadium revenue are the sales of luxury boxes, club seating, and permanent or personal seat licenses. Luxury boxes provide an opportunity for corporations and individuals to entertain clients and friends in lavish style high above the field or court, usually at press box level. The boxes contain wet bars, ample and comfortable seating for eight to twenty people, and closed-circuit television. Some even house bedrooms, game rooms, and elegant marble and gold bathrooms (Michener 1976: 346). Every facility built in the 1980s and 1990s includes luxury boxes, and many older ones have been remodeled to include them.

Club seats are not private and enclosed like luxury boxes, but they are more comfortable than standard seats and offer better food and drink service. In the Rose Garden in Portland, Oregon, which became the home of the NBA's Trail Blazers in 1995, team owner and computer magnate Paul Allen installed fiberoptic wiring in some of his club seats that allows fans to order food and drinks, play music, or see action replays on their own video screens (Laing 1996: 25). In most cases, team owners retain either all or a large percentage of the revenue earned from luxury boxes and club seats.

The most lucrative of all revenue enhancers is the permanent or personal seat license (PSL). A PSL is not a game ticket. It simply grants the licensee the right to purchase a game ticket—usually a season ticket—for that seat and to sell or transfer the license to another individual. Because money earned from PSLs is not actual ticket revenue, it need not be shared with other teams. Therefore, it can be a major factor in determining a team's financial health.

The agreement reached between the Los Angeles Rams of the NFL and the city of St. Louis in 1995 provides an excellent example of how lucrative stadium financing can be for a team. The city of St. Louis, St. Louis County, and the state of Missouri agreed to assume the entire $290 million cost of a new indoor stadium for the team, the 67,000-seat Trans World Dome. The sale of PSLs to fans eager to see a pro football team in their city produced $70 million, which the Rams used to pay for relocation expenses and a practice facility and to absolve debts owed to the city of Anaheim, California, their previous home. The Rams' rent in the Trans World Dome is a modest $250,000 for each year of the thirty-year lease. During that time, the team will receive 100 percent of all food and drink revenue as well as 100 percent of the revenue from luxury boxes and club seats, with a guarantee from the corporate community of St. Louis that 85 percent of those boxes and seats will be occupied for the next fifteen years. Seventy-five percent of all in-stadium advertising revenue will belong to the Rams, as will the $1.3 million paid by Trans World Airlines for the right to name the stadium. Finally, the team was given 1,200 parking spots in the stadium parking lot for each game and a merchandise store near the Trans World Dome, built and paid for by the city. The total value of the financial package to the Rams is estimated to be $700 million. Said one consultant involved in the negotiations: "This will be the best stadium deal ever in the NFL, except for the next one" (Laing 1996: 27).

There will certainly be a next deal—in baseball, basketball, and hockey, as well as football. Any professional team that can convince taxpayers to foot the bill for constructing, upgrading, or maintaining a facility and can negotiate itself a generous portion of the revenue that the facility generates will compete for championships with a decided financial advantage over its rivals. It is an advantage that proves to be quite useful in an environment where players and their agents demand, and usually receive, higher salaries at every opportunity.

ROBBER BARONS OR CIVIC BOOSTERS?

With the cost of retaining or luring a team escalating every year, why do cities and metropolitan areas continue their efforts to attain major league status? Proponents of professional sports, including fans, many politicians, business leaders, and workers in the hospitality industry, answer that a major league team is well worth any investment of public dollars that may be needed to keep or attract it. They maintain that a city reaps huge economic benefits from a sports team because thousands of fans converge on the city for each home game and spend money in retail stores, hotels, restaurants, and other attractions. That vigorous commercial activity can revitalize an urban center that may be suffering from competition from its suburbs. Proponents also maintain that with a well-negotiated stadium lease, a city can make money from rent, parking fees, food and drink concessions, and taxes.

The presence of a major league team also can greatly boost civic pride and community involvement. The thrill of being identified as a major league city may be immeasurable in economic terms, but it plays the key role in every effort to keep or land a major league team. "You don't measure a sports team in just dollars and cents," says Peter Karmanos, who transformed his NHL team from the Hartford Whalers to the Carolina Hurricanes in 1997. "You measure it in cultural spirit. Ask people in Hartford what they think it means to the city when they lost the team, or in Minneapolis–St. Paul. Ask if they'd reconsider subsidizing a team to come back there" (Sandomir 1997: C23).

Opponents of public financing for sports facilities concede that a city's ego and spirit may indeed be lifted by a major league team. But they maintain that the price is far too high. Robert Baade, an economist at Lake Forest College in Illinois, is a prominent critic of public financing. His studies indicate that professional teams have no significant impact on the economies of metropolitan areas. Baade says there is no net increase in spending, but merely a shifting of a finite number of dollars to sports events and away from other forms of entertainment, such as theaters, concerts, museums, and amusement parks. In other words, money spent at a ballpark is money that would be spent somewhere else in the area if the ballpark did not exist (*Barron's* 1995: 63).

Even if there were clear and convincing evidence that economic benefits can be derived from the operation of sports teams, there remains the issue of whether hundreds of millions of public dollars should be used to construct new facilities for the teams. In Columbus, after the spirited campaign of 1997, voters said no to public financing for an arena to attract a hockey team. Two months later, Nationwide Insurance, a corporate titan headquartered in the city, agreed to assume the cost of building the facility. Nationwide's commitment prompted the NHL to award the city an expansion team that begins play in 2000 as the Columbus Blue Jackets. In New York City, complaints are increasing as the city contemplates building a baseball stadium for Yankees owner George Steinbrenner along the Hudson River in Manhattan. It would be the most expensive sports facility ever constructed. "When you have schools crumbling throughout the city, roadways and bridges in disrepair, parks and playgrounds in dangerous shape, it's difficult to provide a rationale for spending almost a billion dollars just for the vanity," says Bronx borough president Fernando Ferrer (*Issues and Controversies* 1996: 433).

Ferrer's reasoning is starting to make sense to more people. There are some indications that the public may be saying that it is time to say no to new stadium requests. That was the sentiment expressed in Pittsburgh, where in 1997 voters turned down a plan to build a new stadium for the Pittsburgh Steelers with an increase in the sales tax. The resounding defeat was a bitter blow to the team and the Rooney family, who have owned the team for over forty years and seen it become the heart and soul of western Pennsylvania. Another defeat was handed to Carl Pohlad, the owner of the Minnesota Twins, who in 1997 was seeking public money for a new ballpark. On November 13, after a long and contentious public debate, the state legislature rejected the Twins' final stadium proposal. Over 500,000 people had called the state capitol in St. Paul in the three days before the vote to express their views. Most of those views were strongly negative. Several lawmakers said the stadium

The Voice of the People: Recent Stadium Ballot Issues

City	Team	Year of Vote	Margin and Result	
Cleveland	Browns	1996	72.3–27.7	Yes
Detroit	Lions	1996	65.7–34.3	Yes
Houston	Astros	1996	51.1–48.9	Yes
Miami	Heat	1996	58.9–41.1	Yes
Tampa	Buccaneers	1996	52.9–47.1	Yes
Nashville	Oilers	1996	62.1–37.9	Yes
Cincinnati	Reds/Bengals	1996	61.5–38.5	Yes
Detroit	Tigers	1996	79.7–20.0	Yes
San Francisco	Giants	1996	66.3–33.7	Yes
Columbus	Blue Jackets	1997	43.7–56.3	No
Seattle	Seahawks	1997	51.0–49.0	Yes
San Francisco	49ers	1997	50.2–49.7	Yes
Pittsburgh	Steelers/Pirates	1997	75.1–24.9	No

Source: Horrow Sports Ventures.

debate was the most emotional they had encountered in their careers, surpassing even abortion in its intensity (Rushin 1997: 138).

It is too early to tell whether the verdicts in Pittsburgh and Minneapolis signal the beginning of a trend or are merely exceptions to the general rule (see table). In the end, it does seem to be vanity that lies at the root of the stadium finance game, and there is an ample supply of that quality among the nation's major cities and the millions of sports fans who live in them. The Washington Redskins opened the 1997 NFL season in a glistening $175-million stadium in suburban Maryland. The Toronto Raptors of the NBA plan to debut the $200-million Air Canada Center in 1999. In the same year, the NBA's Lakers and the NHL's Kings will play in Staples Center in Los Angeles. In 2000, the Milwaukee Brewers will be playing baseball in Miller Park, a retractable domed stadium named after the giant Wisconsin brewing company, and the Houston Astros will have abandoned the fabled Astrodome for the Ballpark at Union Station. And the Florida Panthers are constructing a $212-million arena to play hockey at the southern tip of the Sun Belt. For cities and fans everywhere, the magical allure of major league sports seems irresistible, and no amount of talk about misplaced spending priorities or assaults on the public purse seems capable of changing that.

TOPICS FOR DISCUSSION

1. Do you think that taxpayers' money should be used to finance the construction and maintenance of stadiums, arenas, and ballparks for professional sports teams? Are they wise investments for cities and states? Or are there more vital uses for the money that is spent on sports facilities? If so, what are those uses?

2. Has your city or state ever been involved in a controversy over the construction of a sports facility? What issues were raised by the supporters and opponents of the project? What was the result?

3. The most common argument in support of publicly financed sports facilities is that they give the city and metropolitan area a chance to be "major league." Why is it important to many people that they live in a "major league" town?

4. Critics of publicly financed sports facilities say they have no significant impact on the economies of cities and metropolitan areas. Do you agree with that point of view? Why or why not?

RESOURCES AND REFERENCES

Books

Baim, Dean V. *The Sports Stadium as a Municipal Investment*. Westport, Conn.: Greenwood Press, 1994.
  Examines in detail the construction and operating costs of sixteen football and baseball stadiums from the 1950s to the 1980s and compares the costs of publicly financed and privately financed stadiums.
Coakley, Jay J. *Sport in Society: Issues and Controversies*. Madison, Wis.: Brown & Benchmark, 1994.
  Discusses public financing of stadiums in Chapter 12.
Dudley, William, ed. *Sports in America: Opposing Viewpoints*. San Diego: Greenhaven Press, 1994.
  Discusses the economics of stadium financing in Chapter 3.
Gorman, Jerry, and Kirk Calhoun, with Skip Rozin. *The Name of the Game: The Business of Sports*. New York: Wiley, 1994.
  Two partners in the firm of Ernst and Young, the nation's leading financial services company working with the sports industry, discuss stadium financing, expansion, and other economic issues in the sports world.
Michener, James A. *Sports in America*. New York: Random House, 1976.
  One of America's best-selling authors reflects on many aspects of the country's most popular pastime in a personal and well-researched book.
Quirk, James, and Rodney D. Fort. *Pay Dirt: The Business of Professional Team Sports*. Princeton, N.J.: Princeton University Press, 1992.

Two economics professors offer a wealth of information on the business of sports.

Rosentraub, Mark S. *Major League Losers*. New York: Basic Books, 1997.

A leading analyst of the economic impact of sports franchises, Rosentraub asserts that they have a minuscule effect on the economy of a city or metropolitan area.

Magazines and Newspapers

Babington, Charles. "Foes of Stadiums Getting Blitzed." *Washington Post*, March 30, 1996: H4.

Describes the verbal insults hurled on lawmakers in the Maryland state legislature who opposed state funding for a stadium for the NFL's Baltimore Ravens.

Barron's. "Ground Out." November 13, 1995: 63.

An editorial decrying the huge public expenditures made by taxpayers to support stadium construction and operation.

Becker, Gary. "A Flatter Tax Just Might Keep Fickle Teams at Home." *Business Week*, February 12, 1996: 24.

Comments on the use of tax-exempt municipal bonds to finance stadiums.

Economist. "Football and the Reluctant Voter." June 14, 1997: 26.

An English view of stadium finance referendums in San Francisco and Seattle in 1997.

Fitzsimmons, Kara. "Stadium Bonds Are Finding Tough Going These Days." *Wall Street Journal*, August 20, 1996: C23.

An overview of the uncertainties facing team owners who seek public financing for their stadiums and ballparks.

Forbes, Gordon. "Winning 49'ers, Seahawks Can Thank the Game." *USA Today*, June 26, 1997: 7C.

Cites the emergence of pro football as the nation's leading spectator sport as the major factor in successful stadium referendums in San Francisco and Seattle.

Issues and Controversies on File. "Sports-Stadium Funding." May 31, 1996: 431–435.

An excellent overview of the issues surrounding stadium financing.

King, Peter. "Up in the Air." *Sports Illustrated*, April 28, 1997: 50–51.

Reports on the campaign of computer magnate Paul Allen to win approval of a new stadium for the NFL's Seattle Seahawks.

Laing, Jonathan R. "Foul Play." *Barron's*, August 19, 1996: 23–27.

A detailed look at the numbers, personalities, and politics of stadium financing in the 1990s.

McCormick, John. "Playing Stadium Games." *Newsweek*, June 30, 1997: 55.

Pinpoints civic vanity and the urge to be "major league" as the prime motivating force behind the campaigns to land teams and finance stadiums.

Nawrocki, Tom. "Stadium Wars." *Sports Illustrated*, April 7, 1997: 18.

A discussion of scenarios in Texas and Florida where judges and politicians have said no to stadium proposals.

Price, S. L. "What's Hot, What's Not." *Sports Illustrated*, November 27, 1995: 48–55.

Profiles the city of Nashville, where the NFL and the NHL have come calling with requests for new facilities for new teams.

Rushin, Steve. "Curtains?" *Sports Illustrated*, December 22, 1997: 136–48.

Portrays the changing times in Minneapolis–St. Paul, where citizens have said no to requests by the Vikings and Twins for new facilities.

Sandomir, Richard. "The Name of the Game Is New Stadiums." *New York Times*, June 4, 1997: C23–24.

Reviews pending stadium financing projects, with an emphasis on the proposed ballpark for baseball's New York Yankees on Manhattan's West Side.

Spiers, Joseph. "Are Pro Sports Worth It?" *Fortune*, January 15, 1996: 29–30.

A look at the move made from Cleveland to Baltimore by NFL owner Art Modell in 1995.

USA Today. "How You Pay $$$ for Stadiums Far, Far Away." June 5, 1997: 14A.

An editorial criticizing the use of public money to build stadiums, ballparks, and arenas.

Wright, Steve. "Spinoff Benefits Touted: Arenas, Stadiums Primarily Help Indirectly, Studies Find." *Columbus Dispatch*, April 27, 1997: 1A–2A.

Discusses a report issued by the National Conference of State Legislatures that examines the economic benefits of financing stadiums with public money.

Organizations to Contact

Cleveland Browns
Internet Web Site: www.clevelandbrowns.com
The official Web Site of the Cleveland Browns offers browsers a photographic image of the new stadium being built for the team in downtown Cleveland. The new National Football League expansion team, scheduled to begin play in 1999, will replace the franchise that moved to Baltimore in 1996.

Voters Against Stadium Taxes (VAST)
144 East Kelso Road
Columbus, OH 43202
Richard C. Sheir, the founder and head of VAST, is a prominent opponent of publicly financed sports facilities and has spearheaded several winning campaigns against stadium ballot issues.

12

Fans and Fanatics

Fans are the lifeblood of any sport and a vital ingredient for commercial success. But some fans take their devotion to their games too far, ruining marriages and careers and crossing the line into mayhem and vandalism. What is the difference between a fan and a fanatic?

As a graduate student in sports psychology at the University of Florida, Charles Hillman knew that the school's football fans were passionately devoted to the Florida Gators, the 1996 national champions and a perennial power in the Southeastern Conference. He did not know how strong their devotion was until he conducted an experiment that reached an interesting conclusion. For the most rabid Florida Gator fans, watching their team perform on the football field each Saturday is better than having sex.

Hillman recruited fifty volunteers and classified them according to their interest level—low, moderate, or high—in Florida Gator football. Then he used scientific instruments to measure their heart rate and brain activity while they viewed a series of images. The series included images of violence, neutral objects such as tables and chairs, scenes of Florida football games, and pictures of couples entwined in amorous embraces.

All three groups of volunteers measured similar reactions, except when the football scenes were displayed. At those moments the most fervent Gator fans had reactions that measured very near the top of the two scales that Hillman had devised—one ranging from very unpleasant to very pleasant, the other from calm to excited. To determine how absorbed the volunteers were in the images, Hillman also used a sudden, sharp noise called a startle probe. As they viewed the lovemaking couples, the high-level Gator fans heard the startle probe loud and clear.

But as they watched pictures of their beloved team in action, they became so deeply absorbed that they were much less aware of it. As one professor explained, "There were fewer brain resources available" when the fans were being treated to scenes of their favorite gridiron heroes (*Sports Illustrated* 1997: 29–30).

To anyone who knows or lives with a passionate sports fan, the amusing conclusion reached by Hillman's study does not seem unusual. There are few, if any, other activities in modern America that excite as many people to as great an extent as watching sports events. It makes little difference if the sport being viewed is auto racing, baseball, basketball, football, or ice hockey. Each of those sports has a large and zealous following. For a sizable percentage of the fans, watching sports is the central focus of their lives.

Vicki Tucky of Clintonville, Ohio, knows how strong the passion for sports can be. Her husband David, a Cleveland native, enrolled at Ohio State University because of its successful football teams. He proposed to her with a message on the scoreboard at Cleveland Stadium before a National Football League (NFL) game between the Browns and the Cincinnati Bengals. He planned the conception of their son in 1996 so that the birth would not conflict with the major league baseball (MLB) playoffs, when he would be focused on the fortunes of the Cleveland Indians. Unlike many other spouses, Vicki Tucky accepts her husband's love of sports. She even admits to a love for the Cincinnati Bengals herself. "I put sports above most aspects of my life and I'm not ashamed of it," says David. "As long as I'm not hurting anybody, I plan to keep on doing it" (Fiely 1997: 3I).

Millions of other people plan to keep doing it too. And although a huge majority of today's most intense sports fans are male, interest among women has grown in recent years. The NFL claims that its fan base is 44 percent female, up from 33 percent in 1990. That translates into 40 million fans, 400,000 of whom enter stadiums each week to watch the games in person. "Women are of critical importance to us," says Sara Levinson, the president of NFL Properties, the league's merchandising division. "They control the TV dial on Sunday afternoons and decide what sports their kids will get involved in. We have to make these gatekeepers comfortable" (Meyers 1997: 2A).

Men and women alike can count on plenty of help from the new services and technological innovations that have been developed to meet the desires of hard-core fans. The Entertainment Sports Programming Network (ESPN) began broadcasting in 1979 with the goal of providing sports coverage twenty-four hours per day, seven days per week. It now reaches more than 70 million households in the United States, about 70 percent of all homes with television (Quirk 1997: 17). Viewers also can watch ESPN2, a second network that began broadcasting in 1994, and the Golf Channel, devoted entirely to a sport with the loyal following that advertisers crave. Digital satellite systems such as Primestar and DIRECTV allow fans to view events on hundreds of cable television channels. For a subscription fee paid each season, pro football fans can purchase NFL Sunday Ticket, which provides access to all of the games played each Sunday instead of only the ones telecast in particular viewing areas. Pro basketball fans can enjoy similar viewing options with NBA League Pass. DIRECTV also offers NHL Center Ice for hockey, MLB Extra Innings for baseball, and MLS/ESPN Shootout for soccer. On radio, there are now more than 150 stations that feature sports talk, around-the-clock discussions among the host and the listening audience of all aspects of the sports world.

Fans need not be satisfied with watching games on television or listening to sports talk on radio. There are many other outlets for their passion. Fantasy baseball camps give them a chance to test their skills on the diamond against big league stars of the past. For a die-hard Boston Red Sox fan, there may be no greater thrill than standing in the batter's box trying to hit a knuckleball thrown by former Sox hurler Luis Tiant. Fantasy Leagues allow baseball, football, basketball, and hockey devotees with a bent for statistics and strategy to create their own teams and compete against other league members. Sports Tours, Inc., a Massachusetts-based travel agency, offers vacation junkets to "couch potatoes" who spend most of their time in front of the television watching their favorite teams. Among the most popular destinations are the Baseball Hall of Fame in Cooperstown, New York, and the Babe Ruth Museum in Baltimore, which is one stop on the Bambino Trail, a six-night tour featuring the life and times of the legendary New York Yankees slugger (Magenheim 1997: 16).

Fans with an interest in collecting can enter the $3 billion market for sports memorabilia, which offers jerseys, balls, bats, photographs signed by athletes, and, in the case of at least one superstar, many more items. In 1997, a sale of Mickey Mantle's personal belongings at Leland's auction house in New York City netted $541,880. His passport sold for $9,200, his signed American Express Card for $7,175, and a lock of his hair for $6,900, almost ten times more than the preauction estimate of $700. Mantle's representatives could have made even more money, but they declined to sell many of the late slugger's belongings that were deemed too personal. Those included his bathrobe, prescription medicine bottles, and reading glasses. A second option for the consumption minded is official team merchandise. In addition to popular items like hats and jackets, there are a host of others available for purchase: ties, wastebaskets, mouse pads, duffel bags, earmuffs, comforters, calendars, shower curtains, shaving cream mugs, stuffed animals, telephones, flags, clocks, and rugs.

Why do so many people devote so much time and energy to following sports? British author George Orwell described sports as "war minus the shooting," and the emphasis on aggression and physical violence is clearly a factor in their vast popularity. A second factor is their ability to inspire uplift and hope. Earl Warren, the chief justice of the U.S. Supreme Court from 1953 to 1969, said that the front page of the newspaper reported failures, while the sports page reported accomplishments. In a world overflowing with self-doubt and broken dreams, the ongoing parade of athletic triumph is a source of optimism. But sports offers more than aggression, violence, and the chance for those who lead ordinary lives to experience joy at the achievements of others. In the course of a single contest, a full season, and a lifetime, sports fans can encounter comedy, tragedy, glamor, and high drama. They also can develop a kinship with people who share their devotion, a deep and durable bond that many of them cannot achieve readily in any other aspect of their lives. What effect does that deep devotion have on their spouses, families, careers, and communities? And what price is paid by individuals and by society when fans cross the line between devotion and derangement and become stalkers, arsonists, rioters, and murderers?

THE TIMELESS PASSION

People have loved watching athletic contests since the beginning of recorded history, and fans in the ancient world, like their modern counterparts, often went to extremes in their affection and dedication. The organizers of the Olympic Games in ancient Greece were forced to hire assistants called *mastigophoroi* (whip bearers) and *rabdouchi* (truncheon bearers) to control the unruly crowds who gathered to cheer their heroes (Guttmann 1986: 17). When those heroes returned to their home city-states in triumph, they were showered with trophies and material rewards by government leaders and the adoring public. Fan interest reached even greater heights in ancient Rome, where gladiator fights and chariot races were the two most prominent sporting pastimes. The pay was low for the gladiators who entered the ring to fight each other to the death, but like athletes today, they were granted an exalted status in society and praised for their talents. The savage, bloody spectacle entranced all classes of Roman society, from patricians to slaves, and gladiators were idolized by female spectators as well as male. In 65 B.C., Julius Caesar organized a competition featuring 320 pairs and built a wooden amphitheater especially for the event. Because amphitheaters were flimsy and prone to collapse, they were often replaced by stone structures. The most renowned was the Colosseum in Rome, completed in 80 A.D., with a seating capacity of 50,000. The amphitheater in Pompeii featured its own version of the modern luxury box, where the wealthy and privileged sat high above the masses and were treated to food and drink, awnings, and perfume sprays. The amphitheaters also attracted gamblers, who bet regularly on the outcome of the matches; prostitutes, who plied their trade in the boisterous arcades beneath the stands; and history's first sports merchandisers, who sold clay lamps and statues emblazoned with images of the most popular fighters. And like sports promoters today, those in ancient Rome were willing to arrange an occasional novelty act whenever attendance and interest lagged. The emperor Domitian once sponsored a series of matches between women and dwarfs (Guttmann 1986: 20–25).

Gladiator fights died out after 399 A.D., when they were banned by the emperor Honorius, largely as a result of longstanding opposition from Christians, who objected to the bloodletting. By that time they had been surpassed in popularity by chariot races. The Circus Maximus, one of five hippodromes in Rome, held 250,000 spectators, five times as many as the Colosseum. Commentators noted—and lamented—the passionate intensity of the chariot racing fans. "All over the city you can see them quarreling fiercely about the races," wrote the historian Ammianus Marcellinus. "I can find nothing new in the races," added Pliny the Younger, "that so many thousands of adult men should have such a childish passion for watching galloping horses and drivers standing in chariots, over and over again." The fervor of the fans reached frightening levels. One grief-stricken man hurled himself on the funeral pyre of his favorite charioteer. When the emperor Nero was scolded by his wife for returning home late from an outing at the races, he flew into a rage and kicked her to death (Guttmann 1986: 28–30).

LIVES OF THE SPORTSAHOLICS

Even a quick look at the sports culture of ancient Greece and Rome will prompt readers to ask if things have changed much since the days when gladiators and chariot racers, instead of quarterbacks and stock car drivers, reigned as popular heroes. Of course, in today's sports world, rules are uniform, competitions are standardized, records are maintained, and leagues are formed as partnerships comprising individual players or teams. Those changes are the legacy of England, where in the nineteenth century modern sports were created by aristocrats with a talent for numbers and organization. We also live with the pervasive presence of television and radio, which increases the audience for and the immediacy of sports events by allowing millions of fans across the world to hear and see the same event at the same time. But the "fierce quarrels" and "childish passion" criticized by the historians of ancient Rome seem quite familiar to the wives and families of men who have placed sports at the center of their lives, as does the eagerness of the fans of the ancient world to watch their favorite events "over and over again." Indeed, it is probably the seemingly endless hours of sports viewing that creates the most conflict between fans and nonfans.

In his book *Not Now, Honey, I'm Watching the Game*, Kevin Quirk, a former sportswriter for the *Charlotte Observer* and correspondent for *Sports Illustrated*, profiles the lives of sportsaholics, broadly defined as people who live life through sports or for sports. Despite the book's humorous title, it is a serious attempt to gauge the negative effects of excessive devotion to sports. In an effort to determine the extent of the phenomenon, Quirk conducted a nationwide survey of sportsaholics and the women who love them. The results astonished him. He had touched a raw nerve, and a deluge of responses from tearful, frustrated women and proud, unapologetic men poured into his Charlottesville, Virginia, home by fax, letter, telephone, and e-mail.

Quirk uncovered a colorful gallery of sports-obsessed characters: one Pittsburgh Steelers fan who grew a stubbly beard in imitation of the team's quarterback Neil O'Donnell and another who dropped to his knees in tearful prayer in front of the television during a key playoff game. A University of Kentucky basketball fan who walks his dog during each game because it always seems to increase the team's lead. A man who watches every game with the same amount of change in his pocket—two quarters, one dime, two nickels, and one penny—to bring his team good luck, and another who once paced so nervously during games that he now has taken to hopping on one foot, causing friends to nickname him The Stork (Quirk 1997: 120–125). For these men, a victory for their team creates excitement, giddiness, euphoria, and loud celebration; a defeat leads to despair, sullenness, anger, and an occasional outburst of violence.

Many sportsaholics expand their interest beyond the core activity of watching games. In Fantasy Leagues, a number of fans, usually between eight and sixteen, assemble to conduct a draft of a sport's players through which they assemble their own teams. In the week before the MLB season opens in April, groups of excited men toting clipboards and magazines can be observed holding their drafts in restaurants and bars everywhere. Identical gatherings occur in August before the NFL season and in October before the National Basketball Association (NBA) season. The performance of each fantasy team is then gauged by the statistics that the team's players compile in games actually played in real life. The fantasy player who compiles the best record by the end of the season is the champion. The champion usually wins a significant purse, made up of entry fees paid by each league member. In Fantasy Leagues, fans with strong statistical knowledge can become champions. They also can become fixated on the performance of individual players, a development that concerns some onlookers who believe fantasy owners lose interest in how real-life teams perform as a unit. That concern does not stop many athletes themselves from organizing Fantasy Leagues. During the 1997 NFL season, the most popular diversion in the New York Giants locker room was fantasy basketball, with fullback Charles Way serving as league commissioner.

On radio, sportsaholics can tune into sports talk stations such as WFAN "The Fan" in New York City; WTEM "The Team" in Washington, D.C.; and KTCK "The Ticket" in Dallas, Texas. Cheap shots, insults, put-downs, and macho bluster are the order of the day. The most popular hosts use brutal cynicism to denigrate teams, players, coaches, and even members of the listening audience who sometimes wait hours for a chance to talk on the air for thirty seconds or less. Al Morganti, a member of the sports crew at WIP in Philadelphia, says that when he comes to work each day, he checks his conscience at the door. There is no pretense of reporting facts; the shows traffic in opinions and rumors. "There's no accountability," says a staffer at Morganti's station. "It's dangerous, it's mean-spirited, it's almost a disgrace that it works" (Murphy 1996: 76).

The listeners, phone-in callers, and hosts of sports talk radio inhabit the same world, and through their love of sports they develop a perverse bond of mutual dependency that is tinged with affection, friendship, and even love. It is precisely this bond that alarms Quirk and the legions of women who responded to his survey. The love of sports can become so consuming that it corrodes all but the strongest unions between husband and wife. When a fan pours all of his emotion and energy into baseball, basketball, or football, there is little left for his wife, children, career, and community. That is a recipe for marital disaster. Quirk's first marriage ended in divorce, and he blames the failure on his own excessive sports-viewing habits. (See the Sportsaholism Checklist.)

How can a sportsaholic change? Quirk offers a number of strategies for mapping out a new game plan: rating the importance of each week's sports events and watching only those that are most critical, spending an hour with a wife or other partner for every hour spent watching sports, logging the amount of time spent with sports and then committing to a reduction. He does not recommend that anyone quit the habit completely. For serious fans reveling in what Quirk calls Sports Glut USA, that would be asking the impossible.

CROSSING THE LINE

Some fans' hunger is not satisfied by watching games on television or indulging in other activities like listening to sports talk radio, playing in Fantasy Leagues, or collecting memorabilia or team merchandise. These

Sportsaholism Checklist

1. Do you get annoyed or angry when someone interrupts you while watching a game?
2. Do you get defensive when they question how much time you spend with sports?
3. Do you argue with them about how much time they spend doing something they like?
4. Do you prefer the drama and excitement of sports to intimacy with your partner?
5. Do you often say, "Just one more game," or "As soon as I see the scores update"?
6. Do you feel cravings for the next big game when it's hours or even days away?
7. Do you get more worked up over the game than the daily ups and downs of your life?
8. Does your team's fate affect your mood for days, weeks, or months afterward?
9. Do you experience withdrawal when your favorite season ends?
10. Do you avoid people who don't like sports, or get bored by conversations that don't include sports?
11. Do you sacrifice sleep to see the late game or get the West Coast scores?
12. Do you wake up needing to check the latest scores before doing anything else?
13. Do you know sports statistics better than your budget, family birthdays and anniversaries?
14. Do you neglect household chores or your children to watch more sports?
15. Do you block out disturbing questions of your life with soothing thoughts of sports?
16. Do you daydream about sports when you're unhappy at work, rather than map out a new career?
17. Do you find trying to cut down on sports for someone you love doesn't work?
18. Do you sneak in sports time your spouse doesn't know about, or lie about how many hours you *really* devote to sports, even in the exercises in this book?
19. Do you say you could spend less time with sports but deep down not believe it?
20. Do you fear that life with less sports would be boring, empty and joyless?

Source: Kevin Quirk, *Not Now, Honey, I'm Watching the Game* (Simon & Schuster, 1997).

fans, whether they act alone or in a group, twist their fixation with sports into something far darker that enters the realm of criminality.

Like other celebrities in the public spotlight, sports stars have been stalked by unstable fans. In 1949, a nineteen-year-old woman named Ruth Ann Steinhagen developed an infatuation with Philadelphia Phillies first baseman Eddie Waitkus. She invited him to her hotel room in Chicago when the Phillies were in town to play the Cubs. Once he was inside, she pointed a shotgun at his chest and pulled the trigger. Steinhagen then turned the gun on herself but could not summon the courage to take her own life. Waitkus was critically wounded, but he survived the attack and resumed his playing career. Steinhagen was committed to a mental hospital for three years. Her motive for the attack apparently was unrequited love. When she realized that a relationship with Waitkus was impossible, she tried to end both of their lives. Tainted love also was the motive of a forty-seven-year-old California man who relentlessly pursued Olympic figure skater Katarina Witt in 1992. He sent her nude photographs of himself and sexually explicit letters in an effort to kindle a romance. After being apprehended, he spent thirty-seven months in a mental hospital (Nuwer 1993: 135–136).

Some fans stalk athletes for reasons other than love. An Ohio man who described himself as a devout Christian was arrested in 1997 at the Chicago White Sox spring training camp in Sarasota, Florida. He was there to harass outspoken outfielder Albert Belle, just acquired by the White Sox in a trade with the Cleveland Indians. The man told police he was disgusted by Belle's belligerence and that Belle needed "to atone for his treatment of Cleveland fans" (Antonen 1997: 8C). Another deranged man bolted onto the court at a tournament in Hamburg, Germany, in 1993 and stabbed tennis star Monica Seles in the back with a nine-inch knife. He wanted to injure Seles so that Steffi Graf, a fellow German, could regain the number one ranking in women's tennis. Maryland attorney Robin Feckler, nicknamed the Superheckler, has been a fixture at Washington Wizards' basketball games for many years. He is there to harass the team's opponents from his seat behind the visitors' bench.

There are also fans who simply use sports events as a springboard for vandalism. Writer Joe Queenan believes that "ugly antisocial behavior" is the norm for many New York Jets supporters, whom he calls "the worst fans in America." Jet fans routinely fight with each other, hurl batteries onto the playing field, and fling mounds of garbage into the concrete walkways that surround Giants Stadium, where the Jets play their home games. The most notorious incident occurred at a Monday night NFL game in 1988, when several fans ignited fires in the stands. The resulting mayhem led to fifteen arrests, five hospitalizations, fifty-six ejections from the stadium, and forty fistfights (Queenan 1996: 384–

Fanatical sports fans come in all shapes, sizes, and colors. This Philadelphia Eagles fan dressed as Santa Claus was escorted from the stands at Veterans Stadium in 1997 during the team's crackdown on unruly fan behavior. "We feel very safe," one visiting fan told *USA Today*. "We heard they were bringing in the judges. You've got to do something when things get out of hand." An increasing number of sports teams in the United States share that sentiment. Although fan mayhem has not reached the levels that are common in Great Britain and other parts of the world, over twenty teams have installed video surveillance systems to catch and photograph troublemakers in the act and assist law enforcement officials in prosecuting them. (AP/WIDE WORLD PHOTOS)

89). At the same stadium in 1996, New York Giants fans attacked the visiting San Diego Chargers with a barrage of snowballs and iceballs. Charger equipment manager Sid Brooks was hit in the face and knocked unconscious. Among the fifteen people arrested was a retired police chief. "I'm concerned about the lack of personal responsibility people seem to feel when they come to a sports event," said Robert Mulcahy, head of the New Jersey Sports and Exposition Authority, which operates Giants Stadium. "There seems to be an increased sense that when you buy a ticket you have the right to behave any way you want" (Pedulla 1995: 3C). In 1997, when fighting and alcohol-induced rowdiness reached an unacceptable level at Philadelphia Eagles games, authorities set up a makeshift courtroom in a maintenance room in Veterans Stadium to dispense justice. On the first Sunday of the campaign, Judge Seamus P. McCaffrey fined seventeen fans and expelled them from the stadium. At least twenty teams have installed state-of-the-art cameras in their facilities to zero in on fans who start fights or throw projectiles from the stands. The systems cost about $100,000, an expense that more and more teams are willing to incur in their efforts to curb unacceptable behavior at their games.

The frequency and intensity of fan mayhem in the United States falls far short of what occurs in Great Britain. British soccer fans have a long history of bloodshed and destruction. Sixty-six people died in Scotland in 1971 when fans stampeded during a match at the home stadium of the Glasgow Rangers. On May 29, 1985, in Brussels, Belgium, violence erupted just before the English superpower Liverpool was scheduled to meet Juventus, an Italian team, in the finals of the European Cup tournament. After whipping themselves into a drunken frenzy before the match, the Liverpool supporters attacked the Juventus fans with knives, bottles, chains, and fence posts. Thirty-eight people died, and more than 250 were injured. After the tragedy, English soccer teams were barred from competing on the European continent for six years (Coe, Teasdale, and Wickham 1992: 200–202). In 1989, ninety-four died and 170 were injured at Hillsborough Stadium in Sheffield, England, when thousands of fans without tickets smashed through barricades to see a match between Liverpool and Nottingham Forest.

American writer Bill Buford wrote with accuracy about British soccer violence in his book *Among the Thugs*. At first Buford was repelled by the antics of the "football supporters," but eventually he found himself drawn into their orbit and became a willing participant in their mayhem. In one incident he marched with them to a train station to meet a group of fans of another club who were arriving for a match:

Another minute passed. Nothing happened. The street was filled with Saturday shoppers—families, older women all carrying Sainsbury's shopping bags—but no one knew the nature of the thing forming around them. . . .

I found myself in the middle of the group, which was not where I wanted to be, and I tried to work my way to the front, but it was too late. The crowd was starting to move; it had started off in the direction of the station. It proceeded in a measured way, nothing frantic, at the pace of a steady walk. I could see the confidence felt then by everyone, believing now that they were actually going to pull this thing off. The pace accelerated—gradually. It increased a little more. Someone started to chant, "Kill, kill, kill." The chant was whispered at first, as though it was being said reluctantly. Then it was picked up by the others. The pace quickened to a jog, and then a faster jog, and then a run.

An old woman was knocked over, and two shopping bags of food spilled on to the pavement. There were still no police.

Halfway up the ramp, the group was at a full sprint: a thousand people, running hard, chanting loudly: KILL, KILL, KILL. I was trying to calculate what was in store. The train from London would have arrived by now if it was on time, although it was possible that it was late and that we would burst through the station doors and find no one inside. But *if* it was on time, the West Ham supporters would be clearing the ticket barrier and heading for the main ticket area—that shiny floor where I kept seeing a thick, coagulating puddle of blood. (Buford 1991: 122–23)

Experts in the fields of criminology, psychology, and sociology have labored hard and long to determine the motives of the soccer hooligans. The critical elements the experts have identified are youth, maleness, working-class backgrounds, and a desire to protect territory or turf against encroachers. In the end, the words of one hooligan himself seem as apt an explanation as any: "Football is one tribe against another. We fight 'cos we like fighting" (Coe, Teasdale, and Wickham 1992: 191–95).

The motives of the more passive breed of sports fanatics also have proved elusive. The key attractions are the unending drama of sports and the opportunity they offer to escape, at least temporarily, the burdens and mundanity of daily existence. For every wife who continues to shout, "Get a life!" to her spouse planted on the couch in front of the television set, there will be a husband who continues to reply, "This is my life, and I like it very much!"

TOPICS FOR DISCUSSION

1. Do you have any friends or relatives who fit the description of a sportsaholic? Does their devotion to sports have negative effects on

the people in their lives? Have any of the sportsaholics you know ever attempted to change their behavior? What was the result?

2. The sports talk shows that are so popular on radio have been criticized for dwelling on the mean, negative, and cynical aspects of sports. Have you ever listened to a sports talk show on the radio? Do you agree with that description?

3. Have you ever experienced violence or mayhem while attending a sports event? Did the experience change your mind about attending sports events in the future? Who bears the responsibility for ensuring that fans in stadiums will be safe from the violent behavior of out-of-control fans?

REFERENCES AND RESOURCES

Books

Buford, Bill. *Among the Thugs.* New York: Norton, 1991.
    A compelling account of life among England's soccer hooligans, written by an American who has served as a fiction editor of the *New Yorker* magazine.

Chad, Norman. *Hold On Honey, I'll Take You to the Hospital at Halftime.* Boston: Atlantic Monthly Press, 1993.
    A collection of humorous short pieces about the lives of the sports obsessed.

Coe, Sebastian, David Teasdale, and David Wickham. *More Than a Game: Sports in Our Time.* London: BBC Books, 1992.
    Chapter 11 examines fan violence.

Guttmann, Allen. *Sports Spectators.* New York: Columbia University Press, 1986.
    A professor of American studies at Amherst College explores the history of sports fandom and details its economic, sociological, and psychological aspects.

Harris, Janet C. *Athletes and the American Hero Dilemma.* Champaign, Ill.: Human Kinetics Publishers, 1994.
    An academic discussion of hero worship and star athletes.

Nuwer, Hank. *Sports Scandals.* New York: Franklin Watts, 1993.
    Chapter 8 is entitled "Out-of-Control Fans."

Quirk, Kevin. *Not Now, Honey, I'm Watching the Game.* New York: Simon & Schuster, 1997.
    Using the results of a nationwide survey, Quirk discusses the sportsaholic mind-set and lifestyle and offers strategies for fans seeking to reduce the role of sports in their lives.

Roberts, Michael. *Fans! How We Go Crazy over Sports.* Washington, D.C.: New Republic Books, 1976.
    A sports columnist offers an irreverent look at the pervasive effect sports have on our lives.

Weiss, Ann E. *Money Games: The Business of Sports*. Boston: Houghton Mifflin, 1993.

    Chapter 8 discusses sports fans.

Wolfe, Rich, and Dale Ratermann. *Sports Fans Who Made Headlines*. Indianapolis: Masters Press, 1997.

    A compilation of anecdotes about fans who have gained fame, respect, and notoriety.

Magazines and Newspapers

Antonen, Mel. "Ohio Man Vows Not to Bother Belle." *USA Today*, February 28, 1997: 8C.

    A report on the man arrested for harassing baseball outfielder Albert Belle.

Associated Press. "Sacked for Pack Jersey, Dallas Worker Wants Job Back." *Columbus Dispatch*, January 16, 1996: 5F.

    A news account of a grocery store worker who backed the "wrong" team in the Super Bowl and was fired.

Fiely, Dennis. "An Obsession with Sports Means Relationships Can Come Up Short." *Columbus Dispatch*, November 2, 1997.

    Fiely interviews a rabid sports fan and his wife.

Kessler, Leslie Brown. "When a Fan Is Just a Fan." *Newsweek*, October 7, 1996: 16.

    The author comments on her husband's growing interest in women's sports.

Lopez, Steve. "Put Up or Shut Up." *Sports Illustrated*, March 17, 1997: 84.

    A commentary on the libel lawsuit filed against radio sports talk host Craig Carton and WIP-AM radio in Philadelphia.

Magenheim, Henry. "Sports Tours Courts Devoted Fans." *Travel Weekly*, March 3, 1997: 16.

    A note on the Massachusetts travel agency that sponsors sports-related excursions.

Meyers, Bill. "Football's Female Fans: NFL Sees Women as Key to Its Future." *USA Today*, August 28, 1997: 1A.

    Discusses the popularity of NFL football among women.

Murphy, Austin. "Calls of the Wild." *Sports Illustrated*, September 16, 1996: 72–81.

    Profiles the coarse, uninhibited world of sports talk radio.

Passikoff, Robert. "Pro Sports Needs to Manage Fan Loyalty." *Brandweek*, July 7, 1997: 9.

    A look at pro sports from the perspective of an expert marketer.

Pedulla, Tom. " 'Mob Mentality' Snowballs." *USA Today*, December 28, 1995: 3C.

    A discussion of the changing behavior of fans at sports events.

Queenan, Joe. "The Worst Fans in America." *Gentleman's Quarterly*, November 1996: 384–89.

    Probes the reasons behind the boorish behavior of New York Jets football fans.

Seideman, David. "Caught in the Act of Forgery." *Sports Illustrated*, October 20, 1997: 7.

The results of an investigation into forged sports memorabilia in Chicago.

Sports Illustrated. "Gator Bait." May 19, 1997: 29–30.

A note on the release of a study by University of Florida researcher Charles Hillman.

Tucker, Jamie. "We're Mad as Hell, and . . . You Know the Rest." *Inside Sports,* October 1997: 14–15.

A short profile of United Sports Fans of America, an organization formed to represent the interests of fans as consumers.

Organizations to Contact

Sportsaholism Recovery Circle
P.O. Box 4782
Charlottesville, VA 22905
Author Kevin Quirk invites correspondence from sportsaholics who are attempting to change their lifestyles.

Sports Fans United (SFU)
352 Seventh Avenue
New York, NY 10001
Phone: 212–736–3267
SFU is a consumer organization that represents the interests of sports fans. It is opposed to pay-per-view televised sporting events.

13

Violence in the Ring

In the twentieth century, over 500 men have died from injuries sustained in the savage sport of boxing, and it has been attacked since its inception as an activity that honors violence and glorifies brutality. Why does boxing continue to flourish in a society that considers itself civilized?

The noisy crowd of 16,331 at the MGM Grand Garden Arena in Las Vegas waited restlessly for the main event to unfold on the night of June 28, 1997. Moving among them was an impressive collection of sports and Hollywood celebrities, including Madonna, John F. Kennedy, Jr., Sylvester Stallone, Kevin Costner, Dennis Rodman, Jenny McCarthy, Whitney Houston, Shaquille O'Neal, and Demi Moore. Like millions of other boxing fans who had assembled in record numbers around the world to watch the action on pay-per-view television, the glitterati and the rest of the crowd expected to see an entertaining, evenly matched heavyweight title bout between challenger Mike Tyson and champion Evander Holyfield, a rematch of their clash a year earlier in which Holyfield had knocked out the former titleholder.

What they witnessed instead was one of the saddest and ugliest episodes in the history of boxing, a sport where the sad and ugly are as common as dry heat in the desert. When it was all over, and the pandemonium in the ring had subsided and the MGM Grand lay empty and the world's anger and revulsion had rained down on him with the intensity of a force five hurricane, Mike Tyson offered a simple explanation for ripping out a piece of Evander Holyfield's ear with his teeth. "I just snapped," he said.

Tyson's reasoning seemed as instructive as anyone else's. How else to explain the savage outburst early in the fight's third round, when, with the two boxers standing head to head in a clinch, he bit into the right ear of the champion? How else to explain Tyson's second eruption with thirty-seven seconds left in the same round, when he spit out his mouthpiece and ripped into Holyfield's other ear, taking a piece out and earning a disqualification from referee Mills Lane? The decision sparked a firestorm of chaos. It spread from the ring, where Tyson threw a punch at a policeman who was trying to restrain him, into the grandstands and then to the lobby of the MGM Grand, where forty people were injured and the hotel's casino was forced to close for three hours on what would have been one of its busiest nights ever. The unforgettable evening ended well after midnight, with Tyson bouncing off the window of a Range Rover in a fit of rage, threatening to kill a fan who stood on the street hurling insults at him as his driver burned rubber and peeled away down the Las Vegas Strip (Hoffer 1997: 36–37).

The person who appeared least disturbed by the mayhem was the man missing a piece of his ear. A ring attendant named Mitch Libonati peeled the severed piece of flesh off the canvas and rushed it to Holyfield's dressing room wrapped in a latex glove, but somehow it was misplaced during the ambulance ride to Valley Hospital Medical Center and never recovered. As news of the incident spread and the most outraged members of the media seemed intent on dragging Tyson directly to the gallows, the champion sat calmly as medical personnel attended his wounds. Holyfield himself had once bitten an opponent in the ring as a seventeen-year-old amateur in the Golden Gloves Tournament, an incident that probably helped account for his eerie calm. "I still love Mike," Holyfield cooed. "It's just those demons that possess him and make him do things. He needs to find a new savior" (Hoffer 1997: 36).

Tyson said he bit Holyfield because of his opponent's head butts earlier in the fight, which the referee ruled were unintentional. "I got cheated in the ring," Tyson complained. "This is my career. What am I supposed to do? I gotta retaliate." Others said Tyson bit Holyfield because, bleeding profusely over his right eye and facing an undaunted opponent, he didn't have a chance to win the fight and wanted to end it quickly. And there were still others who said Tyson simply was reverting to his basest instincts, instincts acquired as a violent child on the streets of the ghetto and honed during his meteoric rise to the top of the boxing world.

At one time he had been the most intimidating fighter in the sport. Tyson's power was so frightening that several of his weaker opponents simply surrendered in the ring to avoid the pain of his fists. It had been an incredible journey for the meek, timid kid who was once teased in the Brooklyn ghetto of Bedford-Stuyvesant in New York City as a "little fairy boy" because of his cherubic face and high-pitched voice. The teasing came to an abrupt end one day when Tyson administered a savage beating to an older thug who had torn the head off one of Tyson's pet pigeons. He then embarked on a career in petty crime: he was arrested thirty-eight times before the age of thirteen. His specialty was mugging elderly women. He would volunteer to carry their grocery bags up the steps of their apartment buildings and then beat and rob them in the elevators. In 1978, he was sent to a reform school in Tryon, New York, where he learned to box. After his release, he went to the Catskill Mountains and the training camp of boxing legend Gus D'Amato, who became his mentor, coach, and surrogate father. Tyson fought his first fight outside captivity at age fourteen, carrying a birth certificate with him to verify his age as he competed in "smokers"—unsanctioned events held in sweaty, smoke-stenched warehouses and garages in and around New York City.

Tyson turned professional in 1985, won his first nineteen fights by knockout, and captured the World Boxing Council (WBC) heavyweight crown by beating Trevor Berbick in 1986. The unraveling of his unstable personality lurched into overdrive shortly thereafter. An assault on a parking lot attendant. An ugly street brawl in Harlem with one of his ring rivals. A short and violent marriage to model-actress Robin Givens. A collision between a tree and his sports car that was a purported suicide attempt. A glass-shattering rampage on the roof of his New Jersey mansion. The stunning loss of his heavyweight crown to fifty-to-one underdog James Buster Douglas. And finally a three-year prison term for raping Desirée Washington, a Black Miss America contestant, in an Indianapolis hotel room.

As he waited for the members of the Nevada State Athletic Commission to punish him for his acts against Evander Holyfield, Tyson looked like a forlorn imitation of his former self, a once-overpowering champion laid low by bad companions, bad decisions, and the erosion of his boxing skills. After the commission revoked his boxing license for one year and fined him $3 million, he seemed almost relieved to be out of the ring and away from the hostile glare of the media, the public, and the boxing establishment. It seemed an appropriate time to refocus his energy on raising his pigeons, the lifelong passion that reveals a gentler and largely unknown side of his personality.

The rise and fall of Mike Tyson is a tale that lays bare our fascination with the violent ritual of boxing. All of the elements that repel and attract are there: the climb of the fighter from abject poverty to wealth and fame, the stoic champion who behaves with dignity, the specter of a black superman who threatens mainstream white society, the shameless parasites and promoters who seize on the game as a way to reap riches for themselves, the celebrity revelers and the dangerous crowd, and above all, the sight of two contestants entering the ring wearing nothing but shorts and shoes, each intent on pummeling the other into unconsciousness with makeshift clubs wrapped around his hands.

Jeffrey T. Sammons, who has written the most illuminating history of the sport, calls boxing "one of the supreme anomalies of our time." It seems out of place in a modern, forward-looking society that prides itself on advanced thinking and an ability to cast away the ignoble traditions of the past (Sammons 1988: 235–236). Yet it has entranced many notable authors and intellectuals. Joyce Carol Oates, Norman Mailer, Jack London, and Irwin Shaw all have written about it with the same feelings of attraction and repulsion that can be found in the general public. The very names by which the boxers are known express a fascination with domination and brute force. Jack Dempsey was called the Manassa Mauler, Joe Louis the Brown Bomber, Jake LaMotta the Bronx Bull, Rocky Marciano the Brockton Blockbuster. Later came Thomas Hitman Hearns, James Bonecrusher Smith, Ray Boom Boom Mancini, and Hector Macho Man Camacho.

The game also has been the subject of many classic Hollywood films, including *The Great White Hope, Raging Bull, Fat City,* and *Rocky,* the fictional rags-to-riches saga of the Italian Stallion that parallels the lives of so many real men. In the 1956 film *The Harder They Fall,* Humphrey Bogart portrays a sportswriter who descends to the venal underbelly of the game and comes away horrified. "Boxing," he writes at the end of the film, "should be outlawed, if it takes an act of Congress to do it."

That sentiment has been shared by many others for centuries. Boxing has been called loathsome, indecent, stupid, corrupt, nauseating, repulsive, and monstrous. It celebrates naked aggression. It has been linked to organized crime. It honors violence and has left an uncountable number of men and women dead and permanently maimed. Yet it survives. Why? Harvey Araton of the *New York Times* says that boxing exists because we won't let it die. What are the forces that compel us to keep it alive?

THE VIOLENT SPECTACLE

Crowds have assembled for thousands of years to take in the spectacle of two human beings inflicting pain on each other in an enclosed ring. The stalwart hero Theagenes reigned as the undefeated fighting champion of ancient Greece from 484 to 468 B.C. According to legend, he won 1,400 bouts and killed 800 opponents with his fists. In ancient Rome, gladiator fights attracted all classes of Roman society until they were banned by the emperor Honorius in 399 A.D. Three centuries later, the emperor Thedoric banned the sport of boxing (Berger 1990: 58). It resurfaces again in the history of Western civilization in the eighteenth century, when it became hugely popular in England.

The English advanced the sport by implementing a series of rules changes that distinguished it from simple thuggery. In 1743, Broughton's Rule barred punching in the groin, and in 1838, the London Prize Ring Rules prohibited holding, gouging, kicking, and improper spikes on shoes. Twenty-eight years later, the Marquis of Queensberry Rules called for the use of weight classes, the ten-second count to protect fighters who had been knocked down, and gloves for all contestants. The point of the gloves was not to protect the head and body of the boxer receiving blows. Instead, it was to protect the hands of the boxer administering them. The small bones of the hands had a tendency to break frequently when they came into contact with the larger bones of the face and head. With gloves on their hands, the contestants could hit each other much harder and for a much longer period of time.

In the United States, the sport's popularity surged in the last years of the nineteenth century, the short-lived era of marathon fights. As in all of the eras of boxing that followed, it was the bruising heavyweight fighters who attracted nearly all of the attention. The Boston Strongboy, John L. Sullivan, was the reigning superstar of the day; he fought title bouts of 75 and 21 rounds. In 1892, Andy Bowen and Jack Burke fought 110 rounds over a span of seven hours and nineteen minutes in New Orleans (Berger 1990: 62).

When Jack Johnson battered Tommy Burns in a 1908 bout in Australia to become the first black heavyweight champion, boxing assumed its role as a key element in the nation's ongoing racial drama. Johnson's prowess was seen as a threat to the dominant white culture. The thought of Johnson's besting a white man in the ring aroused great anxiety in civic leaders, boxing authorities, and white supremacists. To make matters worse, Johnson loved to flash a wicked grin and taunt his opponents, especially white ones, and he enjoyed celebrating his many victories in the arms of white women. When he went to Carson City, Nevada, in 1910 and knocked out Jim Jeffries—the Great White Hope who had been persuaded to come out of retirement to challenge him—Johnson ignited a wave of violence. Nineteen people died in nine states; there also were 250 injuries and 5,000 arrests (Berger 1990: 64). The authorities were so fearful of another outbreak of violence that Congress passed a law making it a federal crime to transport prizefight films across state borders for the purpose of showing them to the public (Sammons 1988: 42).

The champion alienated millions of Americans when he married a young white woman just three months after his first wife committed suicide. He was sentenced to a year in prison for violating the Mann Act, which barred the transportation of women across state borders for "immoral purposes." Johnson fled the United States, and in 1915, he lost his title to white challenger Jess Willard in Cuba. Ironically, the same law that was passed to stop fans from viewing Johnson's win over Jeffries also prevented them from seeing Willard's victory—the triumph that "redeemed" the white race.

Despite its popularity, the sport never had the blessing of all factions of society. Antiboxing sentiment was strong, particularly in segments of the legal and religious communities. James Lawson, the only fighter known to have been imprisoned for conduct in the ring, was found guilty of manslaughter after killing his opponent in a bout in Australia in 1884 (Berger 1990: 61). When heavyweights Bob Simmons and Peter Maher were driven out of the United States and Mexico by antiboxing forces in 1896, they fought their title match before a small but enthusiastic crowd of 300 on a sandbar in the middle of the Rio Grande River, 400 miles southeast of El Paso (Oates 1987: 96). The sport was illegal in New York State until the early years of the twentieth century, and it was not a part of the 1912 Olympic Games in Sweden because it was—and still is—banned in the host country. The National Collegiate Athletic Association (NCAA) discontinued the sport in 1961, one year after University of Wisconsin boxer Charlie Mohr died from a brain aneurysm suffered in a bout. In 1983, the *Journal of the American Medical Association* rekindled the reform movement by calling for a ban on the sport. The American Medical Association has adopted an identical position, as has the American Academy of Pediatrics and the medical associations of Canada, England, and Australia. And in 1997, officials in the English borough of Bury in the city of Manchester banned boxing in their small domain, citing the Tyson-Holyfield fiasco as a prime example of the sport's "unacceptable levels of harm."

The critics always have offered three major reasons for their position. The most convincing is the sheer brutality of boxing. When Jack Dempsey captured the heavyweight crown from Jess Willard in 1919, the commentators of the time called it "pugilistic murder." Muhammad Ali described his third match with archrival Joe Frazier as "the closest thing to dying that I know of." Sammons notes that somehow "supporters and fighters have deluded themselves into thinking that boxing, when conducted properly, is safe" (Sammons 1988: 245). It is not. *Ring* magazine has documented over five hundred deaths since 1900; forty-five fighters died between 1982 and 1996. Beyond the risk of death, the principal danger is the high frequency of serious brain damage. *Pugilistic dementia*, better known as punch drunkenness, leaves its many victims battered from thousands of jarring collisions between the soft tissues of the brain and the hard skull that encases them. The condition often develops long after fighters leave the ring, and it is the talented who suffer more severely because they have longer careers and face a longer parade of harder-hitting opponents. A punch-drunk fighter can suffer from staggering, flopping legs, slurred speech, drooling, facial tics, and torn and detached retinas.

The second major objection is that boxing promotes antisocial and criminal behavior in those who watch it. That assertion is difficult for many people to accept, especially in our modern society where video games, television, films, and cyberspace are saturated with graphic images of violence that seemingly have little effect on behavior. It has been statistically validated only once, in a 1984 study by sociologists David Phillips and John E. Hensley. They presented data showing that highly publicized boxing matches have a direct and measurable effect on the homicide rate (Oates 1987: 93).

Antiboxing forces also detest the ruthless economic exploitation of the fighters. Unlike other major sports, boxing has no single, central, controlling commissioner or league that provides some measure of control. There are no players' unions, no long-term guaranteed contracts, no drafts, and no pension plans. The people who call the shots are those who at any given time control the sport's few truly marketable attractions. Most aspiring boxers emerge from the disenfranchised segments of society that have been systematically denied economic opportunities elsewhere. In earlier times, the typical hopefuls were Jewish, Italian, or Irish; today most are African American, Hispanic, or Mexican. They face little chance of any real success. A common scenario finds them leaving the game in their mid- to late twenties after a decade or so of living on the brink of financial collapse. When they leave, they carry with them all of the physical damage that the ring can inflict and none of the skills and education they need to survive outside boxing.

Even the most successful fighters can suffer financially. Legends Joe Louis and Sugar Ray Robinson each earned millions of dollars in their careers, but reckless spending, inept managers, thieving underlings, and unpaid taxes left them both bankrupt. Louis's plight was so extreme that the Internal Revenue Service seized a trust fund that he had established for his two children (Sammons 1988: 239–40). The agency did not end its relentless pursuit until Louis was nearly sixty years old. By that time, he was a greatly sympathetic figure. The Brown Bomber had learned well from the experiences of his predecessor Jack Johnson. Louis never had his picture taken with a white woman. He never went into a nightclub alone. He never mocked a fallen opponent. He never mugged for the cameras (Sammons 1988: 98). His model behavior was a major factor in his huge popularity with white fans. In the end, the world cringed and hid its eyes from the sight of Louis shuffling slowly through the lobby of the Las Vegas casino where he worked as a "greeter" to keep a roof over his head and food on his table.

The urgent need for cash has kept many fighters in the ring for an eternity beyond their prime: George Foreman fought at age forty-eight, Larry Holmes at forty-seven, Jack Johnson at fifty, and Earnie Shavers at fifty-one. The sport also has a history of embarrassing gimmick fights.

Light heavyweight Archie Moore once tangled with writer George Plimpton, and heavyweight Tony Galeno matched up with a kangaroo at Hamid's Million Dollar Pier in Atlantic City. He also fought a bear and an octopus. In 1976, Muhammad Ali fought Japan's heavyweight wrestling champion at Budokan Arena in Tokyo. In the same year, heavyweight Chuck Wepner battled Andre the Giant, a seven-foot, five-inch 430-pound pro wrestler.

In recent years, boxing has brought women into the ring in an effort to boost fan interest. The female role in the sport traditionally has been small because the desire to throw punches at another human being is generally considered a male characteristic. The sight of two women hitting each other in a ring can create discomfort, shock, and even anger. Sammons reports there is a record of at least one match between women as early as the 1880s, but he labels it a freak occurrence, "that period's answer to contemporary, voyeuristic mud wrestling" (Sammons 1988: 54). In the late nineteenth and early twentieth centuries, women were not even allowed to attend boxing matches, let alone participate in them, although some adventurous females gained entrance by disguising themselves as men. The culture of the ring, with its heavy emphasis on violence, gambling, and the consumption of alcohol, was viewed as harmful and unhealthy for females. The nation's antiboxing laws were designed primarily to protect women, as well as children, from contact with the sordid spectacle.

By the 1990s, women were competing in the ring as well as watching from outside it on a regular basis. J'Marie Moore, the daughter of former light heavyweight champion Archie Moore, debuted in 1997 on the night before the Tyson-Holyfield fight. In the first female match shown on network television, Yvonne Trevino scored a first round technical knockout over Brenda Ross. When USA Boxing sponsored its first camp for girls ages eight through eighteen in 1994, five hundred showed up. The organization held its first national championship for girls in 1997.

The reigning queen of the ring today is Christy Martin, the lightweight champion of the World Boxing Council (WBC). A coal miner's daughter from Mullens, West Virginia, and a basketball player at Concord College, Martin entered a fighting contest in 1987 at the urging of friends. Her victory there launched a ten-year apprenticeship that differed not a whit from the male version: exhausting physical training, rank working conditions, dismal wages, ongoing physical risk, and chronic financial insecurity. Today her attitude toward the game is all business, which she says spurs resentment in her less experienced female colleagues. All she wants to do is box. She is not in the sport to make any statements about gender equity or to pose as either a sex symbol or a feminist pioneer. "I try not to ask for special treatment or make waves," she says. "I don't want to change anything. I just want to be the best I can be" (Smith 1997:

Anissa Zamarron, right, plants a left jab on the chin of Jill Matthews in a 1998 flyweight bout in Atlantic City, New Jersey. They fought a ten-round draw as part of the first all-women's fight card ever. Females have not always been welcome in the boxing ring, or even in the boxing arena. In 1897, the wife of heavyweight fighter Robert Fitzsimmons made history by becoming the first woman to stand in a boxer's corner during a bout. Just a year earlier, she had been forced to view her husband's fight through a peephole as she stood in a storage room next to the arena. (AP/WIDE WORLD PHOTOS)

C21). Now married to boxing promoter Jim Martin, she wants to fight as long as she can and then retire and have children.

PRIDE, HOPE, AND FREEDOM

The supporters of the sport have an answer for every objection put forth by the antiboxing forces. Yes, boxing is violent, but there are many other sports in which death and serious injury are regular occurrences, including football, auto racing, and horse racing. Boxing supporters pointedly note that no one in the medical community has called for a ban on any of them. And when the antiboxing forces say that the point of the endeavor is for a fighter to render his or her opponent unconscious, they are exaggerating to make the sport seem more violent than it really is. Boxing matches are tests of athletic skill, and many are won without knockouts. A talented fighter can earn points for footwork, feigning, and defensive maneuvers as well as hard punching. Boxers often say that they feel safer in the ring than they do on the street (Oates 1987: 94).

The premise that boxing promotes violent behavior in fans is countered by the claim that it actually reduces violence by providing a vicarious outlet or safety valve for the legions of young males who have always made up the major portion of its audience. Supporters focus not on the acts of violence that may be linked to boxing but on the untold number of acts that may be prevented by it.

Supporters freely admit that many boxers are economically exploited but insist that, like other athletes, they know the risks of the enterprise when they decide to become involved. In a free society, it smacks of paternalism to bar an individual from pursuing his or her chosen pastime, regardless of how unprofitable it may be. And of course there are boxers who beat the long odds and become brilliant successes; it is they who offer the strongest argument in favor of the sport. One hugely popular figure like Muhammad Ali can obscure the poverty, injury, and despair that are the lot of thousands of lesser talents. When boxers flourish in the ring, especially those from impoverished backgrounds, they become living embodiments of the American dream by demonstrating that success can be achieved by anyone who is willing to work for it. Boxers can become powerful symbols of hope and national pride, like Joe Louis when he defeated the German Max Schmeling during the rise of Nazism, and Sugar Ray Leonard and his Olympic teammates when they outclassed their rivals from communist nations at the Olympic Games in 1976.

The sport also has spawned a number of variations that arouse all of the same passions as boxing itself. Ultimate Fighting, which began in the 1980s as a pay-per-view television event, bills itself as a modern counterpart to a discipline called pankratian, a hybrid of boxing and wrestling that was featured in the first Olympic Games. Contestants fight each other in an enclosure called the Octagon at events with names like the Proving Ground, Clash of the Titans, No Way Out, and Revenge of the Warriors. The desired effect is minimally controlled mayhem; the model is an alley fight or a barroom brawl. There are a few rules: no eye gouging, no throat grasps, no biting, no long toenails or fingernails, no headgear with dangerous straps. Beyond these prohibitions, anything goes, including head butting, scratching, elbowing, kneeing, and hair pulling. Ultimate Fighting has been banned in a number of jurisdictions, including New York State, where state senator Roy Goodman calls it "human cockfighting" (Marks 1997: 48). The American Medical Association also has a position against what it calls "blood-soaked spectacles." The association condemns extreme fighting, which has more rules in the ring to distinguish it from Ultimate Fighting, and toughman bouts, a largely unsupervised activity that pits untrained and unskilled contestants against each other (Lundberg 1996: 1684–1685).

The future of Ultimate Fighting is uncertain. Several pay-per-view television systems, including Time Warner Cable, Intermedia, and Cablevision, have stopped showing the events, which has drastically reduced their potential audience. Those actions have frustrated fans and practitioners, who claim that Ultimate Fighting features legitimate athletes such as Olympic wrestlers and judo experts, former heavyweight boxers, and martial arts champions from Asia, Europe, and South America. They also say the sport's medical safety precautions equal or exceed the most stringent boxing regulations. One form of boxing that seems destined to survive is Muay Thai, or Thai boxing, which has been practiced in Thailand for centuries by young men ranging in age from nine to nearly thirty. The mecca of the sport is Lumpini Stadium in Bangkok, a 10,000-seat contraption of tin, wood, and concrete named after the birthplace of Buddha. Screaming fans massed on bleachers watch the fighters kick, punch, elbow, and knee each other to win purses as small as five dollars. Their goal is the same as that of most American boxers: to escape a life of grinding poverty as an agricultural or factory worker in a country where the average family income is $3,000 (Horn 1997: 61–73). Unlike the United States and Europe, there are few in Thailand who object to the violence. The country's other social problems are so widespread and severe that the abuses of Muay Thai seem almost trivial in comparison.

What does the future hold for the sport of boxing? Its survival in some form seems assured. The public's interest in watching what medical doctors call "intentional blunt force trauma" is too strong and entrenched for boxing to disappear completely from the sports world. Some opponents have called for rules changes that do not constitute a complete ban, such as outlawing blows to the head, banning gloves to reduce the

Ultimate Fighters Tito Ortiz, on top, and Wes Albritton tangle in a 1997 bout in Augusta, Georgia. Their raw, bloody sport has been banned in a number of cities and states, and its critics are trying to ban Ultimate Fighting from the nation's television screens as well. Governor James Edgar of Illinois has called Ultimate Fighting "no-holds-barred street fighting," and Assembly Speaker Sheldon Silver of New York describes it as "barbarism in the guise of sport." The sport's promoters say it is as safe as boxing and wrestling and that it provides a crucial safety valve by allowing a fighter to end a match with honor by "tapping out," or slapping the mat with his hand to signal submission. Most bouts in Ultimate Fighting end in this manner. (AP/WIDE WORLD PHOTOS)

force and number of punches, and requiring headgear. Those reforms seem unlikely to be enacted. Instead, the world will continue to watch men, women, and children in the ring with the same mixture of disgust and amused entrancement that was so evident in the aftermath of the Tyson-Holyfield fight. On one hand, there was a torrent of anger and high-handed sanctimony about the vile nature of Tyson's deeds. At the same time, there was an outpouring of low humor, expressed best by the headline writers of the nation's newspapers and magazines, who were blessed with one of their greatest field days ever: "Ear Today, Gone Tomorrow"; "Bite of the Century"; "Earmarked"; "Feeding Frenzy"; "Undisputed Chomp"; "Champ, Chomp, Chump."

What about the future of Tyson himself? His one-year ban from the sport has been ridiculed as nothing more than a slap on the wrist. One wag said he would be back in Las Vegas before Liza Minnelli. For the time being, he is making appearances as an "enforcer" at professional wrestling matches, which very likely will end once his suspension has been served. Indeed, Tyson remains one of the few marquee names in a game that, like all others, needs star performers to stay financially healthy. In the long run, the biting episode actually may prove to be a boon to the sport. "Tyson and the despicable thing he did made boxing hot," says fight promoter Bob Arum. "I'm not saying this is right and this is good. It's a commentary on the people more than anything else" (Weir 1997: 3C).

Yes, the people have spoken, and their verdict is the same as it always has been. We despise this horrible, ugly, thing called boxing. Please give us more.

TOPICS FOR DISCUSSION

1. Mike Tyson earned a year's suspension from boxing for his ear-biting escapade with Evander Holyfield in 1997. Tyson also was forced to forfeit $3 million, ten percent of the money he earned in the bout. Do you think Tyson's punishment was too light, too severe, or appropriate? Explain your answer.

2. Opponents of boxing say that the sport can increase violent, aggressive behavior in those who watch it. Supporters of the sport say it actually reduces that behavior by providing a way for fans to channel their violent, aggressive tendencies. Which view makes more sense to you? Why?

3. Several jurisdictions in the United States have banned Ultimate Fighting and extreme fighting. Should they take the next step and ban the sport of boxing itself? Why or why not?

4. Opponents of boxing have been labeled as racists because they are seeking to stop a sport that is practiced primarily by African American and Hispanic athletes. Do you think the opponents of the sport are racially motivated? Explain your answer.

5. Boxing promoter Bob Arum has said that the Tyson-Holyfield biting incident actually may increase the sport's popularity because it is a perfect example of the kind of violence that many fans enjoy watching. Do you agree with Arum's point of view? Why or why not?

REFERENCES AND RESOURCES

Books

Berger, Gilda. *Violence and Sports*. New York: Franklin Watts, 1990.
Discusses boxing and wrestling in Chapter 5.

Berger, Phil. *Blood Season: Tyson and the World of Boxing*. New York: Morrow, 1989.
The boxing reporter of the *New York Times* offers a close-up and personal account of the business of boxing and the rise of Mike Tyson.

Collins, Nigel. *Boxing Babylon: Behind the Shadowy World of the Prize Ring*. New York: Carol Publishing Group, 1990.
Dramatic accounts of the triumphs and tragedies of the sport's greatest stars.

Hoffer, Richard. *A Savage Business: The Comeback and Comedown of Mike Tyson*. New York: Simon & Schuster, 1998.
The boxing reporter for *Sports Illustrated* offers an unflinching look at the former heavyweight champion.

Oates, Joyce Carol. *On Boxing*. Garden City, N.Y.: Dolphin/Doubleday Books, 1987.
The prolific novelist and short story writer, a longtime boxing fan, examines the spectacle, lore, and allure of the sport.

Sammons, Jeffrey T. *Beyond the Ring: The Role of Boxing in American Society*. Urbana: University of Illinois Press, 1988.
A comprehensive treatment of boxing and its relationship through history with the law, organized crime, race, and the media.

Sugden, John. *Boxing and Society: An International Analysis*. New York and Manchester, England: Manchester University Press, 1996.
Sugden visits boxing clubs in Hartford, Connecticut; Belfast, Northern Ireland; and Cuba to study their practices and personnel.

Magazines and Newspapers

Araton, Harvey. "The Outcome That Pays Off in 12 Months." *New York Times*, July 10, 1997: C20.
Discusses the license suspension hearing of Mike Tyson before the Nevada State Athletic Commission.

Araton, Harvey. "Boxing's Latest Stench: Holyfield–Tyson III." *Columbus Dispatch*, January 16, 1998: 8E.

Comments on the game's mercenary present and future.

Bradley, John Ed. "Pryor Restraint." *Sports Illustrated*, February 13, 1995: 81–94.

The award-winning novelist draws a moving profile of boxer Aaron Pryor's battle against cocaine addiction.

Fields, Gary. "Tyson's Rage on Street Translates into Death." *USA Today*, July 9, 1997: 17A.

A pointed commentary on the wider social epidemic of violence that found expression in the Tyson–Holyfield fight.

Friend, Tom. "After Biting, Tyson Faces Trouble from All Corners." *New York Times*, June 30, 1997: A1, C14.

Assesses Tyson's boxing future.

Goodman, Ellen. "Tyson's Past Sins Worse Than His Bite." *Columbus Dispatch*, July 5, 1997: 8A.

The noted columnist criticizes the lack of concern about Tyson's rape conviction.

Hoffer, Richard. "Feeding Frenzy." *Sports Illustrated*, July 7, 1997: 32–38.

An eyewitness account of the Tyson–Holyfield bite fight and its violent aftermath.

Hoffer, Richard. "Gritty Woman." *Sports Illustrated*, April 15, 1996: 56–61.

A profile of female boxer Christy Martin.

Horn, Robert. "Marital Madness." *Sports Illustrated*, July 14, 1997: 61–73.

With photographer Walter Iooss, Jr., the author visits Thailand and creates a graphic portrait of Muay Thai boxing.

Kriegel, Mark. "Gentlemen, Start Your Bleeding." *Esquire*, March 1996: 94–108.

An in-depth profile of the lives of Ultimate Fighters.

Lundberg, George D. "Blunt Force in America—Shades of Red or Gray." *Journal of the American Medical Association*, June 5, 1996: 1684–1685.

Calls for a legal ban on all fighting sports.

Marks, John. "Whatever It Takes to Win." *U.S. News and World Report*, February 24, 1997: 46–49.

Features the world of Ultimate Fighting.

Smith, Timothy W. "Martin Is Deflecting the Jabs That Are Aimed at Her Fame." *New York Times*, August 21, 1997: C21.

Female boxer Christy Martin discusses her career as the nation's top female boxer.

Starr, Mark, and Allison Samuels. "Ear Today, Gone Tomorrow." *Newsweek*, July 14, 1997: 58–60.

Describes the Tyson–Holyfield fight in Las Vegas.

Weekly Reader. "Too Extreme." February 10, 1997: 3.

Fourth- and fifth-grade students express opinions about Ultimate Fighting.

Weir, Tom. "Bite Might Help Box Office." *USA Today*, July 22, 1997: 3C.

Assesses the commercial impact of the Tyson biting incident.

Organizations to Contact

American Medical Association (AMA)
515 North State Street
Chicago, IL 60610
Phone: 312–464–5000
Fax: 312–464–5830
Internet Web Site: www.ama-assn.org
The AMA is a partnership of physicians and their professional associations dedicated to promoting the art and science of medicine and the betterment of public health. The association has adopted a position in favor of banning intentional blunt trauma sports like boxing, Ultimate Fighting, and extreme fighting.

International Boxing Hall of Fame
1 Hall of Fame Drive
Canastota, NY 13032
Phone: 315–697–7095
Established in 1989 and opened in 1990, the Hall of Fame is a valuable source of documents and historical archives that illuminate the colorful history of the sport.

14

Fighting Colors, Fighting Words

The colors, team nicknames, and mascots of the sports world, particularly those drawn from Native American culture, have the power to invoke strong emotions and vocal objections from those who view them as racist and derogatory. Are their objections justified?

For Charlene Teters, the call to action came when she took her two children to see a basketball game at the University of Illinois in 1989. As a member of the Spokane Indian tribe who was raised on a reservation in eastern Washington State, she had always felt a strong need to pass the traditions of her people on to the younger generation. On the campus in Champaign-Urbana, where Teters was pursuing a master's degree in art, those same traditions had been a featured part of the school's proud sports program for over half a century. But what Charlene Teters saw that night in the basketball court did not fill her with a sense of pride. Instead, what she saw made her sick at heart.

The source of Teters's pain was Chief Illiniwek, the Illinois team mascot who has performed at thousands of the school's athletic events since 1926, when he was conceived as an impromptu halftime stunt by the assistant band director. As the fans' enchantment with the chief grew, his role expanded. In a costume that includes an elaborate feather headdress, leather skins, and facial paint, the chief now dances in front of the crowd to the thumping beat of drums. At football games, he walks to the fifty-yard line and slowly raises his arms in a sign of victory as the crowd in Memorial Stadium sings "Hail to the Orange," the school's fight song.

To the vast majority of Fighting Illini fans, the chief is a dignified, respected, and revered symbol of the state's history. He also represents what they see as the positive characteristics of Native Americans: bravery, steadfastness, and competitive spirit. To Teters, the chief's costume and performance were an embarrassment and a farce.

"My kids just sank in their seats," she recalled tearfully on the television documentary *In Whose Honor?* which was aired by the Public Broadcasting Service (PBS) in 1997. "I saw my daughter trying to become invisible." Where others saw inspirational celebration, Teters saw trivial entertainment and a mocking of her ancestors. The cruelest aspect of the chief's performance was his dance. For decades, the university claimed that it was authentic and based on a tradition of the Sioux tribe called fancy dancing. By 1992, that claim was no longer being made, and the chief's dance was described by one critic as "M. C. Hammer meets Richard Simmons meets Biff the town idiot" (Pearlman 1997: 19).

Teters's academic adviser in the art department suggested she keep her objections to herself and get on with the business of completing her master's degree. But there was an image embedded in her mind that she could not erase: her daughter trying to become invisible in her seat, surrounded by a throng of white people whooping and applauding the movements of another white man dressed up to look like an Indian. She decided to speak out against the use of Chief Illiniwek as the Illinois team mascot. The backlash against her was immediate and intense. As she stood alone outside Memorial Stadium distributing leaflets and hoisting a placard, she was ridiculed, spit on, sexually harassed, and shoved. Her telephone answering machine soon overflowed with hateful messages. To many Fighting Illini fans, it was nearly inconceivable that anyone could take offense at what they understood to be an honored symbol. They blamed the controversy on protest groups, liberals, college students with too much time on their hands, and "out-of-state foreigners."

When the media began reporting the story, the state's politicians took sides. U.S. Senator Alan Dixon, an alumnus of the university, defended the chief. His colleague, Senator Paul Simon, signed a petition in support of Teters's protest. That prompted the appearance of a small airplane at the next Illinois home football game against Michigan. As the crowd roared its approval, the plane circled the stadium pulling a banner that read "Keep the Chief, Dump Simon" (Davis 1989: 1, 23). Representative Rick Winkel won support for a bill he introduced in the state legislature to ensure that Chief Illiniwek remained as the school's mascot. "We have a rich heritage in this country, especially over the past few decades, of protecting minority rights," Winkel said. "But minority rights aren't always right" (Pearlman 1997: 19). Winkel's bill passed the legislature but was vetoed by Governor Jim Edgar.

The dispute reached a resolution of sorts when university chancellor Morton Weir issued a directive banning "inappropriate derivatives" of Indian symbols such as war paint on the faces of cheerleaders and band members and the painted letter "I" on Chief Illiniwek's face. Weir also said that the university would do whatever it could, within its limited legal authority, to eliminate negative images of Native Americans, such as the drunken Indian who appears on many of the school's sweatshirts. Chief Illiniwek, however, was not sent to the sidelines. He continues to dance at the university's sporting events. Dave Johnson of the University of Illinois athletic department speaks for many Illini fans when he maintains that the chief is not an issue on the campus anymore. The issue is not a real hot one, Johnson says.

The issue has proved to be a hot one in many other places. Charlene Teters, who lives today in Santa Fe, New Mexico, was a pioneer protester who almost singlehandedly created a controversy that has never faded entirely from the sports world. Her stance against nicknames and mascots that demean Native Americans had long been held by many organizations, including the National Indian Education Association and the National Congress of American Indians. But Teters's publicized demonstrations against Chief Illiniwek provided a new forum. They caused many high schools, colleges and universities, and professional sports teams to examine their nicknames and mascots and, in many cases, eliminate them. When Miami University in Ohio changed its nickname in 1997 from Redskins to RedHawks, university president James Garland said the change was an acknowledgment of the power of language. That power is immense. Words arouse intense passions in those who feel a strong allegiance or antagonism toward them. The same can be said for colors, whether they appear on uniforms, on mascots, or in the grandstands. When those colors and words mix with the volatile emotions of the playing fields, they can truly become fighting colors and fighting words.

OUR NAME, OUR TEAM, OUR COLORS

The core objection to the use of Native American nicknames and mascots is that they promote an oversimplified and largely violent image of a vastly diverse people. The magnitude of the oversimplification becomes apparent when one considers that Native American society in the United States consisted of five hundred distinct cultures in which more than three hundred languages were spoken (Johnson and Eck 1996: 76). The portrayal of Native Americans in the sports world, as well as in other facets of popular culture such as movies, television, advertising, and children's toys and games, rarely strays from two deeply engrained stereotypes. In one portrait, Indians are reserved, stoic, and almost dumbly loyal to their white masters. In the other, Indians are angry savages armed with bows and arrows, spears, and tomahawks, poised to attack peaceful white settlers in their encampments and wagon trains. It is this violent image, which is far more dominant, that has aroused the ire of Native American activists.

People who are not Native Americans often have trouble grasping the emotional objections that the nicknames arouse. Kenneth Shropshire, an African American sports attorney who has served as general counsel to major league baseball, tells us that not all of those who fail to grasp the objection to ethnic nicknames are Caucasian. "My high school team's nickname was the 'Dons,' a reference to the Spanish land barons of California. Our mascot was a stereotypical 'sleepy Mexican,' wearing a huge sombrero and poncho with head down and eyes shut," Shropshire writes in his book *In Black and White: Race and Sports in America*. "The high school was nearly 100 percent African-American and none of us ever complained about wearing the uniforms emblazoned with the mascot, or about the African-American elected by the student body to parade around as the mascot with the huge sombrero. It was all good fun, and it was only a mascot. Across town, in Compton, California, a nearly all African-American high school used the nickname 'Tarbabes.' The school was attempting to connect itself with the Compton College Tartars, and the 'Tarbabe' name must have been thought cute" (Shropshire 1996: 13).

The most derogatory term to Native Americans is "Redskins." The National Congress of American Indians calls it a racial slur. Indian activist Tim Giago writes that it derived from a time when America was a British colony and bearskins, deerskins, and beaverskins were among the many items sold and bartered at frontier trading posts. As the nation began its surge westward and the native population faced relocation and extermination, government officials compensated bounty hunters who killed Native Americans. In order to be certain that the hunters had actually completed their tasks, the officials required them to present Native American scalps— "redskins"—in order to receive payment (Giago 1993: A4).

Other popular team nicknames that spring from Native American culture, such as Braves, Indians, Warriors, Blackhawks, and Chiefs, are not as inflammatory as Redskins, but they draw objections as well. Indian activists have waged a number of successful campaigns to eliminate them. In 1997, the Los Angeles school board implemented a policy that forbids the use of Native American nicknames and mascots at the city's high schools. That change followed earlier ones made by Stanford University in California and Dartmouth College in New Hampshire, which both dropped the nickname Indians. At St. John's University in New York, the team formerly called the Redmen is now called the Red Storm.

Opponents also have succeeded in convincing two major newspapers to stop printing Native American team nicknames. In 1992, editor William A. Hilliard of the *Portland Oregonian* told readers that he decided to eliminate the names because they "tend to perpetuate stereotypes that damage the dignity and self-respect of many people in our society and that this harm far transcends any innocent entertainment or promotional value these names may have" (Hilliard 1992: D1). His decision sparked a rash of comments from readers. Some were supportive, others critical. "It's an overdue move," wrote one reader, "and one that should be followed immediately by all media." "You have overstepped your bounds," scolded another. "I urge you to reconsider this decision and opt for accurate reporting of the facts" (Loving 1992: 12).

Two years later, the *Minneapolis Star Tribune* made the same decision as the *Oregonian*. Executive editor Julie Engerbrecht said the move was nothing more than a reflection of the changes that had occurred in the Minneapolis–St. Paul metropolitan area, where the number of high schools with Native American nicknames had dwindled from seventy to fourteen. That reduction is largely the work of Phil St. John, a Sioux Indian who founded Concerned American Indian Parents after taking his two sons to a high school basketball game in Minneapolis in 1983. St. John was hurt and offended by the antics of one of the team mascots during the contest.

In spite of St. John's success in changing the climate in the Twin Cities, Engerbrecht's decision was not greeted warmly by all of the newspaper's readers. A significant number of them angrily cancelled their subscriptions. "I've learned that there are many people in this community—many more than I ever would have thought—who just do not think Native Americans deserve any respect at all," Engerbrecht said (Fitzgerald 1994: 9).

Professional sports teams owners have been more reluctant to make changes than newspaper editors. Only one team has acquired a new nickname in response to concerns raised by Native Americans. In 1993, the Sioux City Soos, a minor league team in the Midwest League, became the Sioux City Explorers. The Iowa team also abandoned its mascot Lonesome Polecat, who was described as a "cartoon Indian clad in a loincloth, flailing a hatchet, and grinning drunkenly" (Johnson and Eck 1996: 80). The teams in the major sports leagues—baseball's Cleveland Indians and Atlanta Braves, football's Washington Redskins and Kansas City Chiefs, and hockey's Chicago Blackhawks—have made no name changes, despite being the target of protests. At Super Bowl XXVI in 1992 in Minneapolis, demonstrators from the American Indian Movement (AIM), the National Association for the Advancement of Colored People (NAACP), and the National Organization for Women (NOW) protested the use of the name Redskins. The biggest demonstration came at the 1995 World Series in Atlanta, where the Braves faced the Indians. Nearly 2,000 protestors objected not only to the nicknames but to Chief Wahoo, the Indians' mascot, and the tomahawk chop, a ritual performed by Braves fans. The chop was first popularized by fans of the Florida State University Seminoles football team in the late 1970s and later adopted by the Braves. It involves moving the hand up and down in a

An Atlanta Braves fan greets the visiting Los Angeles Dodgers with a rude T-shirt and a monster tomahawk at a 1991 game in Atlanta. After originating at Florida State University, the tomahawk chop became a favorite ritual of Braves fans in the 1990s, and it was seen by millions of television viewers nationwide as the team became a superpower and played in four World Series. American Indian activists condemn the chop as a derogatory and violent stereotype of their heritage. The National Congress of American Indians (NCAI) believes that the negative images have serious consequences. "The continued insensitive projection of false stereotypes has resulted in untold harm to, and discrimination against, the American Indian," reads an NCAI statement. "Such portrayals have resulted in real socioeconomic handicaps and loss of self-esteem among members of the Indian population." (AP/WIDE WORLD PHOTOS)

chopping motion to the beat of music. Some fans hold foam tomahawks; others simply pretend to be holding them. With or without the weapon, the ritual conjures up the stereotype of the violent Indian in the same manner as the billboard display that greeted fans entering the stadium. It showed an image of a peace pipe being sliced in half by a three-dimensional tomahawk and the message, "There will be no peace-pipe smoking in Atlanta. Indians beware" (Johnson and Eck 1996: 65).

Braves owner Ted Turner assured the protestors that their concerns would be addressed, but he made no commitment to change the team's name. Nor has that commitment been made by the Washington Redskins. George Preston Marshall, the team's original owner, claimed to have chosen the nickname because he admired Indians and because one of the team's coaches was an Indian. The District of Columbia Council unanimously passed a resolution in 1992 that urged the team to change its name to one that is not offensive to Native Americans or any other minority group. The current ownership has disregarded the resolution, which has no binding legal effect on the team, and says the name symbolizes the positive and honorable characteristics of Native Americans. Professional teams also are wary of the economic impact of any changes. They say it could reduce the amount of revenue they receive from the sale of clothing and other merchandise bearing the well-established nicknames.

Those who defend the nicknames also point out that many Indians do not support Charlene Teters and the others who have worked to eliminate them. The defenders point to a host of more pressing concerns facing the Native American population, including woefully inadequate health care and education services and a dearth of job opportunities. Frank La Mere, a Winnebago Indian who has fought against nicknames and mascots, believes that argument is bogus. "If you can't see me as an individual, how can you understand the problems of my people?" he asks. "We have taken much heat, and the backlash has been tremendous, but we can take it. If our children do not have to endure the insults we have endured, then our efforts will have been worth it" (McCarthy 1993: A21).

WAVING THE FLAG

Native American nicknames are not the only ones that arouse concern and draw complaints in the sports world. The popular nickname Devils, which is used by over three hundred high schools, has been attacked by religious fundamentalists who believe it promotes satanism and is therefore a negative influence on young people. Principals and high school athletic directors say the nickname weathers the criticism because it is a winner with fans, parents, and students. When a group of opponents tried to change the name of the Liberty High School Red Devils in South Carolina, the town "just went berserk," athletic director Joe Burgess told *USA Today*. "The old-timers got so upset at the thought of changing the name, it's never been mentioned again" (Brewington 1997: 7C).

Another nickname with a negative image is Bullets, used by the National Basketball Association (NBA) team that has played in Baltimore and Washington since 1963. In 1997, the Washington Bullets became the Washington Wizards, after team owner Abe Pollan decided that the old name aroused unwanted images of gunfire, street crime, and drive-by shootings. He hopes the new name suggests that the team is made up of players of great skill. Pollan hopes there is no connection in the public mind with the Grand Wizards of the Ku Klux Klan, the white supremacist organization with a long history of violent hostility toward Catholics, Jews, and African Americans.

The Klan was at the heart of another controversy in 1996 at Brentsville District High School in Prince William County, Virginia. Before each baseball game, the Brentsville players drew a symbol called The Well on the diamond to bring them good luck. The symbol represents the view seen by a black man after being thrown down a well by four hooded Ku Klux Klansmen. When the school board learned that baseball coach Matt Ondrof knew the meaning of the symbol and allowed the ritual to continue, they suspended him for the remainder of the school year and assigned him to another school the following season. The incident was a bitter reminder of the South's history and its legacy of racial segregation.

That history remains a source of deep pride for many sports fans in the region. Nowhere is that pride more apparent than at the University of Mississippi, where in 1861 the entire all-male student body left school to enlist in the Confederate Army as the Civil War began. The focal point of the pride is the Stars and Bars, the battle flag of the Confederate States of America. At an institution where over 10 percent of the student body and nearly half of the football team is African American, game days at Vaught-Hemingway Stadium in Oxford feature the fight song "Dixie," the mascot Colonel Rebel, and the waving of the Stars and Bars by thousands of fans.

In 1997, the school banned the presence of pointed sticks in the stadium in an effort to stop the flag-waving ritual. The move came at the request of athletic director Pete Boone and football coach Tommy Tuberville, who said the flag waving made it more difficult to recruit African American athletes. Most blacks view the flag as a hateful reminder of racial segregation and of the resistance in the South to the integration efforts of the civil rights movement. When they see the flag, they have many of the same feelings that Jewish people would have if they were to see thousands of fans in a stadium waving swastikas. The flag had

The Stars and Bars is unfurled at Vaught-Hemingway Stadium on the Ole Miss campus during a 1997 game with Vanderbilt University. Are these flag wavers honoring the men and women who fought and died for the Confederacy during the Civil War? Or are they celebrating the violent and segregated society of the South's past and mocking the struggles of African Americans to end racial discrimination? Whatever the actions of the crowd may signify, Ole Miss athletic director Pete Boone and football coach Tommy Tuberville say they put the university at a disadvantage when they attempt to recruit black athletes. (AP/WIDE WORLD PHOTOS)

already been banned by the university for official business in 1983, an action that sparked bitter resentment and death threats against the university chancellor (Morello 1997: 3A). In 1994, the flag also was yanked from Fulton County Stadium in Georgia, at that time the home of the Atlanta Braves (*Jet* 1994: 48).

Those prohibitions have had little effect on Ole Miss football fans, who view the flag not as a symbol of hate but as one of honor and pride in the men who died defending it during the Civil War. "I love it," says John Crawford, a 1980 Ole Miss graduate. "It's my heritage." Crawford says if the point of barring the flag from the stadium is to help promote a winning football team, "I'd just as soon lose" (Morello 1997: 3A). He is not alone. In the last weeks of the 1997 season, thousands of fans defied the school's ban and continued to wave the flag on Saturday afternoons inside the stadium.

The defiance of the Ole Miss football fans shows how deeply attached people can become to the colors, symbols, nicknames, and mascots of the sports world. And when that attachment involves the tragedies of history, as it does with the Stars and Bars and Native American team nicknames, people will take risks to preserve and protect the things they hold dear. The story of Charlene Teters and her battle against Chief Illiniwek is not only an acknowledgment of the power of language. It is an acknowledgment of the power of the human spirit.

TOPICS FOR DISCUSSION

1. The *Portland Oregonian* and *Minneapolis Star Tribune* are two newspapers that have banned the use of Native American sports team nicknames in their pages. Do you agree with the ban imposed by these publications? Is it appropriate? Or is it too extreme?

2. Some Indians do not object to the use of Native American nicknames by sports teams. They say that their communities have more pressing problems to address, such as poverty, alcoholism, and a severe lack of jobs. Do you agree with their view? Explain your answer.

3. The football fans who wave the Confederate flag at the University of Mississippi say that they are celebrating the South's history and honoring the soldiers who died fighting the North during the Civil War. Do you think this is an accurate view of their motivation? Or are they waving the Confederate flag for another reason? What reason? Explain your answer.

4. People who are not Native American often have trouble grasping the emotional objections that Indians' nicknames and mascots arouse.

What steps, if any, can be taken to sensitize those people to the impact of the nicknames and mascots?

5. Have any of the school athletic teams in your city or conference ever become involved in a nickname or mascot controversy? If so, what were the reactions of the members of your community? Were they similar to the reactions triggered at the University of Illinois over Chief Illiniwek or at the University of Mississippi over the Confederate flag? What was the outcome of the controversy?

REFERENCES AND RESOURCES

Books

Levine, Peter. *Ellis Island to Ebbets Field: Sport and the American Jewish Experience.* New York: Oxford University Press, 1992.
> Uses a wealth of biographical and anecdotal material to detail the achievements of Jews in sports.

Oxendine, Joseph B. *American Indian Sports Heritage.* Lincoln: University of Nebraska Press, 1988.
> An excellent one-volume history of the contributions of Native Americans in the sports world.

Shropshire, Kenneth L. *In Black and White: Race and Sports in America.* New York: New York University Press, 1996.
> Shropshire, a prominent sports attorney, offers a provocative view of the many issues affecting race and sports, including team nicknames and mascots.

Magazines and Newspapers

Banks, Leo W. "The Spirit Moved Him." *Sports Illustrated,* September 19, 1996: 83.
> A retrospective on Hopi Indian distance runner Louis Tewanima.

Brewington, Peter. "Protestor Has Devil of a Time." *USA Today,* September 19, 1997: 7C.
> A report on the use of "Devils" as an athletic team nickname.

Davis, Robert. "U. of I. Won't Send Chief Illiniwek to Sideline." *Chicago Tribune,* November 15, 1989: 1, 23.
> A news report on the Chief Illiniwek controversy at the University of Illinois.

Fitzgerald, Mark. "Downside of Political Correctness." *Editor and Publisher,* June 11, 1994: 9.
> The story documents the fallout from the decision made by the *Minneapolis Star Tribune* to stop using Native American team nicknames in its news and sports coverage.

Giago, Tim. "Vengeance Is Mine Sayeth the Great Spirit." *Indian Country Today,* October 20, 1993: A4.

Giago presents a strong case against the use of Native American sports nicknames and mascots.

Hilliard, William. "To Our Readers." *Portland Oregonian*, February 16, 1992: D1.
The editor of the newspaper explains why he decided to drop the use of sports nicknames that may be offensive to racial, religious, or ethnic groups.

Jet. "Atlanta Stadium Votes to Remove State Flag." March 14, 1994: 48.
A brief note on the removal of the Confederate flag from Atlanta's Fulton County Stadium.

Johnson, Kim Chandler, and John Terence Eck. "Eliminating Indian Stereotypes from American Society: Causes and Legal and Societal Solutions." *American Indian Law Review* 20, 1996: 65–110.
In-depth analysis of the causes and effects of Indian stereotypes in popular culture.

Lofgren, Merle E. "Many Indians Do Not Agree." *Lakota Times*, February 12, 1995: B5.
Defends the use of Native American nicknames by sports teams.

Loving, Paul E. "Native American Team Names in Athletics: It's Time to Trade These Marks." *Loyola of Los Angeles Entertainment Law Journal* 13, 1992: 1–44.
Loving plots a legal strategy for opponents of Native American nicknames.

McCarthy, Coleman. "No New Name, No New Stadium." *Washington Post*, February 20, 1993: A21.
Discusses the debate over the Washington Redskins team name.

Morello, Carol. "Rebel Banner Roils Ole Miss Anew." *USA Today*, October 23, 1997: 3C.
Discusses the popularity of the Confederate flag at University of Mississippi football games.

Nack, William. "Look Away, Dixie Land." *Sports Illustrated*, November 3, 1997: 114.
Criticizes the waving of the Confederate flag at Ole Miss football games.

Pearlman, Jeff. "Righting a Wrong." *Sports Illustrated*, July 14, 1997: 19.
A review of the television documentary *In Whose Honor?* which profiled activist Charlene Teters.

Weinstock, Jeff. "Get Smart about Wizards and Walton." *Sport*, July 1996: 22.
A report on the new nickname of the Washington Bullets of the NBA.

Organization to Contact

National Congress of American Indians
2010 Massachusetts Avenue, N.W., Second Floor
Washington, D.C. 20036
Phone: 202–466–7767
Fax: 202–466–7797
Internet Web Site: www.ncai.org

Founded in 1944, the oldest and largest national Indian organization is dedicated to protecting the rights of Native Americans and improving their quality of life. The group has been active in the campaign against Native American sports team nicknames.

15

Setting Priorities

Many athletes reaching for superstardom neglect their academic duties in high school and college, and the price for that neglect can be steep once their playing days come to an end. Can an appropriate balance be struck between education and athletics?

The big event on the University of Florida campus in June 1996 was a special one for Emmitt Smith, the dynamic running back who led the Dallas Cowboys of the National Football League (NFL) to three Super Bowl championships in the 1990s. Smith was in uniform and waving to the crowd at Florida Field in Gainesville, the very place where he had enthralled Gator fans with his startling cutbacks and superhuman endurance during his college playing days. But on this day, Smith's uniform did not include shoulder pads, helmet, and mouthguard. Instead, it consisted of cap, gown, and sheepskin. Six years after leaving the university to join the NFL, Smith returned to receive his bachelor's degree in public recreation from Florida's College of Health and Human Performance. As he shook hands with university president John Lombardi, the crowd roared its approval, and Smith's mother held up a sign in the stands that read "Proud Mom."

The ceremony attracted attention because Smith, who already has succeeded famously and earned millions of dollars in his chosen profession, made a bachelor's degree a priority in his life. He felt compelled to return to campus and finish the job he had started after graduating from Escambia High School in Pensacola, Florida. For years he had preached passionately to young admirers about the value of obtaining an education. "I always felt a little hypocritical talking to kids when I hadn't accomplished my academic goals myself," Smith said on commencement day. "Now I won't be lying" (McCallum 1996: 73).

Dallas Cowboys running back Emmitt Smith shakes hands with University of Florida president John Lombardi at the school's 1996 graduation ceremony. Since 1991, the National Football League has worked with the National Consortium for Academics and Sports, a group of over 100 colleges and universities committed to providing an education to athletes like Smith who left school to pursue professional careers. About 11,000 former athletes have returned to college since the consortium was founded in 1985. Of those, 4,600 have earned degrees. (University of Florida/Photo by Jeff Gage/All rights reserved. Copyright 1997)

Smith is not the only prominent athlete who has joined the professional ranks and then returned to college to complete a degree. Michael Jordan earned a degree in geography from the University of North Carolina four years after joining the National Basketball Association (NBA). Bo Jackson, the two-sport star from Auburn University who played for both the Kansas City Royals of major league baseball and the Oakland Raiders of the NFL, earned a degree in family and child development. Sportscaster Ahmad Rashad, who left the University of Oregon in 1971 under the name Bobby Moore, got his diploma from the school twenty-four years later. These stars heeded the words of Ricky Barden, a less renowned football player who graduated from the University of North Carolina at age thirty-eight, long after a knee injury ended his professional career. "I started thinking, 'I need that piece of paper,' " he told *USA Today*. "You want to look in the mirror and feel good about yourself. I'll probably be the oldest-looking guy at graduation, but it will be one of the proudest days of my life" (Carey 1997: 14C).

There are thousands of athletes who earn scholarships in high school and then enroll at colleges and universities and succeed on the playing field as well as in the classroom. Like most other members of the student body, they graduate in four or five years and go on to lead productive lives. But those athletes typically receive little attention or publicity. Instead, the spotlight often focuses on the underachievers who fail academically or hover on the edge of eligibility. These athletes reinforce the stereotype of the college jock that has persisted since the earliest days of the twentieth century, when humorist James Thurber poked fun at the academic efforts of a classmate at Ohio State University: "He was a tackle on the football team, named Bolenciecwcz. . . . In order to be eligible to play it was necessary for him to keep up with his studies, a very difficult matter, for while he was not dumber than an ox he certainly was no smarter. . . . 'Name one means of transportation,' the professor said to him. No light came into the big tackle's eyes. . . . Bolenciecwcz was staring at the floor now, trying to think, his great brow furrowed, his huge hands rubbing together, his face red" (Thurber 1933: 65).

What name should be given to young men and women who enroll in colleges and universities with scholarships that provide them with tuition, room, board, and books in exchange for their athletic skills? Are they student-athletes, whose first priority is the classroom, or are they athlete-students, whose first priority is the playing field?

The frequently asked question implies a conflict, and the root of the conflict is the unwieldy alliance between sports and education. It is an alliance that is stronger in the United States than anywhere else in the world. In many other countries, the development of young athletes and the promotion of sports competitions is largely a private function, with the costs borne by organizations that have no direct connection to educational institutions. There are exceptions. In England, the universities of Oxford and Cambridge field outstanding rugby teams that compete at the national level. Their annual varsity match, which has been played since 1870, draws 70,000 spectators. But most talented soccer and rugby players in England, Germany, Italy, and elsewhere do not hone their skills at high schools or universities. Instead, they join organizations that receive no public funding and often are affiliated with professional teams. There is no controversy about what to call them. They are neither student-athletes nor athlete-students. They are students *and* athletes. The spheres of activity are separate and distinct.

In the United States, Little League Baseball and the Amateur Athletic Union are two of the many private groups that promote sports. But these groups generally play second fiddle to the sports programs of high schools, colleges, and universities. Those programs sponsor the teams that attract the most fans and generate the highest level of revenue, interest, and tradition.

Of course, the argument can be made—and frequently is—that sports deserve their place in an education system that includes any number of extracurricular activities that extend beyond the traditional classroom setting. Participating in sports is little different from playing in the school band, joining Junior Achievement or the Future Farmers of America, or taking a field trip to Washington to learn about the operation of the federal government. Sports can offer students a magnificent experience that teaches teamwork, discipline, self-sacrifice, and perseverance. There is nothing inherent in the alliance of sports and education that makes abuses automatic or that prompts so many derisive snickers toward characters like Thurber's Bolenciecwcz. Problems arise only when individual athletes make the choice to place sports above all else, including the opportunity to obtain an education that can serve as the groundwork for earning power and financial stability later in their lives.

The response to this view is that many young athletes, for whatever reason, do sacrifice their education for sports. And regardless of who is to blame—the athletes themselves, the competitive and commercial enterprise that produces them, or the larger society that envelops both the athletes and the enterprise—they likely will continue to do so in large numbers. Who are the athletes who throw away so much to play sports? Is it accurate to call them underachievers? And if the answer to that question is yes, how can things be changed to raise their achievement level in the classroom?

STARTING YOUNG

The challenge of setting priorities begins early in the lives of young athletes. By the time they reach high school, they face competing demands for their time, particularly if they participate in the high-profile sports of football and basketball. In many high schools, football can be as rigorous and demanding as the college version of the game. Author H. G. Bissinger profiled one prominent high school team in his classic book, *Friday Night Lights*. At Permian High School in Odessa, Texas, football is taken seriously. The Panthers have won four state championships. They play on artificial turf in a stadium with 19,032 seats, a two-story press box, and a full-time caretaker. The school even has an organization called the Pepettes, a group of senior girls who provide support and encouragement to the team. Each girl in the group is assigned to a varsity football player each year.

In the world of Texas high school football, finding time for school work can be difficult. Since 1985, the state has had a "no pass, no play" law that requires athletes to meet prescribed academic standards to remain eligible to participate. The campaign to pass the law was spearheaded by H. Ross Perot, the Texas business tycoon who ran for president in 1992 and 1996. The law requires students to maintain a minimum grade of seventy in each class during each six-week-grading period to retain eligibility. A score below seventy during a grading period will trigger ineligibility in the next grading period (Wong 1994: 254).

Nearly every other state has academic requirements for high school athletes similar to those in Texas. Some are contained in laws passed by the state legislature. Others are included in the rules of state high school athletic associations. Regardless of which body imposes the requirements, the intent is the same: to ensure that athletes make sufficient academic progress during high school. Former governor Mark White of Texas, who designated Perot as the point man in the campaign to pass the Texas law, sees the issue as an economic one. "The issue is not no pass, no play," White says. "The issue is no learn, no earn. . . . We must have an educated work force in order for Texas to attract the business, industry and jobs to our state that are vital to keeping Texas a leading economic force" (*CQ Researcher* 1995: 838).

The courts have upheld no pass–no play rules against challenges from athletes who were denied the opportunity to play because of low grades. Their reasoning has been that, unlike classroom instruction, participation in sports and other extracurricular activities is not a legal right. Instead, it is merely a privilege that may be granted or withdrawn at the discretion of the state legislature or the local school board (Wong 1994: 257).

No pass–no play rules have wide support among lawmakers, educators, and the public. There are, however, some dissenters. When former

Ohio State University football coach Woody Hayes was asked to endorse a bill in Ohio that created no pass–no play rules, he refused. Later he explained his position by telling a story about one of his players. "He was one of the finest young men I ever had the honor of coaching," Hayes said. "A big, tough, tackle who was ferocious on the field—and a leader off of it. But as a kid he had a horrible home life. In high school his father beat him up every time he brought home his report card. The kid wasn't getting F's. He was getting A's and B's. His dad hit him because he believed getting good grades was the white way to do things and he didn't want his son doing things the white way. So the kid started to fail on purpose to keep his dad from beating him up. What kind of help would this law give a kid like that? It would take away the only worthwhile thing he had. Football is what saved him" (Hayes 1987).

The coach's story graphically illustrates the concern that has always been at the heart of the debate over athletics and academics: what is the best way to bolster the chances of success for students who grow up in deprived environments? Like the football tackle who played for Woody Hayes, many athletes are raised in homes where the value of a high school or college education is not only dismissed but brutally mocked. They battle the prejudices of their elders, who often failed in school themselves and have scant respect for the life of the mind. The cycle of defeat and denigration flourishes in the poorest segments of the African American community, where decades of racism, neglect, and inferior public schools have turned education into an empty dream. When psychologist John Osborne of the State University of New York at Buffalo conducted a national study of 15,037 white, African American, and Hispanic teenagers, he discovered that the self-esteem of young black males was tied not to academic achievement but to popularity and athletic ability. Osborne says young blacks were telling him, "Academics are irrelevant. Whether I'm failing or on the honor roll doesn't affect how I feel about myself" (Elias 1997: 1D).

ATHLETES ON CAMPUS

Osborne's survey findings are played out regularly in the world of college athletics. When many African American basketball and football stars arrive on campuses, they step into an environment radically different from the one in which they grew up. Their fellow students and their teachers are overwhelmingly white, as are the fans who fill the arenas and stadiums and the coaches and assistant coaches who serve as their mentors. Those coaches expect the athletes to contribute to the success of their teams, a task that demands thirty to forty hours of time each week during the season.

Just as demanding is the academic load, particularly for those who struggled in high school. At the same time, adoration is no longer the only emotion directed at the stars. Their popularity takes a serious hit. On campus they can be viewed with scorn by peers and professors who do not regard them as serious students, but as modern counterparts to Bolenciecwcz. The stubborn stereotypes about race and academic achievement remain, and young black athletes often "allow the lingering doubts of others to become modern-day shackles" (Funk 1991: 104). They are expected to fail, and in the face of that expectation, they often do.

The classroom challenges seem especially great to the many athletes chasing the dream of a professional sports career. Except for the most talented, the odds of playing in the NFL or the NBA are exceedingly slim. And because the average career in those leagues lasts only three or four years, there is no long-term financial security even for those who are fortunate enough to advance to the next level. Despite the long odds against success, the professional dream dies hard—very hard. If a basketball guard has convinced himself that he is the heir apparent to Michael Jordan, it can make activities like composition, biology, history, and mathematics seem pointless.

Standing at the center of the conflict between academics and athletics is the National Collegiate Athletic Association (NCAA). Its member institutions establish admission and eligibility standards for student-athletes. Proposition 48, which became effective in 1986, required high school students to attain a minimum score of 700 on the Scholastic Aptitude Test (SAT) or 15 on the American College Test (ACT) in order to practice or compete during their freshman year in college. Student-athletes also needed to earn a minimum grade point average (GPA) of 2.0 in eleven core high school courses. Those who did not meet the minimums were required to demonstrate satisfactory academic progress in their freshman year in order to rejoin their teams. If they failed to do so, they lost their athletic scholarships.

The NCAA also reviews the transcripts of high school students to determine if the courses they have taken can be designated as "core courses" for the purpose of determining initial eligibility. The review process, which has always been slow and cumbersome, was streamlined in 1998. Instead of requiring principals to forward the entire curriculums of their high schools to the NCAA's clearinghouse for approval, the NCAA now allows principals to decide which of their own courses meet the eligibility standards and which do not. The change in procedure has two points. The first is to ease the confusion that generates more than 11,000 phone calls to the clearinghouse each month in Iowa City, Iowa. The second is to allow educators, not the NCAA, to determine which courses are considered college preparatory. Educators resented the ability of workers at the clearinghouse to refuse a core-course designation simply because they did not like the sound of the title or had never seen a course like it before. "If anyone is qualified to make these kinds of decisions, it's a principal," says John A. Lammel of the National Association of Secondary High School Principals. "They know what the curriculum is all about" (Richardson 1998: 8C).

The goal of Proposition 48 was to increase the academic achievement levels of student-athletes. The numbers indicate that it did so. Fifty-seven percent of all student-athletes who entered college in 1987 graduated within six years, a percentage that was one point higher than the figure for all incoming students that year. In 1987, the graduation rate for black athletes entering college was 43 percent, an increase from 33 percent for black athletes entering in 1984, 1985, and 1986 (Judson 1995: 49).

Controversy over NCAA standards intensified in 1989 when the member schools passed Proposition 42. It went a step further than its predecessor by allowing institutions to withhold athletic scholarship money from entering freshmen who had not met academic guidelines. Under Proposition 48, athletes were able to receive aid during their freshman year as they attempted to improve their standing. Georgetown University basketball coach John Thompson walked off the court before a 1989 game with Boston College to protest the passage of Proposition 42. He viewed it as a naked attempt to limit the number of black athletes in college, many of whom could not afford to be there without scholarship aid. Proposition 42 was repealed in 1990.

In 1993, the schools of the NCAA imposed another set of more stringent standards for entering student-athletes. Proposition 16, which became effective in 1996, raises the minimum SAT score from 700 to 820 and the minimum ACT score from 15 to 17.5. It also requires a minimum GPA of 2.5 in thirteen core high school courses in science, math, English, and social studies. As with Proposition 48, the goals are to emphasize the need for preparedness and promote academic achievement in college.

Are the NCAA's standards unfair to minority athletes? Critics argue that the higher cutoff figures, particularly on standardized tests, translate into fewer educational opportunities for disadvantaged students. The NCAA responded to that charge by passing Proposition 68 in 1997. It allows athletes who lost their freshman season of eligibility because of poor academic work to regain that season later in their playing careers, providing they graduate from college in four years. Supporters say minority athletes are responding well to the challenge of raised expectations. That is the view of Harry Edwards, a professor at the University of California at Berkeley and the dean of American sports sociologists. Edwards could barely read or write when he left his ghetto high school to pursue a college athletic career. He believes the NCAA standards are not stringent enough and would like to see the bar raised, not lowered (Hu 1995: 69). Supporters also say that access to college for minority athletes has not declined significantly since the passage of Proposition

48. They continue to receive about 25 percent of the scholarships that are offered (Ethier 1997: A38). And the NCAA itself frequently notes that the standards do not bar anyone from attending college. They are only the hurdles that must be cleared to receive an athletic scholarship. They do not in any way restrict the ability of student-athletes to obtain need-based financial aid like other students (Peoples 1997b: 66).

The NCAA's campaign to raise academic standards for athletes on campus can best be described as a partial success. The upside is documented. One hundred percent of the student-athletes at Prairie View A&M University in Texas who entered in 1991 had earned degrees by 1996, according to the NCAA's 1997 Division I graduation report. Twenty-nine other universities boasted graduation rates of more than 80 percent, including Boston College, Bucknell, DePaul, Duke, North Carolina, Notre Dame, Stanford, and Virginia.

The downside is just as apparent. The same report shows that only 46 percent of African American football players earn degrees within five years, well below the figure of 67 percent for white football players (Ethier 1997: A38, A39). Three of the teams that reached the Final Four of the 1997 NCAA basketball tournament—Minnesota, Arizona, and Kentucky—had graduation rates below 35 percent (Feinstein 1997: 15A). "It's unnerving when you see that whites are graduating and blacks are not," says Charles S. Farrell, director of the National Rainbow Coalition's Commission for Fairness in Athletics. "We still seem to have a high percentage of schools that seem not to care about blacks . . . unless they can score 20 points a game and pull down 12 rebounds" (Peoples 1997a: 82).

SEEKING CHANGE

Those who support strong academic standards for college athletes have proposed a number of reforms that extend beyond requiring minimim test scores and GPAs. Some of the proposals are conventional, such as ending spring football practice, eliminating eligibility for all freshman athletes, and increasing the number of academic tutors who provide individual instruction to those needing help. Others are more radical in nature. One would link the number of available athletic scholarships at a school to its graduation rate for athletes. Schools that fall behind in their academic efforts would then have to compete with smaller teams against their rivals. Another proposal would hit schools directly in the pocketbook. It would require them to graduate at least 75 percent of their scholarship athletes within five years in order to ensure that financial contributions to their athletic departments remain tax deductible (Funk 1991: 21).

Some reformers have tried to force change in the courts. Lawsuits alleging "educational malpractice" or "educational exploitation" have been filed on behalf of athletes at Arizona State, Creighton, Michigan, and other universities. The lawsuits contend that the schools broke their promises to provide athletes with educations in exchange for their playing skills. The promises were broken by enrolling the athletes in courses designed only to keep them academically eligible, denying access to tutors and academic counselors, and instructing athletes to accept grades for courses they never attended. The most publicized case involved Kevin Ross, a Creighton University basketball star who left the team after three years and returned to a Chicago middle school to improve his reading skills, which stood at the second-grade level. As in the other lawsuits, the court ruled against the athlete, rejecting Ross's claim that there had been an explicit contract between him and the school that had been broken. Ross did receive a payment of $30,000 from the university (Wong 1994: 338).

The most far-reaching proposal for change has been offered by sportswriter John Feinstein. He asks a simple question: Why is it necessary for football and basketball players to attend college at all? When Deion Sanders of the NFL's Dallas Cowboys was starring at Florida State, he was once asked if he wanted to be in college. "No," he replied, "but I have to be." What Sanders meant was that there is only one path available for athletes, like him, who have the talent and ambition needed to play in the NFL or the NBA. That path runs directly through the higher education system. The major college sports programs function today as farm systems for the NFL and the NBA, relieving those leagues of the burden of developing players with their own resources.

That state of affairs is starting to change in basketball, where an increasing number of players are bypassing college altogether and entering the NBA directly out of high school. In 1998, high school seniors Korleone Young, Rashard Lewis, and Al Harrington leapfrogged into the professional ranks. They followed Kevin Garnett of the Minnesota Timberwolves, Kobe Bryant of the Los Angeles Lakers, and Tracy McGrady of the Toronto Raptors. At the moment, the option to go pro is reserved only for the most talented high school performers. Most players need the years of seasoning that college basketball offers before their skills are strong enough to compete effectively in the NBA.

Feinstein would like to change the system to give even more basketball players the chance to go pro immediately. He proposes the creation of a developmental league for basketball players leaving high school, to be funded by the NBA. Each player would be paid $75,000 to $100,000 per year and could play up to four years. Twenty percent of each player's salary would be placed in a trust fund. At the end of the four-year period, a player would have three choices: advance to the NBA or another professional league, find a job other than playing basketball, or attend college with the money in his trust fund (Feinstein 1997: 15A).

The details of the proposal are sketchy, but its point is crystal clear. It may be time to loosen the century-old alliance between academics and athletes by offering promising young athletes another route to the big time. If that happens, the serious athletes who also are serious students can follow the traditional path through college, and the athletes who are not serious students can avoid the tensions that arise in college when they have to pretend to be. Feinstein's plan may be seen by some as an admission that times have changed and by others as simply another attempt to deny educational opportunities to minority athletes. In either case, the rocky alliance between books and balls is not likely to get any smoother in the future.

TOPICS FOR DISCUSSION

1. Many star basketball and football players now leave college early to pursue careers in the National Basketball Association (NBA) and the National Football League (NFL). Do you think they are making the correct decision by forgoing their education for athletics? Why or why not?

2. Does your school district have a no pass–no play policy that prohibits students from playing sports if they fail to maintain a minimum grade point average? If so, do you think it is an effective way to force students to make academics, instead of sports, their primary focus? Why or why not?

3. High school and college athletes have been denigrated for decades as "dumb jocks" who need special assistance in the classroom in order to maintain passing grades. Do you think the "dumb jock" stereotype is an accurate one? Does that description fit the athletes you know personally?

4. Critics charge that the eligibility standards of the National Collegiate Athletic Association (NCAA) are unfair to minority students because of their emphasis on standardized test scores. They say that minority students, who generally fare less well on standardized tests than their white counterparts, are denied scholarship opportunities at colleges and universities. Do you think that is a fair criticism? Why or why not? Explain your answer.

5. What do you think of John Feinstein's call for the creation of a minor league for basketball players who have neither the ability nor the interest to pursue an academic career in college in order to play their sport? Is it a good idea to offer aspiring professional basketball players another route to the NBA other than college? Why or why not? Who would object to such a league? Why?

REFERENCES AND RESOURCES

Books

Berlow, Lawrence H. *Sports Ethics*. Santa Barbara, Calif.: ABC-CLIO, 1994.
A guide to sports ethics issues that includes biographies of major figures, documents, and a bibliography of resources.

Bissinger, H. G. *Friday Night Lights: A Town, a Team and a Dream*. Reading, Mass.: Addison-Wesley, 1990.
The life and times of the Permian High School Panthers football team of Odessa, Texas.

Dudley, William, ed. *Sports in America: Opposing Viewpoints*. San Diego: Greenhaven Press, 1994.
Chapter 2 is a discussion of whether and how college athletics should be reformed.

Flowers, Sarah. *Sports in America*. San Diego: Lucent Books, 1996.
Chapter 2 deals with the athlete-student conflict.

Funk, Gary D. *Major Violation: The Unbalanced Priorities in Athletics and Academics*. Champaign, Ill.: Leisure Press, 1991.
The director of the Academic Support Center at Southwest Missouri State University offers cogent insights into the problems faced by student-athletes.

Hu, Evaleen. *A Level Playing Field: Sports and Race*. Minneapolis, Minn.: Lerner, 1995.
Chapter 5 concerns the academic challenges faced by African American athletes.

Judson, Karen. *Sports and Money: It's a Sellout!* Springfield, N.J.: Enslow Publishers, 1995.
Chapters 3 and 4 discuss academics and sports in high school and college.

Miracle, Andrew, Jr., and C. Roger Dees. *Lessons of the Locker Room: The Myth of School Sports*. New York: Prometheus Books, 1994.
Two college professors challenge the widely accepted notion that participation in high school sports builds character.

Thurber, James. *My Life and Hard Times*. New York: Harper and Brothers, 1933.
The humorist reminisces about college football in the chapter entitled "University Days."

Wong, Glenn M. *Essentials of Amateur Sports Law*. 2d ed. Westport, Conn.: Praeger, 1994.
An excellent source on the many legal issues that affect student-athletes, including no pass–no play laws, NCAA eligibility standards, and education malpractice claims.

Magazines and Newspapers

Brownlee, Shannon, with Nancy Linnon. "The Myth of the Student-Athlete." *U.S. News and World Report*, January 8, 1990: 50–52.
A thorough discussion of the conflict between academics and sports.

Carey, Jack. "Ex-Athletes Hit Books Again." *USA Today*, October 22, 1997: 14C.
Profiles degree-completion programs for former college athletes.

Chambers, Marcia. "An Athlete Challenges a Stealthy Rule." *New York Times*, November 19, 1997: A22.
Discusses the controversy surrounding the NCAA's stance on athletes with disabilities.

CQ Researcher. "High School Sports." September 25, 1995: 825–48.
Published by *Congressional Quarterly*, this issue examines many aspects of high school athletics, including eligibility requirements. The publication formerly was known as *Editorial Research Reports*.

Dodd, Mike. "Winning One for the Admissions Office." *USA Today*, July 11, 1997: 1A, 2A.
Includes stories of how athletic success has boosted the academic standing of several universities.

Elias, Marilyn. "Academics Lose Relevance for Black Boys." *USA Today*, December 2, 1997: 1D.
Findings from a study that reveal a lack of interest in academics on the part of young African-American males.

Ethier, Marc. "Male Basketball Players Continue to Lag in Graduation Rates." *Chronicle of Higher Education*, July 3, 1997: A38–A39.
Dissects the latest NCAA report on graduation rates for athletes.

Feinstein, John. "Not Every Athlete Needs to Go to College." *USA Today*, November 13, 1997: 15A.
Proposes an alternative to business-as-usual in college sports.

McCallum, Jack. "Better Late Than Never." *Sports Illustrated*, June 13, 1996: 72–73.
A report on football player Emmitt Smith's graduation from the University of Florida.

Moran, Malcolm. "Win a Few, Lose a Few, and Get a Few to Graduate." *New York Times*, November 19, 1995: 29.
Laments the low graduation rate among major college basketball players.

Peoples, Betsy. "Blocked Shots." *Emerge*, February 1997a: 80–83.
A discussion of African American basketball players and NCAA eligibility standards.

Peoples, Betsy. "No Access." *Emerge*, November 1997b: 64–67.
Peoples unveils her "Bottom 50"—the colleges with the lowest graduation rates for football players.

Richardson, Sandee. "Principals Gain Say in Eligibility." *USA Today*, April 22, 1998: 8C.
A report on the NCAA's new procedures for determining the academic eligibility of incoming college athletes.

Rooney, Charles. "Rules Unfair to Minorities." *USA Today*, September 19, 1997: 24A.
An editorial opinion on the NCAA's academic standards for athletes.

USA Today. "Texas Tech Audit Reveals Infractions." October 3, 1997: 3C.
Details widespread academic abuses in the athletic department at Texas Tech University.

Wolff, Alexander. "School's Out." *Sports Illustrated*, February 24, 1997: 60–66.

An account of the travails of Oklahoma City University basketball player Marcus LoVett.

Interview

Hayes, Woody. Personal interview by author, January 6, 1987.
The former Ohio State University coach discusses his stance on no pass–no play laws.

Organizations to Contact

National Collegiate Athletic Association (NCAA)
6201 College Boulevard
Overland Park, KS 66211–2422
Phone: 913–339–1906
Fax: 913–339–0030
Internet Web Site: www.ncaa.org
The NCAA's guide for the college-bound student-athlete includes information on academic eligibility, core courses, and the initial-eligibility clearinghouse.

National Collegiate Athletic Association Clearinghouse
2255 North Dubuque Road
Iowa City, IA 52243
Phone: 319–337–1492
The NCAA Clearinghouse is operated by the American College Testing organization for the NCAA. It makes determinations regarding initial college eligibility for high school athletes by reviewing transcripts submitted by the students' high schools.

16

Sign on the Dotted Line

The commercialization of sports exploded in the 1990s, with Nike and other athletic footwear companies leading the charge up the mountain of cash. Has commercial sponsorship harmed our sporting traditions, or has it been a key factor in their survival and popularity?

In a style worthy of royalty, the deal of the century was rolled out before the start of the 1997–1998 season of the National Basketball Association (NBA). Michael Jordan, the reigning king of roundball and perhaps the world's most famous athlete, was about to become a brand name in the international consumer marketplace. The superstar guard of the Chicago Bulls would not merely be lending his name to Air Jordan basketball sneakers, already positioned among the most popular lines of athletic footwear on the planet. His new venture went well beyond that. With the blessing and support of Phil Knight, founder and chairman of the athletic footwear and apparel company Nike, Jordan was in line to head his own enterprise within the giant Nike empire. Known simply as Jordan, it opened shop with its own logo, the Jumpman, five types of athletic shoes, and five rising NBA stars handpicked to endorse the products.

Jordan holds no formal title in the organization, nor is he investing any money in the venture. His assignment simply is to be himself, and his goal is to establish a presence in the athletic footwear marketplace on a grand scale as he begins his retirement from basketball. For Nike, the arrangement offers a chance to keep the greatest name in the game in its own camp and retain a competitive edge over sportswear rivals Reebok, Adidas, and Fila.

Jordan's record of achievement is incomparable. In his freshman season at the University of North Carolina, he drained the jump shot that gave the Tar Heels the National Collegiate Athletic Association (NCAA) title. In 1984, he was college basketball's player of the year and the leader of America's Dream Team, Olympic gold medalists in Los Angeles. After joining the Chicago Bulls of the NBA, he led the team to league titles in 1991, 1992, 1993, 1996, 1997, and 1998 and won five Most Valuable Player awards and eight league scoring championships. Many call Jordan the greatest basketball player ever—greater than any of his contemporary rivals and greater than Bill Russell, Wilt Chamberlain, or Kareem Abdul-Jabbar, the imposing centers who dominated the NBA for three decades from 1960 to 1990.

Jordan is certainly the most renowned man ever to play the game. His fame cuts a wide swath across the landscape of the sports world. In 1997, the *Sporting News* named Jordan the most influential person in sports, the only player ever to top that annual list. He travels with a six-man security force made up of former Chicago policemen, and he receives 6,000 pieces of mail each month. Not all of those items are letters; his fans have sent him shoes, curtains, Bibles, ice cream, paintings, drawings, and poems. When he took a year's leave of absence to play minor league baseball with the Birmingham Barons of the Southern League, the club smashed its season attendance record. The Barons celebrated Michael Jordan Poster Day—more than a year after he left the team to return to the Bulls. In 1997 at the McDonald's Championship in Paris, an international tournament in which the Bulls competed with five top European teams, over 1,000 news reporters and photographers recorded the event. As usual, Jordan found himself mobbed by autograph seekers. In Paris, however, the mob included not only spectators but players from the other teams in the tournament. In Jordan's home base of Chicago, Japanese tourists who have paid up to $2,000 each to take "The Michael Jordan Tour" spend an average of $300 apiece on "Michael-bilia." Among the tour's stops are the eleven-foot, 2,000-pound statue of Jordan outside the United Center, the Bulls' home arena; Michael Jordan's Restaurant north of downtown, which serves up to 15,000 customers each week; and Michael Jordan Golf, an apparel and equipment shop in the tony Water Tower Place shopping mall on Michigan Avenue. Some fans are lucky enough to catch a glimpse of Jordan's mansion in suburban Highland Park, where the town police chief says he maintains a low profile and asks to be treated like a regular guy (Bonkowski 1996: 3C).

Jordan has parlayed his athletic skills and fame into a career as the premier endorser of commercial products in the sports world. He plays the endorsement game in the same rarefied air in which he plays basketball—a mile above the rim. He earned an estimated $47 million in 1997 touting the merits of Nike shoes and apparel, McDonald's hamburgers, Gatorade, and other products. The only other athlete who approaches Jordan's commercial clout is Tiger Woods, the young golfer who won the Masters Tournament in 1997. He raked in $24 million in 1997; the total value of Woods's endorsement deals with Nike, American Express, Titleist, and Rolex is estimated at $95 million. In an effort to boost sales of its golf clothing and footwear, Nike signed Woods to a five-year contract just after he won his third United States Amateur title in 1996 and before he turned professional.

"Tiger has a chance to have an even broader appeal than Michael Jordan," sports agent Leigh Steinberg told Roy S. Johnson of *Fortune* magazine, "because we live in a time when communications is so instant and so universal that a guy on an island in the Pacific could have watched him win the Masters live." Steinberg believes Woods could have the most profound impact inside and outside of sports of any athlete since Muhammad Ali (Johnson 1997: 74).

Jordan and Woods stand on the summit of the mountain of cash that has been created by the commercialization of sports. The world has changed greatly since the days of the Fort Wayne Zollners, the pioneer NBA players of the 1950s who served as a living advertisement for Indiana auto parts maker Fred Zollner before he moved them to Detroit and renamed them the Pistons. But the desire of companies to link their products in the public eye with individual stars and popular teams remains the same. The best-known players in the endorsement game are the athletic footwear giants Nike, Reebok, and Adidas. They compete for upcoming and established stars and sign them to multiyear contracts in exchange for the right to outfit those stars in their own brands of shoes. For the companies, the key benefit is authenticity. When a player is seen wearing Nike, Reebok, or Adidas shoes in competition, it signifies to potential buyers that the shoes meet the rigorous standards demanded by professional athletes.

Many of the endorsement battles are waged in professional basketball, one of the most popular sports with consumers under age eighteen who purchase about 70 percent of all basketball sneakers sold (Meyers 1997b: 2A). In a volatile world where fashion rules and styles change frequently, the quest for teen dollars is tough and competitive. Shoe companies are learning that only the stars with the highest profiles can help their bottom line. In addition to Jordan, Nike counts Phoenix Suns forward Charles Barkley, Utah Jazz guard John Stockton, and Minnesota Timberwolves center Kevin Garnett in its camp. Reebok shoes are endorsed by Los Angeles Lakers center Shaquille O'Neal and Philadelphia 76ers guard Allen Iverson. In 1997, Adidas signed Toronto Raptors forward Tracy McGrady before he had played in a single professional game. The six-year agreement could pay him as much as $12 million, the most lucrative endorsement deal ever for a player who entered the NBA directly out of high school without attending college. Fila, an Italian company, signed Detroit Pistons star Grant Hill as its principal spokesman and watched footwear sales more than double from 1993 to 1996. "The Hill" is Fila's fastest-selling product ever (Goldberg 1997: 38).

Endorsement money flows to athletes in less visible sports as well. The swimwear company Speedo outfitted thirty divers, swimmers, and beach volleyballers at the 1996 Olympic Games in Atlanta. In 1996, IBM signed an athlete for the first time, pro golfer Phil Mickelson, to endorse its hardware products. Drag racer Kristen Powell, known as the world's fastest teenager, signed with Reebok in 1997. American soccer stars Eric Wynalda and Alexi Lalas are under contract to Reebok and Adidas, respectively, and Mia Hamm, the mainstay of the women's national team, endorses Pert Plus shampoo, Power Bars, Pepsi, and Earth Grains cereal. The Women's National Basketball Association (WNBA), which began play in 1997, has attracted a host of sponsors, including Sears and Lee Jeans, and corporate sponsorship of women's sports in the United States soared from $285 million in 1992 to $600 million in 1997 (Horowitz 1997: B1). "Women couldn't sell a car unless they were wearing a bathing suit," says WNBA center Rebecca Lobo. "Now the stigma is gone. People see us as athletes" (Bhonslay 1997: 61).

Corporate sponsors are finding ways to spend their money in the corners of the sports world where the amateurs compete too. Youth sports leagues, which always operate on slim budgets, have offered sponsors access to the millions of children and parents who participate in their games in exchange for operating revenue. Rawlings Sporting Goods, Lever Brothers, Sunkist, and Quaker Oats are among the many consumer goods companies that have signed on. Their goal is to create loyalty to their products early in the lives of the young athletes in the hope that that loyalty will endure for a lifetime. Commercial sponsorship in youth leagues is not a new phenomenon. When Little League Baseball launched its first season in 1939, a pretzel company, a lumber yard, and a dairy in Pennsylvania each paid $30 to place their names on team uniforms. That quaint practice, which is still common, has been expanded to include sophisticated and targeted mailings to the upper-middle-class, affluent families that participate most heavily in youth sports leagues (Johnson 1998: A1).

Outside the United States, aided by an infusion of American cash and cachet, the commercialization of sports has blossomed. In China, the Marlboro League, underwritten by the Philip Morris Company, attracts 100 million soccer fans to its televised contests each week, and American tennis star Michael Chang pitches Procter and Gamble's Rejoice shampoo and Eveready batteries (Tanzer 1997: 96–98). With Tiger Woods playing tournaments around the world and pointing with pride to his Asian ancestry, Nike has been flooded with unsolicited orders for shoes and clothing from Africa, Japan, and other countries in Asia. Coca-Cola, in the words of its former marketing chief, Sergio Zyman, is "moving slowly, inexorably into every sport," including soccer's World Cup, cycling's Tour de France, and cricket in India and Pakistan (Greising 1996: 36). Great Britain's foremost soccer team, Manchester United, boasts Sharp electronics and Umbro sporting goods as its two main sponsors and reported $83.1 million in revenues in fiscal year 1997, more than any other European soccer team. The NBA sponsors school basketball programs in Great Britain, France, and Germany, and a survey by the league revealed that 88 percent of the teenagers in Western Europe recognized the league's logo.

THE SAGA OF THE SWOOSH

Most prominent of all the companies in the endorsement game is Nike, founded by Phil Knight, a self-described "track geek" who ran as a miler on the University of Oregon team in the 1960s. Knight began his career selling inexpensive, high-quality Japanese running shoes out of the trunk of his car at high school track and cross-country meets in Oregon. "We were the children of Holden Caulfield," says Knight. "Nobody liked the phoniness or hypocrisy of the establishment, including the business establishment" (Lane 1996: 44).

Today, Nike is a major part of that establishment, operating with a philosophy that springs from Knight's youthful outlook. Nike athletes are presented to the world as confident, competitive, rebellious individuals, and the company is proud of its willingness to embrace controversial figures such as flamboyant football and baseball star Deion Sanders, outspoken tennis legend John McEnroe, and figure skater Tonya Harding, who was banished from her sport after being implicated in a knee-bashing attack on archrival Nancy Kerrigan. Indeed, the original Nike athlete was Steve Prefontaine, the Oregon runner who became a counterculture icon after he died in a car crash in 1975 at the age of twenty-four. Knight openly paid Prefontaine to wear Nike shoes in 1973, and it caused a furor in the track and field world, where endorsement deals had always been concealed to preserve the facade of amateurism. The same willingness to take risks is evident in Nike's aggressive television advertisements. They have featured former presidential adviser James Carville touting baseball slugger Ken Griffey, Jr., for the White House, film actor Dennis Hopper portraying a crazed football fanatic, and Charles Barkley defiantly proclaiming to children and parents, "I am not a role model!"

The company's attraction to controversial players and in-your-face advertisements has not hurt its bottom line. Nike ranks with Coca-Cola, Disney, and Hallmark as one of the world's most recognizable brand names. In 1995, the company surpassed Reebok as the market share

Running legend Steve Prefontaine, who died in 1975 in a car accident at age twenty-four, was the first athlete to endorse Nike shoes. He ran for the University of Oregon a decade after Nike founder Phil Knight. Ever an intense competitor, Prefontaine ripped the swoosh off his shoes in one race to reduce wind drag. (AP/WIDE WORLD PHOTOS)

leader in athletic footwear and has remained firmly entrenched at the top ever since. Its worldwide revenues surpassed $9 billion in 1997, and Knight has become one of the world's wealthiest individuals. He has made his fortune by understanding that in modern America, millions of people define themselves by what they purchase and by transforming athletic shoes from exotic luxuries for star athletes into everyday items that could be bought up to ten times each year by status-hungry shoppers (Lipsyte 1996a: B11).

The focal point of Nike's market presence has been the swoosh, the ancient Greek symbol of winged victory that resembles a check mark. Knight paid Carolyn Davidson, a graphic designer from Portland State University, $35 to create the swoosh in the early 1970s. "I don't love it," he told her when he first saw it. Knight thought the design might grow on him. It did. Football fans see the swoosh on the shoulder pads of more than forty college and professional teams that Nike sponsors, including perennial powers like Ohio State, Michigan, Penn State, and Tennessee, and Super Bowl contenders like the Pittsburgh Steelers, Green Bay Packers, Dallas Cowboys, and Denver Broncos. Basketball fans see it on sneakers worn by fifteen major college teams and uniforms worn by ten NBA teams. Hockey fans see it on the jerseys of eight teams in the National Hockey League (NHL). Rick Reilly of *Sports Illustrated* describes the symbol as "so huge that the name of the company that goes with the Swoosh doesn't even appear anymore" (Reilly 1997: 78).

Nike itself apparently believes the swoosh may have become too big for its own good. In 1997, when it faced declining revenues and stiff challenges from competitors, the company began featuring a new advertising slogan, "I Can." The swoosh and the popular slogan "Just Do It" are not being eliminated. They simply will receive less attention as Nike attempts to solidify its grip on the top rung of the ladder. The I Can campaign also is part of an effort to reconnect with amateur athletes in a time when the professionals are generating negative feelings with their high salaries and off-court antics.

Regardless of which slogans and symbols it may display, Nike is using its track record and cash reserves to push its products into new and expanding markets. The latest target is soccer, the world's most popular spectator sport and a game now played by nearly 18 million Americans. In 1997, Nike promoted soccer to core sport status alongside basketball and running. It has signed sponsorship agreements with the Netherlands, Italy, Russia, South Korea, and Nigeria and pledged $200 million over a ten-year period to the national team of Brazil. In the United States, it is providing $120 million through 2006 to the national team. "We're the No. 1 sports and fitness company in the world and we want to be No. 1 in soccer in the world," says Nike spokesman Jim Small (Sandomir

1997: C22). Given the company's track record of success, it is not hard to believe that Nike will reach that goal.

HOW MUCH IS TOO MUCH?

Endorsement contracts seem like a good thing for all of the parties involved: the players and teams that receive millions of dollars in fees, the companies whose products receive a high degree of visibility, and even the fans, who are treated to close-up and personal views of many of their favorite stars in their latest television commercials. But the practice raises a number of concerns, many of which deal with the effect that commercial endorsements have on young people. Most alarming is the fact that teenage males—most of them African Americans residing in or near the nation's largest cities—have been robbed at gunpoint and killed by thieves who coveted the shoes and clothing they were wearing.

The list of victims from the Sneaker Wars of the 1980s is long and depressing: a Baltimore youth wearing a Georgetown University warm-up jacket, a high school football quarterback in Detroit wearing Nike sneakers, a fifteen-year-old in suburban Washington wearing Air Jordans, a seventeen-year-old in Atlanta wearing Avia hightops. Police in one area of Chicago say they deal with over sixty incidents involving jackets and sneakers each month. Even more disturbing is the bonanza that some retailers reap from drug dealers, who often purchase large quantities of shoes and clothing from stores in Los Angeles and other large cities. Some dealers get a kick out of dressing their runners— youths who make drug deliveries to customers—in matching sneakers. One gang of teenagers in Boston dressed themselves exclusively in Reebok hats, jackets, sweatpants, and shoes and even devised a Reebok handshake patterned after the three stripes that appear on the products (Telander 1990: 38–43).

Critics charge that athletes and sportswear companies contribute to the violence by helping to create a demand for their gear in poverty-stricken inner cities. In those locales, Air Jordan sneakers have little to do with fitness or athletics and a great deal to do with status and self-esteem. Driven by peer pressure and the prospect of empty futures, black teenagers seek fulfillment by indulging in a crass materialism that values the latest hot sneakers above all else, even human life. And while the athletes soar above the squalor with their multi-million-dollar endorsement deals, teenagers are murdered in the street for the very products those athletes are endorsing. Are any athletes bothered by the accusation that they are contributing to the cycle of violence? At least one is. "I'd rather eliminate the product than know drug dealers are providing the funds that pay me," Michael Jordan told *Sports Illustrated* (Telander 1990: 49).

Another concern is the promotion of sports events by alcohol and to-bacco companies. They market products that cannot be purchased legally by consumers under the age of eighteen, but that does not stop them from courting the millions of young people who watch sports. Many of the largest breweries, including Miller, Anheuser-Busch, and Coors, maintain a pervasive advertising presence in football, baseball, and bas-ketball, and tobacco companies have been major sponsors of the National Association for Stock Car Auto Racing (NASCAR). RJR Nabisco pays between $20 and $30 million annually to promote the Winston Cup, NASCAR's premier competition that is named after one of the com-pany's cigarette brands (Associated Press 1997: 3B). The strategy is to link tobacco use with the exciting action on the track, where drivers and vehicles surge in a heated pack at 160 miles per hour. The ongoing ne-gotiations between tobacco manufacturers and the federal government on the product's future presence in society may signal an end to to-bacco's fruitful alliance with NASCAR. One proposal under discussion would ban brand-name tobacco sponsorship of sports events. If that ban takes effect as proposed, other big-name sponsors will have the oppor-tunity to tap NASCAR's swelling attendance figures, rising television ratings, and strong merchandising growth.

In 1996, another spate of negative publicity erupted over the working conditions at several of Nike's factories in Indonesia, where 70 million pairs of shoes are made each year. Reporters from *Business Week* visited one facility operated by a Nike subcontractor and found employees working for an average wage of $2.46 per day. At the same time, they endured mandatory overtime, physical abuse, verbal humiliation, and intimidation by law enforcement officials used by the factory owner to quell union organizing (Clifford 1996: 46).

Nike admits that its Asian operations are far from perfect, but it staunchly defends its efforts to improve workplace conditions. The com-pany's stated goal is to provide a fair, safe, and legal environment for all of its workers. In 1997, Nike severed ties with four Indonesian com-panies that refused to comply with its standards for pay and working conditions. Then on May 12, 1998, Knight announced that Nike would raise the minimum age for workers at its shoe factories to eighteen and would require its overseas manufacturers to meet the same health and safety standards in effect in the United States. Those standards are par-ticularly vital in maintaining air quality in an industry that uses dan-gerous raw material and chemical solvents. Knight also said he would allow representatives of labor and human rights groups to join the in-dependent monitors who inspect its facilities.

Knight did not promise a pay raise for Nike's overseas workers. The company's critics say workers need to make at least $3 a day to maintain an adequate living standard in China, Indonesia, and Vietnam. Nike and other American companies pay their workers less than $2 in those countries. Medea Benjamin, director of the human rights group Global Exchange, told the *New York Times* that the lack of a pay raise was a big gap in Nike's pledge to reform its workplace environment. "A sweatshop is a sweatshop is a sweatshop unless you start paying a living wage," Benjamin said. "That would be $3 a day" (Cushman 1998: C5). Other commentators find it disheartening that not one of the athletes who endorses Nike products has felt compelled to criticize, let alone condemn, the company's workplace environment in Asia. One writer called their silence a sign of "social and spiritual impoverishment" (Livingston 1997: 1D).

Do Nike and its counterparts exert too much influence in the sports world? That thought probably occurred to some who read of the threat posed by Los Angeles Lakers center Shaquille O'Neal before the start of the NBA's 1997–1998 season. As a Reebok endorser, O'Neal vowed to place tape over the Nike swoosh on his new warm-up pants, which appears because Nike has become the official uniform supplier of ten NBA teams. O'Neal's move could be viewed as a response to Michael Jordan's action at the 1992 Olympics. As a Nike endorser, Jordan refused to appear on the victory stand for the gold medal ceremony wearing the Reebok warm-up suit supplied to each member of the team. Jordan changed his mind and participated in the ceremony, but with an American flag draped over his shoulder to conceal the Reebok logo.

"They influence the coaches' salary, they influence who wears what, and they prescribe what logo is worn," says Bill Friday, former president of the University of North Carolina. "I think they've gone too far" (Miller 1995: 65). Distance runner Joan Nesbit agrees. She was overwhelmed by the rampant commercialism of the 1996 Summer Olympics in Atlanta, which she and others dubbed the "Coke Olympics." Corporate sponsors provided $540 million, or 32.7 percent of the event's operating budget. "The athletes and fans won't be trading country pins," she wrote. "They'll be trading company pins" (Nesbit 1996: 37).

In another effort to resist commercial influence, faculty members at the University of Wisconsin fought an attempt by Reebok to insert a "non-disparagement" clause into its endorsement contract with the school's athletic department in 1996. The clause barred any employee speaking on behalf of the university from criticizing Reebok or any of its products. When the faculty members labeled the clause a threat to free speech and academic freedom, it was removed. Basketball coaches complain that the summer camps sponsored by shoe companies have become the major showcases for high school superstars seeking to impress college recruiters. The camps diminish the importance of high school coaches and even the high school basketball season. They also may pressure athletes who attend a camp sponsored by one shoe company to enroll at a university

Nike is paying golfer Tiger Woods $40 million over a five-year period to wear and endorse its products. Even at that price, the deal has proved to be an excellent investment. During his historic victory at the Masters Tournament in 1997, Woods's swoosh appeared on the television screen for nearly fourteen minutes. Advertisers called it the greatest single exposure of a corporate logo. In 1997, Woods earned an estimated $24 million in endorsement income, placing him second behind Michael Jordan's $47 million among professional athletes. Following Jordan and Woods on the endorsement earnings list were golfer Arnold Palmer ($16 million), NASCAR driver Dale Earnhardt ($15.5 million), tennis player Andre Agassi ($14 million), golfer Greg Norman ($13 million), basketball players Shaquille O'Neal ($12.5 million) and Grant Hill ($12 million), Formula One racecar driver Michael Schumacher ($10 million), and tennis player Michael Chang ($9.5 million). (AP/WIDE WORLD PHOTOS)

sponsored by the same company. Sonny Vaccaro, who runs a summer camp in New Jersey for Adidas, bristles at the complaint: "Who gave them the wisdom to say that we who run summer basketball are the bad people and they're the good people?" (*Sports Illustrated* 1997: 23).

Phil Knight believes the effects of commercialization in general, and of Nike in particular, are grossly exaggerated. He says his company is no different from a company that sponsors a Little League Baseball team, and he flatly rejects the notion that Nike has the power to create an unlevel playing field by rewarding endorsement contracts to some players, coaches, and teams and not to others. He prefers to see Nike as a powerful force for good in the world, a force that can generate goodwill and optimism by creating products that can allow every athlete to achieve maximum potential, regardless of skill level. In Knight's view, Nike cannot dictate the future; it can only capture a piece of it.

Nike's piece of the present is huge. Its piece of the future—with or without the swoosh—may be even bigger.

TOPICS FOR DISCUSSION

1. Phil Knight, the founder and chairman of Nike, Inc., dismisses the claim that his company exerts too much influence on the sports world. He says his company has far less clout than people think. Do you agree with Knight's view?

2. Has Nike's use of low-cost and underage workers at its Asian production plants affected your personal opinion of the company? Has it been a factor in your decisions about which sneakers to buy? Why or why not?

3. Do you think that tobacco companies should be barred from advertising their products at auto races and other sporting events? Or do you think they should be able to promote tobacco in the same manner that other companies promote noncontroversial products?

4. Do you know anyone personally who has been robbed of his or her sneakers, warm-up jacket, or other piece of sports apparel? What does such an incident say about the values of young people and society at large? Is there an effective way to de-emphasize the importance that so many young people attach to athletic apparel?

REFERENCES AND RESOURCES

Books

Coe, Sebastian, David Teasdale, and David Wickham. *More Than a Game: Sport in Our Time*. London: BBC Books, 1992.

Cowritten by two-time Olympic gold medalist Coe, the book is based on an acclaimed British Broadcasting Company television series. Chapter 10 discusses endorsements.

Flowers, Sarah. *Sports in America*. San Diego: Lucent Books, 1996.
Chapter 1 discusses the business of sports.

Lupica, Mike. *Mad As Hell: How Sports Got away from the Fans and How We Get It Back*. New York: G. P. Putnam's Sons, 1996.
Lupica, a newspaper columnist and television commentator, takes no prisoners in this frank appraisal of greed and hypocrisy in the sports world.

Weiss, Ann E. *Money Games: The Business of Sports*. Boston: Houghton Mifflin, 1993.
A provocative and highly readable look at the influence of money on sports. Chapter 4 discusses player endorsements.

Magazines and Newspapers

Armstrong, Jim. "Three Stripes You're In." *Sport*, September 1997: 84–87.
A profile of Sonny Vaccaro, an Adidas promoter and public relations man.

Associated Press. "Sports May Have to Do without Tobacco's Millions." *Columbus Dispatch*, June 21, 1997: 3B.
A discussion of how stringent antitobacco regulations may affect sponsorship efforts by tobacco companies.

Bhonslay, Marianne. "Women for Sale." *Women's Sports and Fitness*, September 1997: 60–62.
Details the boom in corporate sponsorship of women's basketball and other sports.

Bonkowski, Jerry. "Fans Go for Michael-bilia." *USA Today*, May 17, 1996: 3C.
A tourist's guide to Michael Jordan's Chicago.

Clifford, Mark L. "Pangs of Conscience." *Business Week*, July 29, 1996: 46–47.
A report on a visit to a Nike shoe factory in Indonesia.

Cushman, John H., Jr. "Nike Pledges to End Child Labor and Apply U.S. Rules Abroad." *New York Times*, May 13, 1998: C1, C5.
A report on Nike's plan to revamp hiring practices and working conditions in its Asian assembly plants.

Dixon, Oscar. "Air Apparent Executive." *USA Today*, September 9, 1997: 3C.
A look at Michael Jordan's role as a corporate leader.

Goldberg, Karen. "If the Shoe Fits . . . Endorse It." *Insight on the News*, March 3, 1997: 38.
An overview of the sneaker wars waged by Nike and other manufacturers.

Greising, David. "Run, Jump and Sell." *Business Week*, July 29, 1996: 36–37.
A report on the impact of corporate sponsors at the Atlanta Olympic Games.

Horovitz, Bruce. "Big-League Advertisers Line Up To Sponsor Women's Sports." *USA Today*, June 20, 1997: B1.
Reports on the growing number of corporate sponsors in women's sports.

Johnson, Greg. "Youth Leagues Play the Sponsorship Game." *Los Angeles Times*, April 3, 1998: A1.

Surveys the new, sophisticated techniques used by companies to attract customers from youth sports leagues.

Johnson, Roy S. "Tiger! Now the Sky's the Limit for Golf—the Game and the Business." *Fortune*, May 12, 1997: 73–84.
Discusses the effect of Tiger Woods on golf's booming international popularity.

Lane, Randall. "You Are What You Wear." *Forbes*, October 14, 1996: 42–45.
A profile of Nike founder Phil Knight.

Lapchick, Richard. "Sharing the Wealth." *Sporting News*, September 29, 1997: 5.
Comments on how growing salaries and endorsement contracts may affect female athletes.

Lipsyte, Robert. "Mere Companies Chasing an Icon." *New York Times*, February 8, 1996b: B15, B21.
Nike founder Phil Knight discusses the role his company plays in the sports world.

Lipsyte, Robert. "One Fell Swoosh: Can a Logo Conquer All?" *New York Times*, February 7, 1996a: B9, B11.
A look at Nike's dominance of the sportswear market.

Livingston, Bill. "Bottom Line Clouds Vision of Athletes." *Cleveland Plain Dealer*, April 18, 1997: 1D.
A criticism of the indifference of Nike athletes to working conditions in the company's Asian shoe factories.

Meyers, Bill. "Jordan, Inc." *USA Today*, September 9, 1997b: 1A, 2A.
A front-page profile of Michael Jordan's newly created business enterprise within Nike.

Meyers, Bill. "Prep Star Signs $12M Adidas Deal." *USA Today*, June 19, 1997a: 1C.
A report on the endorsement contract signed by high school basketball star Tracy McGrady.

Miller, Annetta. "Just Doing It." *Newsweek*, October 2, 1995: 64–65.
Examines the growing influence of commercial sponsors in sports.

Nesbit, Joan. "Looking for Magic in the Coke Olympics." *Business Week*, July 29, 1996: 37.
An Olympic distance runner offers a wry look at commercialism in the 1996 Summer Games.

Reilly, Rick. "The Swooshification of the World." *Sports Illustrated*, February 24, 1997: 78.
A satirical view of Nike's overwhelming presence in sports.

Salfino, Catherine. "You Can't Tell the Players without an Endorsement Card." *Daily News Record*, August 19, 1996: 48–50.
Includes interviews with several marketing experts from shoe companies.

Sandomir, Richard. "A $200 Million Soccer Bid to Sell the Swoosh." *New York Times*, April 30, 1997: C22.
A report on Nike's bid to become a major player in international soccer.

Solomon, Jolie. "When Cool Goes Cold." *Newsweek*, March 30, 1998: 36–40.
An account of the troubles encountered by Nike during its sales slump in 1998.

Sports Illustrated. "Summer Stock." October 13, 1997: 23.

A brief note on concerns raised by college basketball coaches about summer camps sponsored by shoe companies.

Tagliabue, John. "Europe Enters the Big Leagues." *New York Times*, September 10, 1997: C1, C4.
An in-depth look at the growing commercialization of European sports, particularly soccer.

Tanzer, Andrew. "Tiger Woods Played Here." *Forbes*, March 10, 1997: 96–98.
The surging popularity of golf in Asia is linked to the rise of Tiger Woods.

Telander, Rick. "Senseless." *Sports Illustrated*, May 14, 1990: 36–49.
Telander's sad tale attempts to make some sense of the "sneaker killings" that have plagued America's inner cities.

USA Today. "O'Neal Says No Go to Nike Uniform Logo." October 17, 1997: 3C.
A report on the planned refusal of basketball center Shaquille O'Neal to display the Nike logo on his warm-up suit.

Organization to Contact

Nike, Inc.
One Bowerman Drive
Beaverton, OR 97005–0979
Phone: 503–671–6453
Internet Web Site: www.info.nike.com
Nike's Web site includes a section entitled "Responsibility," which provides information on the company's labor practices and the working conditions in its Asian factories.

Index

About the Author

DOUGLAS T. PUTNAM is a Fantasy League Commissioner and attorney who works for the County Commissioners Association of Ohio in Columbus. He is a former contributing editor of *The Lincoln Library of Sports Champions* and a member of the Professional Football Researchers Association.